LIVING
THE GREEN PLATFORM

LIVING
THE GREEN PLATFORM
LIFE-CHANGING STORIES

DECLAN COYLE

Ballpoint Press

About The Author

DECLAN COYLE is the author of the bestselling book *The Green Platform* — a book that has changed the lives of thousands for the better since it was first published in 2013.

He is one of Ireland's top internationally-known leadership training and development consultants. Declan is also a director of the award-winning media communications company Andec Communications and a much sought-after executive coach and conference keynote speaker.

His success as an inspirational speaker for business leaders has in recent years been harnessed in the sports arena. He has given regular goal-setting and mental strength motivational sessions to many Irish teams, including the successful Kerry, Cork, Cavan (football), Tipperary and Dublin (hurling) teams. He worked closely with Kilmacud Crokes, who won the 2008 All-Ireland Senior Football Club Championship. He himself played senior football with Cavan and is a former Ulster Championship medal winner.

In the United States, he works regularly with the legendary Coach Calipari and the Kentucky Wildcats. In 2012, following a number of losses, the team went on to win the national basketball title.

Declan is a member of the Irish Institute of Training & Development. He is also a Master Practitioner in Neuro-Linguistic Programming and a certified Enneagram teacher.

A former Columban missionary for 27 years, Declan is married to Annette and they live with their three children in Bray, Co Wicklow.

I'd like to dedicate this book to two families
to whom I owe an enormous debt of gratitude:

Firstly, to the family I grew up with in Dungimmon,
who shaped, enriched and nurtured my mind, body and soul —
my brother Vincent and Annette, my sister Kay and Sean
and their family and extended families, my brother Norbert
and Brigid and their family, my brother Finbarr and Petria
and their family, and in memory of Daddy, Mammy and my
brother Noel, who all smile down at us eternally.

Secondly, to the Columban missionary family all over the globe,
who continue to find joy in their lives and bring joy to others.

Published in 2016 by Ballpoint Press
4 Wyndham Park, Bray, Co Wicklow, Republic of Ireland.
Telephone: 00353 86 821 7631
Email: ballpointpress1@gmail.com
Web: www.ballpointpress.ie

ISBN 978–0–9932892–1–7

While every effort has been made to ensure the accuracy of
all information contained in this book, neither the author
nor the publisher accepts liability for any errors or omissions made.

Book design and production by Joe Coyle Media&Design,
joecoyledesign@gmail.com

Cover photography: Dermot Byrne Photography

Printed and bound by GraphyCems

Contents

Foreword
Dr. Pearse Lyons
FOUNDER AND PRESIDENT
OF ALLTECH

THE purpose of one's life is surely to have a life full of purpose. When you start a business with $10,000, and after 30 years it has grown to be in excess of $2 billion in revenue, with a target of $6 billion, is that what life is all about?

No. It's not about revenue. It's not about profit. It's about having a positive impact on as many lives as you possibly can.

Living The Green Platform is about enthusiasm, it's about hope, and it's about avoiding naysayers and 'energy vampires'.

These people constantly remind you that if it could be done, then it would have been done before — giving you that horrible feeling of bringing you back to average. *Living The Green Platform* is not about average; it's about fun, it's about excellence and it's about encouragement.

I've had the privilege of running with Declan Coyle throughout the years in many places around the world. Wherever we go, we have the same message. Whether we meet a local homeless person on the street and listen to his or her story, or a university professor at the local coffee shop or call out to those elite runners who pass us like Olympic stars — it's all about retaining the common touch.

"Live on the Green Platform" has become a mantra for Alltech and for our 4,700 people around the world. We've shared it with college basketball coaches, using its simple message to transform their athletes from a group of talented individuals into a cohesive team, who then believe they can do, and go on to make that belief a reality.

I recommend that you read *Living The Green Platform*, underline its messages, write them down and tie them into your own objectives. We at Alltech do this, and it has worked for us. I have no doubt that it will work wonders for you too.

Dr. Pearse Lyons
May 2016

Preface

HOW did the Green and Red Platform come about? Over the years, I wanted to develop something that would be powerful, challenging and deep, and at the same time achieve this inner shift in people and teams striving for peak performance. Something that would create change, and be easy to absorb, understand and implement.

Most courses and development programmes can be complicated and my challenge in terms of peak performance always was to make things extremely simple to understand, implement and embed in a team culture.

That's where I got the idea of the Green and Red Platforms. The colours came from an inspired moment at traffic lights one morning. The subliminal idea of Red for 'Stop,' and Green for 'Go,' with the Green connotation of spring, new growth, fresh starts and new beginnings.

Green also seemed to contain that sense of our ancient Celtic spirituality that was always so full of wisdom, insight and good humour. I wanted it to embody the pure joy of living life to the full.

The Green Platform is an inner place where we consciously choose all that is positive, uplifting, creative, joyful, inspiring, compassionate and generous. It's where we radiate positive energy and choose actions that bring joy to others. It's where we live our lives with passion, excellence and fun; where rather than making excuses, we make things happen.

The Green Platform is the empowered platform and has the

ten most powerful words in the English language, no word more than two letters: 'If it is to be, it is up to me.' People on The Green Platform are energised but also calm, enthusiastic, confident and optimistic. They are 'Energy Transformers.' You meet them and they contribute to your energy and increase your inner joy.

The pronoun on the Green Platform is 'I.' I am responsible. People on the Green Platform have 'response-ability,' the ability to choose their response at any given time.

Underneath the Green Platform is the field of all possibilities.

The Red Platform is the home of the victims, the whingeing, whining, moaning, 'poor me' people who are constantly blaming others. They're the 'Energy Vampires' who drain you in every encounter. They suck the energy out of you like a vacuum cleaner. They're the robbers and thieves of your inner joy, peace and happiness.

Underneath the Red Platform is a septic tank of fear, procrastination and limiting beliefs that all lead to personal and team sabotage. The Red Platform is a place of complaining, blaming and finger pointing.

The pronoun on the Red Platform is 'you.' I blame you. You are responsible for all my problems. It's all your fault.

The key to choosing your Platform is totally in your hands. You have in your hands the last and the greatest of the human freedoms — the freedom to choose your response in any given set of circumstances.

On the Green Platform your mind is your best friend and your brain is working positively to serve you. On the Red Platform your mind is your worst enemy and your brain is working negatively to sabotage you.

How does it work?

For many years, I was against negative thinking and I didn't know why, because as Irish people we saw ourselves as negative, but real, whereas we viewed Americans as being positive, but maybe not so real.

Later on I realised that we have to be emotionally honest, and that struck at the core of what my problem was. For example, if I suffer a terrible tragedy or disappointment, then I can't turn around and just say "be positive, have a positive mental attitude and the problem will disappear." That's not realistic or honest. There's an important step in between.

I discovered this 'missing step' during my postgraduate studies in Ottawa while listening to a visiting professor, legendary psychiatrist and Holocaust-survivor Viktor Frankl. Frankl had been tortured in Auschwitz and he talked about his horrific experiences in the death camps. But instead of being destroyed by these experiences, inside, he chose peace, joy and happiness. He learned that in any situation he had the freedom to choose his response. Even in the torture chambers of Auschwitz. "They could break my body," he said. "But they couldn't touch my spirit."

This was a defining moment for me — a moment when I realised the great power we have 'to choose our response,' no matter how challenging the situation.

Between stimulus and response there is a space, I call it the 'White Space.'

In that space we have the power to be aware and on the one hand to proactively consciously choose the energy with which we want to respond — kindness, compassion or empathy on the Green Platform — or to automatically react negatively to negative things on the Red Platform, with a guaranteed negative outcome.

If we consciously choose the Green Platform, then that awareness and choice of response is what saves us from being just another bunch of predictable reflexes constantly being triggered by people and events into predictable outcomes. We can choose our response rather than being mere 'reactors'. A curious and compassionate awareness is the key. What if in this situation when someone says something mean to me that I could have the ability and the awareness to choose the energy of kindness from the Green Platform rather than automatically snapping back at the person with by saying something even meaner from the Red Platform?

What I had been grappling with for years suddenly came together — you have a human experience, an emotional experience, you honour it, you feel it fully. If it's tragedy you cry the tears. If it's loneliness you turn on the tap. There can be no healing without a real and genuine feeling. Total emotional honesty. Then within that 'White Space' you have the freedom to choose your response — and even from a negative experience, we can choose to take positive actions, which will in turn deliver more positive outcomes. This, then, is what'll transform the quality of our lives.

When bad things happen to good people, good people respond differently. But it's all based on a foundation of absolute emotional honesty. You cannot just pour positive pink paint over human suffering.

On the Green Platform acceptance — 'it is as it is" — is followed by positive action now, but on the Red Platform that acceptance can easily turn to apathy or indifference.

We cannot argue with reality or we will lose, but only 100% of the time. The formula on the Green Platform is 'Acceptance + PAN.' Acceptance — 'It is as it is' — and then Positive Action Now. Of the 100 things, what one thing can I do now to make matters better? Then just do it.

Is it possible to train Red Platform people to become Green?

Yes, I've seen it happen over and over — once people get the tools and become aware, then they change. Think of it as an ABC choice: Red Platform people will respond with Anger, Blame and Complain.

Green Platform people respond with people with Awareness, Belief and Commitment to do what needs to be done, long after the mood in which you planned to do it has gone.

I ask people to aim for PAR's as much as possible: Positive Affirming Remarks in all situations. In other words catch other people doing things right and mention it to them. That's taking a Green Platform approach. Shining a light on what is right.

Almost by default we catch people doing things wrong and ignore all that they're doing right.

The greatest poison in a family or team or organisation is the pervasive presence of NBRs. Negative Belittling Remarks. The put-downs. By the time the average child is 12 they have received 100,000 NBRs. We then wonder why 98% of children at the age of 14 have a negative self-image.

An eight-year-old was asked one time: "How do you know if two people are married or not?" He replied: "You might have to guess, based on whether they're yelling at the same kids."

Is it about interpretation, meanings?

Yes, it's all about interpretations, meanings or stories that we tell ourselves. If you go into any company you'll find a lot of Red Platform stories. For example, an event has no meaning, a fact has no meaning and a situation has no meaning unless I make up an interpretation or meaning or a story about it.

On the Red Platform, the response is dis-empowering stories where the interpretation of events becomes poison to the organisation, for example: "This is a disaster, we can't succeed," etc.

On the Green Platform, meanings, interpretations and stories become energising and powerful. The interpretation of what would be a Red Platform 'disaster' is: "This is a great opportunity, let's see what we can do here to succeed. What are the three gifts contained in this situation?"

On the Red Platform people feel bad because of the negative story or interpretation they're telling themselves, whereas on the Green Platform their empowering stories help them to feel good and increase their energy to take positive action. Feelings follow meanings.

In life we do two things over and over. We think and we feel. We either think and feel about what we want to create and attract into our lives on the positive inner Green Platform, or we think and feel about what we don't want to create and attract into our lives on the negative inner Red Platform.

It's always a choice. And choice is power. Decisions shape destiny. The choices you make make you. Where attention goes energy flows.

My question is this: "Why should we be making up negative stories on the Red Platform like — 'Woe is me' — that make us feel bad, when we can just as easily make up positive stories on the Green Platform like — 'I can handle it' — that make us feel good?"

Then there are Green Platform and Red Platform questions. Green Platform PowerQuestions and Red Platform PoisonQuestions.

The questions in the canteens and offices of organisations around the world are also often full of Red Platform PoisonQuestions such as:

"Why me? What else will go wrong? Why does this always have to happen to me?"

It's 100% certain when you ask a PoisonQuestion question, you'll get a poison answer.

"Why you?"

'Because you're a slob. Because you lacked early life love. Because your mother loved your sister more than you."

Instead ask "How can I ...?" "What can I ...?" Green Platform PowerQuestions like:

"How can I turn this around and enjoy the process? How can we double our productivity and halve the time? What's the most important thing to focus on at this meeting and where can we get the biggest breakthroughs in the coming months? How can I be the best that I can be today?"

If I'm a salesperson and I don't get a sale, instead of asking a Red Platform PoisonQuestion such as: "Why me, what else can go wrong?", the salesperson is more likely to achieve a better outcome by asking a Green Platform PowerQuestion like: "What can I ..."

such as: "What can I learn from this and what can I do differently next time?"

Likewise, if you don't get a promotion, instead of asking: "Why am I being left behind?", ask instead: "How can I add value to the company."

Even with a child not doing well at school, instead of asking the PoisonQuestion: "Why can't the teachers do better?" ask a PowerQuestion instead like: "How can I help my child with his or her homework."

PowerQuestions are powerful because they imply action.

Then we have beliefs. The Red Platform person with the PoisonBelief says: "I can't do it" versus the Green Platform PowerBelief person who says: "We can do it, we'll find a way." As Henry Ford said: "Whether you think you can or think you can't, you're right."

Is that not just putting a gloss on stuff?

No. Positive thinking on the Green Platform is based on reality. It's not seeing the weeds in the garden and saying: "There are no weeds, I must be positive." Instead it's rolling up your sleeves, taking action and responding with a plan, a strategy to get rid of the weeds and a vision of how your garden will look afterwards.

The Green Platform is not driving down the road and seeing that your fuel gauge is at 'E' and then getting a green Smiley Face sticker and putting it over the fuel gauge, saying: "I must be happy, happy, happy. I must be positive." That's denial. The Green Platform approach is to get your car to a petrol station and fill the tank

The Green Platform is not about denial. It's about taking positive action now.

The Green Platform is always honest, realistic ... but challenging and stretching getting you out of your comfort zone into your excellence zone.

What's the impact on organisations?

I've been bringing the Green Platform approach into organisations at every level for more than 25 years.

Transformations occur because on the Green Platform people have autonomy. They're motivated to make things happen because they understand what they're doing and why it's important. So managers need to communicate more effectively to ensure employees find meaning and purpose in what they do.

I asked the head of HR in one of the major multinational companies in Ireland to explain the impact of the Green Platform, and she said: "It's simple, in 2007 if you asked people to do something, you'd get a big sigh and a roll of the eyes. Now, because of the Green Platform, they say, 'Okay, let's see what we can do and how we can do it more efficiently and effectively.' Now they think about the whole plant, about customers and how they make a positive difference. This more positive Green Platform culture has become embedded throughout the organisation."

I always insist that things are measurable, because what gets measured gets done. This client has placed Green and Red Platform goal achievement measurement signs around the site, so they can clearly see whether they're leading on the Green Platform or lagging on the Red Platform. The programme has given them a language and imagery for change which is very practical, visual and powerful.

In one organisation they even have a piece of green carpet and invite people to step on it to say something from a different perspective — to give a Green Platform analysis rather than Red Platform view of a challenge, to focus on a creative solution rather than getting bogged down in the problem.

Another great thing is that after the training programme everyone in the company has a common language that everyone easily understands, so they're able to embed the Green Platform thinking and move forward more quickly.

I have worked with a number of multi-billion dollar companies in the USA, where the transformation in the top leadership has been profound, with a massive trickle down effect and impact.

How can something so simple have such a big impact?

It's because it IS simple that it's effective — people get it. Also the Green Platform's way of achieving goals is by bringing people with you. If you achieve or exceed your goals, but there's so much blood on the floor and you have tired and miserable employees, you've taken a Red Platform approach. Then you may get ready for exit interviews.

But on the Green Platform, people become more joyful, innovative and inspiring when working towards goals. This radiates out to the customers. There's that emotional connection that great branding craves.

It's back to the inner world of people. When people feel good about themselves, they achieve incredible results. If people feel bad about themselves, they neither deliver good results nor do good work.

Is it not all a bit tree-huggy and touchy-feely?

My response to this is to look at the huge cost of negative behaviour and attitudes in the workplace. Research has shown the cost of Red Platform negative attitudes and behaviours to the US economy in just one year is half a trillion dollars (one thousand dollar bills on your hand 38 miles high) in lost productivity — and that's without taking into account absences, illness and other problems that result when workers are disengaged from their work and their companies. So the cost of Red Platform negative thinking and behaviour is enormous, *Harvard Business Review*, May 2014, p. 62)

Whereas on the Green Platform, another Harvard study showed that when people are positive in the present every single business outcome improves. Specifically across a range of trials, productivity went up 31% and sales went up 37%.

Research has also shown that when people are positive in the present on the Green Platform, they have enhanced immune system functioning, lower levels of stress-related hormones, lower blood pressure, less pain, fewer colds, better sleep and a smaller likelihood of having hypertension, diabetes or strokes.

That, in a nutshell, is the power of the Green Platform.

Introduction

SOME years ago, the *Irish Independent* decided to bring out with its Thursday newspaper a magazine concentrating on fitness for everybody.

Fit magazine wanted to get every man, woman and child out exercising — a laudable sentiment in times of widespread obesity in Ireland.

The editor of the magazine asked me to write a weekly column; he wanted me to motivate people to get up off the couch, get out into the fresh air and take exercise.

As sitting had become the new smoking, I was only too happy to take up his offer on a trial basis. I was unsure as to the response there might be to the life-changing power of the Green Platform principles that I would use as part of these weekly pieces.

To say I was astonished at the response would be an understatement. It was extraordinary what happened. Within a matter of weeks, the columns had got a kind of cult following throughout the country, and I ended up contributing columns for over two years.

Teachers would get the magazine on a Thursday and read the column out for the class. Then they would challenge the students to find three ways to implement the content of the column in their daily lives.

Mothers were cutting out the columns and posting them to their adult children overseas. Others were cutting them out and sticking them up on their fridges.

I got stories of people coming home at Christmas and getting a shoebox full of the carefully cut out columns with their Christmas presents.

Boxing champions, footballers, hurlers, rugby players, tennis players, basketball players and athletes have all told me that they used them as motivational tools to achieve peak performance.

The editor was delighted with the response, as was the *Independent* with the increased sales on the day. The most satisfying feedback for me, however, came from people all over the country who said that one particular column came at the right time to get them through a life crisis.

Just recently, after delivering a keynote presentation at a conference in a hotel in Dublin, I was over in a corner signing copies of my book *The Green Platform*.

Waiting patiently at the end of the queue was a quiet woman. She asked me to sign two books for her two friends. Then she said: "I just wanted to thank you for all the motivation, inspiration and inner strength I got from your *Fit* magazine columns. Some years ago I went through two years of horrific suffering. I could barely cope. I lived from Thursday to Thursday when I would go out and buy the newspaper and read your column.

"Each week the column just gave me enough inner strength, resilience and courage to go on. To keep on keeping on during a really tough time in my life. I don't know if I would have made it through those two awful years without your inspirational *Fit* magazine columns. I came here today specially to thank you. You have no idea the difference those columns made in my life. I kept every one of them and I keep going back and rereading them any time I go into a bit of a dip."

That's what she told me.

She understood that the columns are really about being fully alive and living life to the full. They are about bouncing back from setbacks and turning stumbling blocks into stepping-stones.

Sure the columns are about getting fit and taking exercise, but they are no more about fitness and exercise than Moby Dick is about a whale.

The stories are about life; and they're life changing.

They're about your growth and development. They're about you being the best that you can possibly be. They're about finding joy, purpose and meaning in your life and bringing that joy to others.

They're about the greatest currency there is in this life, which is the positive effect you have on other people. Along with *The Green Platform* book, they form an inner software peak performance manual for the mind.

For this book, we've narrowed down the 116 columns to just 90. I hope you enjoy reading them and I thank you for the feedback that made us decide to print them in book form.

Enjoy all of these wonderful life-changing stories and from today on, I hope you'll make the right choice — to live only on the Green Platform.

Declan Coyle
May 2016

1

The Miracle Walks
Of Ali And Alex

DEEP and lasting change is a heroic journey. Sometimes in our efforts to complete a particular journey in our life, we bite off more than we can chew and end up disappointed when we fail.

Other times, though we find the hero inside ourselves and this is witnessed in the growing numbers who are exercising at a time when ironically we also see a huge rise in obesity in our country.

Everything is relative — for some a 5k or a 10k might be that goal to feel good and for others, it might be to complete shorter, personal journeys that are absolutely immense victories for them.

I've seen some of those achievements by people over the years where these journeys were completed with both courage and conviction. Some were just over 26 miles long and others were only five steps long.

I had the privilege of introducing the great Muhammad Ali to an Irish audience in Dublin at a charity dinner organised by Dr Pearse Lyons, president and founder of the Alltech company some years ago.

I was with the great boxing legend and his wife, Lonnie, backstage as the MC was talking to the audience. Ali was sitting in a chair, shaking with his Parkinson's disease. My script was simple. Just say, with as much power and passion as possible: "And now, ladies and gentlemen, a big warm Irish céad míle fáilte for the greatest, Muhammad Ali."

The directions were clear. Give Ali the nod to stand up and walk to the curtain as I was bellowing out, boxing ring-like, the introduction.

I looked at Ali and nodded to be sure he was okay. He nodded back. When he stood up, he smiled. Chin up. Head back. He was ready. As he started to walk, I began my introduction. I could have been in Madison Square Garden introducing a world championship fight. But I saw clearly within a millisecond that my speaking was much quicker than Ali's ability to put one foot past the other.

I just got as far as saying: "And now ladies and gentlemen a big warm Irish céad míle fáilte for ..." but Ali had only moved two steps.

His jaw was square. He had that same steely determination he needed in those nights he fought Joe Frazier, George Foreman and Sonny Liston. He had refused to use a wheelchair and was fighting harder than he did against those opponents inside the ring to walk out and greet his Dublin audience.

He had moved only two steps, and I was stuck. I had totally overestimated his walking speed. He takes the third step and I say: "A living legend." I pause. He takes a fourth step. I go on: "The most recognised face on the planet ..." and then he takes his fifth step and just before he splits the curtain I say: "The greatest, Muhammad Ali."

He got a standing ovation. The longest one I've ever seen or heard. By the time it was over he had been helped to a chair where he was happy to sit down.

Those five steps had taken an awful lot out of him but he has been fighting for a bigger cause than just a boxing payday for these past three decades since he retired.

His wife, Lonnie, said that boxing was only ever a vehicle for him to do what he's doing now; raising millions for his charity as he continues to encourage every man, woman and child in the world to be the greatest they can be.

I was humbled to be beside him as he completed those five steps with immense courage and conviction. In those five steps, I saw the 'Rumble in the Jungle,' and the 'Thrilla in Manila'. He did it not because he had to do it but because he wanted to do it. It gives him purpose and meaning every day. With those five steps he conquered yet again his personal Everest.

Alexander is our third child. He has a rare medical condition called Mowat-Wilson syndrome. He was the first child in Ireland discovered to be suffering from it as a baby.

He is now 11 years old. He will never talk. He can do a little walk if heavily assisted by Annette, his mother, or Genevieve or Fionn (his sister and brother) or by his godmother, Mary, or his visiting nurse, Liz, who all help make his life so worthwhile.

He hasn't eaten for over eight years because he gets his food into his system through a tube into his stomach. He's also doubly incontinent.

We are all in awe of him in our house. He is the most magical and magnetic child you could ever imagine. Every morning he goes on his special bus to St Catherine's in Newcastle, Co Wicklow where the people there do amazing work with him and with all his special needs friends.

Before Christmas a few years ago they even staged a nativity play. Alexander was St Joseph. In the rehearsals, he was great at knocking on the doors of inns that were full and closed to weary travellers with a donkey.

However, during the play itself, as soon as he saw the audience he became more interested in waving at us and clapping his hands on the stage than knocking on inn doors.

All the actors in the nativity play had members of the staff helping them move around as some were in wheelchairs and some needed assistance to stand upright.

In the midst of it all, Alexander turned around and took off. He walked five steps across the stage on his own. Unaided.

Jane, who looked after his class was so excited afterwards. "Did you see him walking five steps on his own. Could you imagine him doing anything like that last year?"

Like Ali, he conquered his own personal Everest that day in the nativity play by walking those five steps.

So if you've given up on exercise or working harder to get promotion or any other personal challenge, think of Ali and Alex and then realise what you are capable of doing in your life.

Their 'marathons' were just five steps each but what a magnificent achievement for the two of them. Your journey of 1,000 miles begins with just five steps.

In the book, *The Green Platform*, chapter 11 is about Alexander and the positive impact he has on everyone he meets. The chapter is called *Meet Alexander the Greatest*.

Every day is a new beginning only waiting for you to start your own heroic journey and be inspired by "The Greatest, Muhammad Ali" and "Alexander The Greatest" so that you too can become the greatest you can be.

RED PLATFORM: "What's the point? It's only five steps. Where's that wheelchair? Where's Jane?"

GREEN PLATFORM: Every step in the right direction matters. Five or five thousand. "I can do it, one step at a time."

2

Just One More Degree To Greatness

AT 211 degrees Fahrenheit water is hot, but it does remarkably little by way of achieving anything for the world in this state.

However, if you turn the heat up by just one degree until it hits 212 degrees, then it reaches boiling point.

Boiling water creates steam. And steam can drive a train across a continent or light up a city.

One degree is the small difference that makes all the difference.

Small things make a big difference. It just depends on how you harness them.

That one degree extra effort is what separates champions from also-rans and leaders from losers.

That one degree extra of effort in your pursuit of a fit and healthy body will make all the differnce between the old you and the new version of you. That one degree, that one small step could be your tipping point.

The Olympic margin of victory in the 2004 men's 800 metres was 0.71 seconds. Often fractions separate a gold medal from a 'no medal.'

The Olympic margin of victory in the women's 1,000-metre speed skating is 0.7 seconds. In the Indianapolis 500 the average margin for victory in the past 10 years was 1.54 seconds. The average winner took home $1,278,813 in prize money. The person in second place got $621,321 in prize money. A difference of $657,492 all because of 1.54 seconds.

That extra degree of effort is so often what achieves victory and separates the good from the great.

Al Pacino in his role as Coach Tony D'Amato understood the power of those small steps in the film *Any Given Sunday*.

"Inch by inch, play by play, till we're finished ... you find out that life is just a game of inches ... the inches we need are everywhere around us."

It's the same for your mental state. You can stay the way you are or you can decide to improve yourself in a small way and see huge results. Just look at what happens at boiling point, that one degree extra, your tipping point. You'll take off.

Triumph is always nearest when defeat seems inescapable. It's all down to that extra degree of vigorous effort at the last moment. You dig deep. You think there's nothing left until you just dig deeper. You empty the tank.

Imagine if you spent all your life just that little degree or two below your best. Imagine you were a rose that forgot to bloom.

That could be any of us right now. So use today to consider the choice you have to tap into the magnificent person that you were born to be.

There is an old Chinese proverb that says: "It is better to make many small steps in the right direction than to make a great leap forward only then to stumble backwards."

So take those small steps today because pretty soon they will add up to something substantially new for you.

Martin Luther King had a graphic way of illustrating this concept of progress one step at a time: "You don't need to see the whole staircase, just the first step. Take that first step in faith," he stressed.

If there is a big tree out there in the forest and I have only a small axe to cut it down, how do I do it? If you swing at it with five strikes every single day, then one day, that tree is going to come crashing down.

If you go out in the dark at night for a walk with just a torch, you can only see five feet in front of you. Take those five steps and another five feet of light will emerge.

Many small, private victories precede the large public victories. "If you always do what you've always done, you'll always get what you've always got." If you want different results in your life, you need to start doing different things than you normally do.

If that's not working, then don't be afraid to change that as well. And if you find the newer approach still not working, be brave enough to change again. But don't work harder at what's not working.

To get what you've never had, you must do something that you've never done before. To succeed at a new level you must start with 'one degree extra' of effort.

A slight change in a golfer's grip can make a huge difference in a shot, never mind in 18 holes.

Take small steps in the direction of your dream, but don't get caught up in destination addiction. Have a dream, a goal or an outcome. Then detach from it, and enjoy every single step of the journey, no matter how small. The joy is in the journey.

Those inches are all around you. As Andy said to Red in the film *The Shawshank Redemption*: "Get busy living or get busy dying."

It just takes a slight change in your own determination to bring you to the next level as a sports achiever, a family person or as an employer or employee.

If you cross that one degree threshold to creating 'steam' in your life, just watch how that vortex of energy that will be at your disposal to propel you forward on a joyous and rewarding journey.

RED PLATFORM: Small improvements make no difference. Forget the inches. What's the point? Stop at 211 degrees.

GREEN PLATFORM: One degree extra makes all the difference. Create the 'steam' breakthrough. Find the inches everywhere. By the yard it's hard, by the inch it's a cinch.

3

The Blessing Of Motivation

WHEN it comes to living a fit and healthy life, probably the most common problem people have is staying motivated.

Sometimes they talk about losing focus, being discouraged, having too much to do, but what it boils down to is that they aren't achieving their exercise goals as much as they would like.

We all have things that are important to us. Some people work hard for a while, and then slacken off. Others procrastinate and never get to it. Some don't know how to get started or are too tired, weary and worn out. At the core of it all is motivation.

The fact is that we always do the things we are intensely motivated to do. How many times have you worked through the night to pass an important exam or to complete a term paper in college or to get all the hay baled on a sunny day?

Think about the times you've worked really hard to achieve something you just had to get done. You dug deep and found the motivation.

There's a wonderful story about a young man who travelled the world to get an interview with a famous Indian guru with a long white beard. When they finally met, the man said: "I'll do anything to find God. Will you help me?"

Without a word, the guru silently led the young man to a nearby river and suddenly jumped on him, pushed him into the river and pressed his head under water.

After the man thrashed and fought for a while, the guru let him up and he immediately gasped for air. Then once more the guru smashed his head down under the water.

The young man was surprised at the guru's strength and almost passed out but with a huge effort he threw the guru off him and gulped in the fresh air as soon as he got his head out of the water. But one more time the guru jumped on his back and forced the young man's head under the water.

He was on the point of drowning when finally with a massive effort he threw the guru off his back and crawled panting to the bank.

"What was that all about?" asked the young man: "All I asked you was how could I find God."

The guru then settled himself down, sat cross-legged, smiled and said: "When you desire God as badly as you wanted that breath of air when you were under the water, you'll find God."

Isn't that the truth?

When you are motivated, nothing stands in your way. When something fires your soul, impossibilities vanish. Within each of us there are places where we have never gone. Only by breaking through your perceived limits will you ever find those places.

So, how do you stay motivated? Here are five things that will help you break through and find those places:

1. Clarity and Focus

You can hit almost any target if you define it and see it clearly enough. Like a blindfolded archer, you cannot hit a target that you cannot see. It's hard to stay motivated for a vague, fuzzy or distant goal. That kind of goal contains little energy. Be specific. Be precise. Be concrete. You will be far more motivated to lose 10lbs a month than to lose "more weight" in that time. Without a clear goal you cannot score. Underpin it with a powerful passionate purpose. A 'why.' Give it a cause as strong as the man's need for air when his head was under the water.

2. Have A Massive Action Plan (MAP)

When you know the next step, you are much more motivated to

do it. Baby-steps are less sexy and exciting, but are always easier and more do-able than giant leaps. Have a clear action-oriented plan. Then, consistently take one step after another.

3. Have A Pool Of Positive Energy
Surround yourself with positives. Positive people, positive stories and positive books or CDs. Surround yourself with people who energise you — find Energy Transformers, and avoid the Energy Vampires who drain you with their complaining.

4. Begin Well Each Day
Re-commit to your most important priorities, goals and plans every single day. In the rush of the day, minor emergencies will beat strategic action every time. What are your one or two or three things that must get done today? When you make something an absolute 'must,' it tends to happen.

5. Great Supportive Friends
Have lots of enthusiastic friends who will hold you accountable, support and encourage you. Pick their brains for good ideas, and report back to them regularly.

If it is important to you, you'll find the motivation to do it.

If it's not, you'll find an excuse. So, make it important. Deeply desire it and want it like the man in the river wanted air. Then, make it happen.

RED PLATFORM: The blindfolded archer. How can she hit a target that she cannot see? Goalless. Drifting like a leaf on a pond.

GREEN PLATFORM: A clear goal, a MAP, a passionate purpose and supportive friends. Wanting it bad enough like that man in the river wanted air. A leaf heading in a clear direction to a definite destination with an outboard motor and a tiller attached to a steering rudder.

4

Overcoming The Half-Lived Life

For as this appalling ocean surrounds the verdant land,
so in the soul of man there lies one insular Tahiti,
full of peace and joy, but encompassed by all of the horrors of the half-
lived life.
From *Moby Dick*, by Herman Melville (1819-1891)

O h, the horrors of the half-lived life. I have no problem with dying but I have a huge problem with dying without having lived.

I'm writing this column from Vietnam, in the middle of the bustling city of Hanoi. Many are still wearing those conical straw hats, with those famous black pyjamas and they are riding bicycles. They have cartloads of stuff for the market on the backs of their bicycles.

I've noticed two things about these people:

1. I didn't see one obese or overweight person on a bike.

2. I'd say I got more genuine smiles before breakfast here than I'd get in a week in Ireland.

From the slums of this Asian city, Ireland looks like a never-ending Celtic Tiger. Materially, we have 10, or maybe 100 times more than they can ever aspire to have.

Yet they are so happy.

I heard Irish psychologist and author Maureen Gaffney a while back talking about the 20 per cent of us who are floundering, living with a kind of permanent, low-grade depression. Most of us at this level are sucking the energy from you like a vacuum cleaner. Every day is a dreadful day. We're your famous Energy Vampires.

She said another 60 per cent of us are at the ordinary functioning dial in life. We turn up for work. We try not to get sick. Mediocrity rules. The problem is not absenteeism; it's "presenteeism" (going to work, just turning up). We are into compliance, but not full engagement. You can't say we're not there.

The final 20 per cent of us are flourishing. We are full of energy. We are creative, innovative and good-humoured. We are fully alive. In a word, we are happy. How do we become fully alive, joyful and happy?

Some years ago I remember seeing a programme on television about the London psychologist Robert Holden, nicknamed the 'Happiness Psychologist', called *How To Be Happy*.

The challenge was to see if he could take three clinically depressed people, and in a short period, make them happier. As part of the process they participated in a university study to measure the activity in the left prefrontal lobe of the brain, a reliable indicator of the level of happiness they were experiencing in their daily lives.

He simply asked them to do three things:

1. Daily Exercise

The first was a daily habit of physical exercise. He knew that the body is the greatest pharmaceutical plant in this world and that exercise is a natural antidote to depression. It does this by using up the adrenaline and other chemicals released in our bloodstream by stress and also by relieving tension in the muscles.

Regular exercise releases the body's natural opiates, giving you a warm, relaxed feeling afterwards. The only way you'll feel afterwards is better. Gradually this habit of exercise becomes your new normal, your body's natural default setting.

2. Laughter

Secondly, he opted for laughter. Genuine laughter is the single biggest boost for the immune system. Like exercise, laughter produces endorphins to make the body feel good. Even just smiling releases serotonin (a happy neurotransmitter) into the bloodstream and acts as a powerful anti-depressant.

Robert asked them to laugh for 20 minutes a day, even if they had to force it at first. A real case of: "Fake it until you make it."

Norman Cousins in his book, *Anatomy Of An Illness — How One Man Proved Your Mind Can Cure Your Body* used laughter to great effect to boost his immune system in the process of his healing. Since Cousins' ground-breaking subjective work, scientific studies have shown that laughter has a curative effect on the body, mind and emotions. Norman saw laughter as a kind of inner jogging: "Hearty laughter is a good way to jog internally without having to go outdoors."

3. Positive Thoughts

Thirdly, they had to consciously decide to have positive thoughts. They all had to place coloured stickers around their work areas and homes. Every time they saw one they had to think of something positive that made them feel good.

This strengthened the neural pathways in their brains and reinforced the happy chemicals (the endorphins) in their bodies. They actually developed new synaptic patterns in their brains and changed their brains' inner physical landscapes. The newly discovered 'plasticity' of the brain makes these physical changes possible.

By the end of the first month, each of these new behaviours had become automatic and habitual. At the end of the study, the people had their brains measured.

The results stunned the university researchers. The differences in the levels of happiness were so astonishing that one of the scientists demanded to have the equipment checked.

All three people moved from being classed as 'clinically depressed,' to being classed as 'extreme optimists.' They had moved from one end of the scale to the other. They had literally rewired their inner software and changed the inner physical landscape of their brains to become happier.

So if you want to accelerate the process to your own personal happiness, follow Robert Holden's simple three-step formula.

1. Daily Exercise

Simply decide to exercise for about half an hour each day with a friend.

2. Laughter

While you're doing it, decide to have a good laugh. Cut yourself a bit of slack and have a bit of fun. Let go and release that tight-lipped, teeth-clenched, tight-fisted determination fuelled by destination addiction.

3. Positive Thought Reminder Stickers

Step into positive mode and keep thinking positive thoughts. That only takes one extra thought to happen. You decide that, come what may, you are going to be positive and enjoy this day. Put up your positive thought reminder stickers around your home. If you want to be happy, you have to be happy on purpose. When you wake up you don't have to wait to see what kind of a day you'll have. You have to decide what kind of a day you'll have. It's a choice.

The good news is you can then turn around and do the same tomorrow. And the day after. It has all the appearance to me of the daily life of a person living on The Green Platform.

Forget the horrors of the half-lived life. Don't swim in that appalling sea. Be the best that you can be. Find your inner Tahiti, full of peace and joy by taking exercise, laughing and smiling like the Vietnamese and by replacing the Automatic Negative Thoughts (ANTS) with Positive Automatic Thoughts (PATS).

Then you'll be catapulted into that top flourishing 20 per cent of people who are flourishing, free and fully alive.

RED PLATFORM: No time to exercise. Far too busy. No fun in my life. Definitely no laughter. I swim in a sea of automatic negative thoughts. "The horrors of the half-lived life."

GREEN PLATFORM: Exercise. Laughter and a bit of fun. Positive thought reminders all over the place. Flourishing, free and fully alive.

5

Make A Good Habit In Less Than A Month

THE Chinese say that "habits are cobwebs at first; cables at last." I was reminded of this old saying following a great chat I had with a very happy woman recently. She had made a dramatic change in her life for the better.

She explained that what had finally got her to change her habit was the line we talked about from Melville's *Moby Dick*: "All the horrors of the half-lived life."

Ryder Cup captain José María Olazábal touched on this same idea of the horrors of a half-lived life in his victory speech in Medinah at the Ryder Cup some years ago. He said: "All men die but not every man lives — and you made me feel alive again this week."

It sparked her into action. She said: "I didn't want to continue my life living with a backpack of "If onlys."

"If only I got up early and went to the gym every day."

One of the most empowering questions you can ask yourself begins with "What if ...?" So she asked herself instead: "What if I just made a decision to get a fit and healthy body, and actually did it?"

She changed her daily mantra from "If only ..." to "What if?" and felt immediately empowered.

So the next day she went to the gym before work and completed her workout. Afterwards she felt fantastic. She had, as she said, that morning "conquered ordinary everyday human laziness."

All was going great for a while. But then came a morning when she just didn't feel like it. Then she thought: "There are people who make excuses and there are people who make it happen. Can I make an excuse to go to the gym?"

Yes, she flipped her excuse and went to the gym. She changed her inner software. Life was no longer happening to her, she was happening to life.

She packed her bag and headed out the door. "I was like a recovering alcoholic," she said. "I don't know about tomorrow but just today I'm going."

Then, after a month, something magical kicked in. Going to the gym in the morning became automatic. It had become a habit. It was embedded in her subconscious. She had nailed one of the most powerful tools for human development that we have in our inner software arsenal.

She had formed a good habit. It takes motivation to start us, but it takes a habit to keep us going.

Bad habits are easy to do, easy to be faithful to, and extremely hard to break. Good habits are hard to do, hard to be faithful to, and extremely easy to break.

Aristotle once said: "Excellence is not an act, but a habit".

According to award-winning New York Times business reporter Charles Duhigg's *The Power of Habit*, it turns out that every habit starts with a psychological pattern called a "habit loop," which is a three-part process.

1. Trigger Automatic Mode

First, there's a trigger that tells your brain to go into automatic mode and let a behaviour unfold.

2. Routine. The Daily Behaviour

Then there's the routine, which is the behaviour itself. That's what we think about when we think about habits.

3. The Reward. The Habit Loop. The Feel Good Factor Afterwards

The third step is the reward; something that your brain likes that helps it remembers the "habit loop" in the future. The feel-good factor afterwards.

The English poet John Dryden puts it this way: "We first make our habits, and then our habits make us".

This lady I mentioned put in 28 days going to the gym and made a new habit. Now this new habit is making her very happy and excited with a feel-good factor that lasts all day.

Can you make a similar habit around your life? If you make it, it will make you. Dump the backpack of "If onlys."

Replace them with "What ifs." Now, what if you just started tomorrow morning?

RED PLATFORM: Dying without ever having really lived. Trapped in bad habits. Lots of "If onlys."

GREEN PLATFORM: Making excuses to make it happen. Starting a life-changing good habit. Lots of "What ifs."

6

Discovering The Fun Factor In Your Life

A DOCTOR in the US gave me an amazing statistic when I met up with him a few years ago. He told me that every month he sees 300 patients and asks each of them the same question: "Have you been having any fun recently?"

He faithfully records an answer scoreboard ... 299 times a month so far he receives the same answer. "Nah, just working."

But not having fun? Just one out of 300 having fun? How did we get it all so wrong? Seemingly, it's the same with exercise. I met another man who was really fit. He had a well-sculpted body but he didn't look that happy. I was chatting with him about his training regime and here's what he said: "I don't really like lifting weights but I love the results of doing those things."

He didn't enjoy doing the workouts; he endured them. He was totally missing the point that the real joy is in the journey, in every step of the journey, not the destination. It's in not succumbing to destination addiction.

That evening while in the US I got an email from a lady who had read one of these columns. She, too, seemed to be missing the fun and the joy on her exercise journey.

She wrote: "Three months ago I joined a gym and was doing quite well with the treadmill and weights. Then I decided that for some variety I would go to classes — kettlebells, Pilates, step aerobics and spinning.

The classes are full of extremely fit people who make me feel bad about myself. In every class I go to I'm the worst in it, even after attending them consistently for a number of weeks. The difference between me and the others is so vast I'm close to giving up."

First of all comparisons are odious. We should never compare, because we usually compare ourselves negatively with other people. The problem with comparison is that you always feel either better than someone else or worthless in comparison. If we compare, we should only do it to model someone else's good points.

"Be yourself," Oscar Wilde said, "because everyone else is already taken."

But to be yourself in a world where everyone else is hell-bent on making you somebody else is one of the toughest battles you'll ever fight. You don't want to be better than anyone else. You just want to be better today than you were yesterday. Compare yourself with your previous self. It's not how good you are compared to anyone else; it's how good you are compared with how good you could be. It's a case of finding your unique hidden untapped potential.

Secondly, the key to any form of self-improvement comes with self-acceptance first. The Green Platform formula is: Acceptance + Positive Action Now (PAN). Without the positive action, acceptance could easily degenerate into indifference or apathy.

Self-acceptance comes before self-improvement. First and foremost, you must accept and love yourself as you are.

Another woman had a question for me recently: "I get up at five every morning, I go for a half hour jog down by the river, I come back and I do 15 minutes Pilates, then I meditate for 20 minutes. Next I have a very healthy breakfast ... now why am I not happy?"

When I explained to her that self-acceptance comes before self-improvement, then she got it. She kept postponing happiness until she got to this ideal picture of herself that she had in her mind.

If you don't love yourself when you are 180 pounds, there isn't a chance you'll love yourself when you are 150 pounds. Most of us live one of the commandments back-ways. "Love your neighbour instead of yourself."

There's a huge difference between taking good care of yourself, accepting yourself and being selfish. Change the story in your head. Your energy will follow your story. Why are you making up a story that makes you feel bad when you can make up a story that makes you feel good?

Change the way you look at things and the things you look at change. It's an inside job. If an egg is broken from the outside, life ends; but if an egg is broken from the inside, then life begins. All real and lasting change comes from the inside and works its way out. Go back to the gym and have fun. If you go for a run, make sure it's a fun run.

And if you really want to have fun exercising, remember what Mark Twain once said: "Comparison is the death of joy."

RED PLATFORM: Comparing yourself negatively to everyone else. Ensuring "the death of joy."

GREEN PLATFORM: Accepting yourself and striving to be better today than you were yesterday. Taking yourself lightly and having some fun.

7

A Great Body Of Work

YOUR body is the most amazing gift you've ever received. There is an amazing intelligence that runs your body. You have a heart that pumps over two gallons of blood a minute, over 100 gallons an hour. It pumps over 100,000 times a day through 60,000 miles of blood vessels. It pumps over three billion times in a lifetime without any stops for repair or time out.

Scientific studies show that you replace 98 per cent of all atoms in your body in less than one year. You make a new liver every six weeks. You make a new skeleton every three months. Your make a new stomach lining every five days. You make new skin once a month. Even the brain cells that you think with now weren't there last year.

Some time ago scientists asked the Dali Lama if they could borrow eight of his monks to do a mind-body experiment. These were monks who had completed over 40,000 hours of meditation. Then they got a group of 'ordinary' people to do the same test. They used an EEG to scan their brains so that they could see what was happening on a computer.

They asked the monks to "pay attention to compassion." Immediately their frontal lobes (the seat of emotions and judgments related to sympathy — also the happiness part of the brain to the left) lit up like Christmas trees.

They asked the other group to do something similar, but nothing happened. Ordinary people normally focus on three things:

1. The body — that pain in my back
2. The environment — this room is too stuffy
3. The time — how long more before we can get out of here?

When Dr Joseph Dispenza studied people who got remissions from life threatening diseases, he found a number of things in common with all of them.

1. An Intelligence, A Force That Loves You More Than You Love Yourself

First, they all believed that within them there's an intelligence that gives life to every human being, some mind greater than their mind, a force much greater than themselves that loves them more than they love themselves.

2. Change Attitude. Change Thinking. Leading From Their Minds

The second was that they all decided afterwards to change their attitude, their thinking. They now understood that our thoughts create chemicals in our bodies. Happy thoughts, happy molecules. Unhappy thoughts, unhappy molecules.

If you think you're insecure, you'll feel insecure. Then the loop begins to spin. You begin to think the way you feel. That's disaster.

Feeling becomes a way of thinking. The tail starts wagging the dog. The body is now determining your thinking based on how it's feeling. You wake up in the morning feeling bad and through the day this bad feeling is on a roll and by day's end, you begin to believe the feeling. Your body convinces you.

The body should serve the mind but with most of us the mind is serving the body. We're putting the cart before the horse. Now those in Dr Dispenza's study were determined to lead from their minds and not just react to feelings coming from their bodies.

3. A Wish To Reinvent Themselves. Positive Questions To Change The Inner Landscape of Their Brain

The third thing they all had in common was that they wanted to reinvent themselves. They started asking new positive questions:

- What would it be like to be a happy person?
- What would I have to change about myself to live with joy?
- Who in history do I most admire who was really great?

When they scanned the brains of those people when they were asking those empowering questions, guess what part of the brains lit up? The frontal lobes, the happiness parts, just like in the monks' brains.

They found that repeatedly asking these positive empowering questions actually rewired their brains and changed the feelings in their bodies. They literally reprogrammed their bodies. They changed the physical inner landscape of their brains.

What would a body manual say? You have a mind to control your body, not the other way around.

Keep asking questions like: "What would it be like to live with joy today?"

"How can I fuel every moment with the best that's in me now?"

"How can I choose more actions that bring joy to others?"

Eat good nutritious food. Get enough sleep. Take lots of exercise and, oh yes, lead from your mind and don't just react to feelings coming from your body. Your mind is the dog that wags the tail, not the other way around.

RED PLATFORM: No Inner Loving Force or Intelligence. Body leading, with feelings leading thoughts. Staying stuck in the same rut. Tail (body) wagging the dog (mind).

GREEN PLATFORM: Powerful Loving Inner Force of Intelligence. Mind leading with thoughts leading feelings. Mind controlling the body. Reinventing and renewing yourself always with positive questions. Dog (mind) wagging (body) tail.

8

A Strange Kind Of Magic

OVER weekends when I am working in the US, a small group of us gather at six o'clock on Saturday mornings out in the Keeneland horse park in Lexington, Kentucky. Then we run together for about an hour.

Now when I say, 'run', we are no Usain Bolts. We may be slow but we're still running rings around those who are lying in their beds or sitting on their couches at that hour.

When we finish our run we always feel fantastic. It's one more morning we've conquered ordinary human sloth. We then head for breakfast (in our running gear) to a country coffee shop, and for an hour or so we share great stories that generate much laughter.

It's a magical time. Everyone is full of serotonin and on a runner's endorphin high by nine o'clock.

They say that it takes 17 muscles to smile and 43 muscles to frown. While the jury is still out on the exact levels of that statement, there's no doubt about the benefits to your body of a genuine smile or spontaneous laughter. It's also a very inexpensive way to improve your looks.

Some time ago, one of the professors at Harvard University invited 132 students into a room and got them to wear the technological gear to measure the responses in their bodies to various stimuli. At the same time in another room there were video screens to measure these responses coming from the students' bodies.

When they got students thinking positively, their immune

systems were boosted. When they were thinking negatively, their immune systems plummeted. Then they tried another experiment. They got them all to watch a movie of Mother Teresa working with the poor in Calcutta. The students were from many different faith traditions and some with no faith tradition at all. While they were watching the movie all of their immune systems were boosted. Just seeing love in action was enough to deliver the boost. The people at Harvard call this the 'Mother Teresa Effect.'

The positive effect of kindness on the immune system and on the increased production of serotonin in the brain has been proved in research studies. Serotonin is a naturally occurring substance in the body that makes us feel more comfortable, peaceful and, in general, happier.

They discovered that a simple act of kindness directed towards another person improves the functioning of the immune system and stimulates the production of serotonin in both the recipient of the kindness and the person doing the act of kindness.

Even more amazing is that persons observing the act of kindness have similar serotonin boosting beneficial results. Kindness extended, received, or observed beneficially impacts the physical health and positive feelings of everyone involved.

Kindness is a win-win-win scenario for the giver, the receiver and the observer. They call it the 'Helper's High.'

Now back to the Harvard experiment where they found that the biggest boost to their immune systems came from genuine laughter. If you want to really increase your levels of this happiness serotonin, then combine your laughter with exercise.

In numerous studies, exercise like running, swimming and cycling has been shown to increase both the production and the release of serotonin.

Interestingly, though, if you do too much exercise or feel forced into doing it, it may not have the right effect.

The fact that you're proactively choosing to exercise changes its neurochemical effect. This may be a result of our ancient hunting instincts. There's a huge difference between running because you're hunting something for your supper, or running because something's hunting you because you for their supper.

The biggest problem with exercise is that when people don't feel like doing it, they don't do it. That's normally because their serotonin levels are low. "When I feel better about myself, I'll go out and do it." No, go out for that run or walk, and then you'll feel better about yourself.

So it's important to go against what you're feeling at the moment, and remind yourself of the benefits of that boost of happiness serotonin by taking your daily exercise, doing an act of kindness or laughing with good friends until the tears run down your cheeks.

RED PLATFORM: When I feel better about myself I'll go out and do it. Few friends. No acts of kindness. Not much conversation. No fun.

GREEN PLATFORM: Go out and do it and you'll feel better about yourself. Many acts of kindness. Great conversations with great friends. Lots of laughter.

9

Hard Work — The Most Underrated Talent

SOME years ago I gave a presentation to a group of young U-16 Leinster hurlers in Croke Park along with some star players such as Eddie Brennan, Jackie Tyrrell (both Kilkenny) and Wexford's Damien Fitzhenry. Afterwards there were questions from the floor for the three hurling legends.

One young hurler asked Jackie: "What is the secret of your success?" Jackie recalled what his father had told him when he was a young hurler aspiring to play on the great Kilkenny team. "Hard work will always beat talent when talent won't work hard," he recalled.

Hard work is at the heart of all great achievements. Every day, through our work, we get to invent and build and use our resources to create a world that our grandparents could never have imagined.

Through work our motorways are built, hay is saved, potatoes are planted, pigs are fed, cows are milked, dinners are cooked and cakes are baked. Through work the Mona Lisa was painted, Beethoven created beautiful music and we humans visited the moon. Through work we have the Internet, heart operations and ice cream 99s. Because people work, we have modern medicine, nutritious food and we can talk to and see people at the other side of the planet. There is tremendous dignity in human effort, in hard work. As George Bernard Shaw said: "I want to be thoroughly used up when I die, for the harder I work, the more I live."

As I write this column I'm on a train in France coming home to Ireland from the Alltech FEI World Equestrian games in Normandy. The amount of work that went into making the games such a huge success has been enormous. But then there's that massive satisfaction, that sense of achievement and that great feeling of a job well done on all the faces of these wonderful hard working people.

I was speaking to a former equestrian world champion. Remembering Jackie's answer, I asked her what was the secret of her success. She pondered the question for a while and then told me there were a number of things that had contributed to her becoming a world champion. She actually gave me nine things. She said that you must have:

1. An Inspiring Vision

You need to have an ability to see yourself as a champion. A clear and focused vision helps you not only to predict — but also to create reality. Without a goal you cannot score.

2. Hard Work

You cannot cheat the training routines or the horse won't consistently deliver peak performances.

3. Smart Work

An ability to work hard by all means, but above all work smart. What's giving you your greatest training leverage? Twenty per cent of the time we spend at training in the paddocks accounts for 80 per cent of what a horse will deliver in a competition. Be smart and focus like a laser beam on that 20 per cent of your training and preparation work that will deliver 80 per cent of your results.

4. Rest and Recovery

An understanding of the need to build in time for rest and recovery for both your horse and yourself.

5. Proper Nutrition
Recourse to eating nourishing, nutritious and healthy food. Both you and your horse have two 'engines' that both need top class fuel.

6. Positivity
Positivity and uplifting thoughts at all times. Have rhythmic inspiring mantras, affirmations or PowerTalk that you repeat to yourself.

7. Chemistry
You're a team like any team. You must trust your horse and your horse must trust you.

8. Confidence
Confidence rooted in your competence. Your competence comes from your hard work — your smart work.

9. A Dream
That lovely feeling of natural tiredness that comes from a hard day's work in the paddocks doing all the training. A feeling of being totally fulfilled as you chase the big inspiring dream. When is work really 'hard?' Work is really hard when you're working without an inspiring, motivating and compelling vision at what you don't love. When you do what you love and love what you do, when you do what makes your heart sing, you'll never work a day again in your life.

Your work makes a huge contribution to this small planet. In some small way, each of us contributes our energy, our talent and our skills to making life better for everyone.

In his book, *Players First*, legendary coach John Calipari says to his new Kentucky Wildcats players: "You tell me you want to be challenged. Okay, I'm going to do that. Every single day. Playing for me is going to be the hardest thing you've ever done."

He added: "You've got to love the grind. Embrace the work, Embrace the pain."

Coach Cal's approach is very similar to that of Muhammad Ali. "I hated ever minute of training but I said: 'Don't quit. Suffer now and live the rest of your life as a champion.'"

If hard work will always beat talent when talent won't work hard, imagine what happens when you work hard, you work smart and you combine that with your natural unique talent.

RED PLATFORM: Talented but lazy. Busy fool. Headless chicken. Wallowing in the 80 per cent trivial tasks that deliver few results.

GREEN PLATFORM: Clear vision of success and hard smart work focused on the vital few 20 per cent tasks that deliver real results.

10

Shape And Sculpt Your Day

DOES a day happen to you, or do you happen to a day? Does life happen to you, or do you happen to life?

There was a sculptor who knew how to look at a block of marble and see a statue within the marble. Instantly he knew what he had to chip to release the statue trapped inside.

He admired Michelangelo. He remembered once reading that when Michelangelo was asked how he carved his beautiful statue of David, he replied: "I just saw David in that lump of marble without blemish, and all I did was remove everything that was not David."

This sculptor knew how not only to sculpt and shape a piece of marble but also how to sculpt and shape his day. He fully understood how his freedom to choose either the Green Platform or the Red Platform also shaped his day for better or for worse. This is his morning self-talk.

• Today on the Red Platform I can complain because the weather is rainy or I can be thankful on the Green Platform that the grass is getting watered for free. My choice.

• Today I can feel sad on the Red Platform that I don't have more money or I can be glad on the Green Platform that my finances encourage me to plan my purchases wisely and guide me away from waste. My choice.

• Today I can grumble on the Red Platform about my health or I can rejoice on the Green Platform that I am alive and that I can take exercise and become fit. My choice.

• Today I can lament like an "Energy Vampire" on the Red

Platform over all that my parents didn't give me when I was growing up, or I can feel grateful on the Green Platform that they allowed me to be born. My choice.

• Today I can cry on the Red Platform because roses have thorns or I can celebrate on the Green Platform that thorns have roses. My choice.

• Today I can mourn my lack of friends on the Red Platform or I can excitedly discover new relationships on the Green Platform. My choice.

• Today I can whine on the Red Platform because I have to go to work or I can shout for joy on the Green Platform because I have a job to do. My choice.

• Today I can complain because I have to go to school on the Red Platform or eagerly open my mind and fill it with rich new knowledge on the Green Platform. My choice.

• Today I can murmur dejectedly on the Red Platform because I have to do housework or I can feel honoured on the Green Platform because I have a house to work in. My choice.

• Today stretches ahead of me, waiting to be shaped. And here I am, the sculptor who gets to do the sculpting and the shaping. What today will be like is up to me. I get to choose what kind of day I will have. I can shape my day. I can sculpt my day. My choice.

What'll you choose to do with today? When you plan your day, when you shape and sculpt your day, make sure you start on the Green Platform and build in some exercise. A jog. A swim. A bicycle ride. Or just a walk out in nature.

Make sure you happen to life; that you happen to your day. Choose to have a great day on the Green Platform.

RED PLATFORM: The day happens to you. You believe you don't have control. You complain that roses have thorns.

GREEN PLATFORM: You choose to sculpt and shape your day. You rejoice that thorns have roses.

11

Avoid Energy Vampires

A YOUNG boxer asked me recently: "Is there a cure for negativity?" Well, there is. It's all about flipping an inner switch. Making a choice.

Automatic Negative Thoughts (ANTs) come easily to us. They sting, hurt and thwart any possibility of us achieving our true potential. But we can flip that inner switch from ANTs to Positive Automatic Thoughts (PATs).

What pollution is on the outside, negativity is on the inside.

Negative people we meet are like Energy Vampires because they are constantly knocking everybody and everything around them. You know these people. It's not their bad breath or their body odour, but their non-stop whining and complaining.

Look up from your desk or across the yard and I bet you see one in your line of vision. Just become aware of who are the whingers, the complainers and blamers around you. Generally, we are so immersed and surrounded by negativity that we're not even aware of it. It's like our normal default mode.

There are two kinds of such negative Energy Vampires. One is internal and the other is external. Internally, that negative voice of our inner Energy Vampire insists: "You're not good enough. You'll never make it; give up. They'll only laugh at you if you try that."

Then there is the toxic external Energy Vampires who also keep knocking you. They suck energy from you like a vacuum cleaner. Our inner Energy Vampire starts early in the morning. "That's a dreadful day."

What's really dreadful is the negative story you've told yourself in your head. The day has its own energy. As the Scandinavian saying goes: "There's no such thing as bad weather, there is only inappropriate clothing."

It's important to remember once again that your subconscious is your unquestioning slave and won't process the words 'not,' 'don't,' 'instead of,' or 'without.' It just goes like a laser beam for the picture or image, and the emotion contained with the picture.

"Don't think of a white elephant," and there's the white elephant. Now watch how, even in our everyday greetings, we condition ourselves to be negative with these automatic autosuggestions.

"How are you doing?"

"Not so bad."

Bad.

"Could be worse."

Worse.

"Hanging in there."

Hanging? By what? Your fingernails.

"Can't complain."

Complain.

"Surviving."

But not flourishing.

"Keeping the wolf from the door."

Ravaging wolf at the door.

"Keeping the head over water."

Drowning.

"Two steps ahead of the hearse."

At death's doorstep.

"Ah, sitting up and eating a bit."

Sick, the hospital bed image.

I met an old man recently.

"How are you today, Mick?"

"Ah, sure the worms are winking up at me now."

How often do you hear people saying instead?

"Great."

"Wonderful."

"Fantastic."

You cannot say "great" with emotion and feel bad.

So if you have a job to do, do it with positive uplifting people.

These people are not Energy Vampires. They are Energy Transformers. They affirm people in their gifts in a way that is specific, genuine and sincere. They continually catch people doing things right. They shine a light on what is right. These Energy Transformers see the light in others before they see it in themselves and treat them as if that is all they see.

You are the average of the five people you hang out with.

Make a list of your five friends. Are they positive or negative? Put a plus or a minus beside each name.

If you have five minuses you need a new set of friends.

If you eat food from the fridge that's gone off, and you vomit all over the floor, do you put that toxic food back in the fridge and say: "Oh, I'll have another good feed of that tomorrow as you wipe up the floor."

No, you throw it in the bin. You protect yourself. If you are bleeding you don't go swimming with the sharks. You protect yourself. If you are walking on a roof you don't step off it to test gravity and see whether or not it's still working. You protect yourself.

Then why do you work with toxic people who will fill your head with belittling remarks, put you down at every turn and poison your performance?

Protect yourself.

A friend got very excited the other day showing me a text he'd received. It was about a mutual friend in hospital who was breathing with the aid of a machine.

The text simply said: "Great news, John. He took two breaths on his own today."

What a text to get. The one sure way to cure negativity I told the young boxer, was to focus on gratitude because gratitude and negativity cannot co-exist. You cannot be truly thankful and negative at the same time.

How many breaths did you take on you own today? That alone could kick-start your attitude of gratitude and instantly banish the energy-draining ANTs and replace them with energy transforming PATs.

RED PLATFORM: Energy Vampires: Two steps ahead of the hearse. Sitting up and eating a bit. The worms are winking up at me now. Poison ANTs.

GREEN PLATFORM: Energy Transformers: Fantastic. Great. Wonderful. Energising PATs. The best.

12

Catching The Whole Of The Moon

MY work takes me regularly to Lexington, Kentucky, in the United States and on one of my visits Dr Pearse Lyons invited me to a live recording of the famous Woodsongs Radio Hour. It was a one-off broadcast dedicated to the work of the poet W.B. Yeats. Dr Lyons was a special guest on the show and he recited *The Lake Isle of Innisfree*.

The Waterboys were the other special guests and they sang many of Yeats's poems, which their lead singer, Mike Scott, had turned into beautiful songs.

They also sang one of their former hits: "The Whole of the Moon." They got a fantastic reception from the audience. "I saw the crescent, but you saw the whole of the moon." The lyrics of that song kept playing around in my head all week. They really nailed the two sides of the struggle that all of us face as we strive for success, victory and happiness. Most of us see and achieve only the crescent, but not the whole of the moon and then we wonder why we're not happy. The crescent alone will never deliver happiness.

The great tennis player Andre Agassi was utterly frustrated with achieving the crescent, which he mistook for the whole of the moon. "What the hell is wrong with me ... I'm the number one tennis player on earth, and yet I feel empty ... I've had the wrong goals," he says in his autobiography *Open*. He continued: "I've been let in on a dirty little secret. Winning changes nothing."

External achievement, in and of itself, will not and cannot fill the basic needs we have as human beings.

What did Agassi mean by "I've had the wrong goals?" We can chase dreams, goals, titles and achievement, but real goal achievement has to ask and answer the fundamental question: "Who do you become, what kind of a person do you become as a result of your goal achievement, of winning the title, of lifting the cup?"

Are you a happier, healthier, more creative, joyful, innovative, contributing-to-humanity goal achiever, or are you a tired, cranky, empty, fatigued, black-eyed, sleep-deprived selfish clod of a goal achiever? Who do you become in the process of achieving your goals and your dreams? Who have you become as a person as a consequence of the chase?

If, in fact, success did breed happiness, then Andre should have been the poster boy for happiness. The fact was he gained no real pleasure or peace from all his celebrated tennis achievements. He even tried to force-feed himself happiness with his self-talk: "I tell myself you can't be unhappy when you have money in the bank and own your own plane."

Then in 1997 he fell to number 141 ranking in the world. He tried crystal meth, failed a drug test and then lied about it. At his lowest he decided to reinvent himself and dump the "wrong goals." He had enough of the crescent. Now he was going for the whole of the moon. He wanted new goals that would sustain him regardless of whether or not he ever won another Grand Slam or tournament.

Here's what he came up with: "This is the only perfection there is. The perfection of helping others. This is the only thing that we can do that has any lasting value or meaning. This is why we're here. To make each other feel safe."

When Andre dedicated his tennis to helping others feel safe, a transformation occurred. The game he hated became a priceless gift. He started a school for disadvantaged children and since then he has raised over $60 million to create the space where those children can grow, flourish and become fully alive as they achieve their hidden potential. He had come up with a way to leverage his tennis, money and fame for a worthwhile purpose, a caring cause, and a meaningful "why." He was still playing tennis, but with a completely different mind-set.

In 1998 he bounced back with a new conditioning programme and new purpose that was about using tennis to make a difference in the lives of the most vulnerable children. He ended 1999 as the number one ranked player in the world. He had found his 'why,' his burning desire, his passionate and powerful purpose and now he could achieve any 'how.'

He discovered that nothing in the world can make us happy, but everything in the world can encourage us to be happy.

He discovered that happiness breeds success, and not the other way around.

He discovered that happiness in not in *things*, it's in you and in your relationships and friendships.

He discovered that the happiest people don't *have* the best of everything; they just *make* the best of everything.

He discovered that happiness is not getting what you want; it's wanting what you get.

He discovered that happiness is a by-product that comes from helping others. The 'pursuit' of happiness is a myth; happiness 'ensues' as you set out to make somebody else's life better.

As Viktor Frankl says: "Don't aim at success. The more you aim at it and make it a target, the more you are going to miss it. For success, like happiness, cannot be pursued; it must ensue, and it only does so as the unintended side effect of one's personal dedication to a cause greater than oneself or as the by-product of one's surrender to a person other than oneself." Happiness "ensues".

In a speech following his final match at the US Open in September, 2006, Andre said: "The scoreboard says I lost today, but what the scoreboard doesn't say is what I've found. Over the past 21 years I've found loyalty, inspiration, generosity and I've found you. I'll take you and the memory of you with me for the rest of my life."

More importantly, he found himself through using his incredible tennis talents to help vulnerable children feel safe. He had discovered not just the crescent, but also the whole of the moon.

Are you living in the crescent or are you finding the whole of the moon through reaching out and helping the vulnerable ones in whatever way you can?

If you are, you are like Andre seeing "the whole of the moon." You'll also discover that you are bit by bit becoming a host to happiness.

RED PLATFORM: "Winning changes nothing. You can't be unhappy when you have money in the bank and own your own plane."

GREEN PLATFORM: "The perfection of helping others. This is the only thing that we can do that has any lasting value or meaning. This is why we're here. To make each other feel safe."

13

What Gets Measured
Gets Done

WHAT'S the most important task of a newspaper boss every day?" an editor once asked students at a journalism college.

"To break news stories."

"To get everything right, to be accurate."

"To be fair."

"To make sure there are no typos."

Through each answer he drew a line. Finally, when their guesses were exhausted, he gave his answer.

"It's simple. It says it right here on the front page." He then picked up the newspaper, and pointed to a small word under the masthead.

It said simply: "Daily".

"It means you promise this paper will be there every morning when people wake up. Daily. That's the biggest and first promise you make to readers. That's the one thing you can't compromise on. And if any of these other things get in the way of that," he said, and pointed to their rejected answers: "They have to go."

"And so, your job as an editor is this: Put out the best paper you can in the time you have."

This is something we all struggle with, no matter what we're doing. 'Daily,' is absolutely the key word to apply to your own life. They say that motivation doesn't last. Neither does a shower or a bath. You need to take one or the other daily. Motivation is the same. We need to motivate ourselves daily. It's motivation that starts us but it takes a habit to keep us going.

What separates the winners from the losers, the fit from the unfit, the healthy from the unhealthy is that the winners have a habit of taking daily action to achieve their goals.

When I lived in Taiwan learning the Chinese language was a huge challenge for me.

To get mentally ready for the daily encounter with new words, tones and characters I used to go for a 30-minute run every morning. I called it the long way around to the shower.

I told myself that I didn't deserve a shower unless I was sweating. The shower was the reward for the wake-up run. My brother Vincent used to always say: "You should sweat at least once every day, but never out of fear."

If you want to live your dreams, you must also start taking 'daily' action. If one of your goals is physical fitness, make a commitment to do some sort of exercise — walking, bicycle riding, jogging, running, swimming, weight training, or stretching — every day for a minimum of 20 minutes.

If you simply went for a 30-minute walk four times a week, that would put you in the top one per cent of those people getting exercise.

Then make your exercise trend your friend. You don't need a crystal ball or special powers to predict the future if you have the courage to track and monitor a few key daily exercise trends.

Human beings tend or 'trend' to gain weight. If you've gained a pound a year for several years, it's not difficult to predict your future waistline. It's a trend. Most things in life change along observable and predictable trend lines.

Years ago, the famed management expert, W. Edward Demming, noted: "What gets measured, gets done."

When we track our exercise and put the graph where we will see it everyday, things improve. When we 'wish' or 'hope' or 'try' to change things, but refuse to document the data, our results seldom live up to our desires.

What gets measured does, in fact, get done. Then when the graph begins to show a trend — either upward or downward — we can begin to predict the future.

One of the most powerful positive motivational techniques for people is when they can see and measure their progress.

Get the habit of 'daily action' into your exercise trend or your work trend and then make that trend your lifelong friend. You'll then be really living the mantra of the great psychologist and pharmacist Émile Coué de La Châtaigneraie: "Every day in every way, I'm getting better and better." (Tous les jours à tous points de vue je vais de mieux en mieux.)

Not some days. Every day. 'Daily.'

RED PLATFORM: No measurement. Yo-yo up and down inconsistent graph with overall downward trend.

GREEN PLATFORM: Daily small incremental pattern of improvements. Upward trend. Able to see, measure and be encouraged by your progress.

14

A Daily Mile Makes Children Smile

WE'VE got some stark reminders recently about the state of fitness of the modern world. In Ireland, some 61 per cent of us adults are overweight or obese and what's worse is that our children are catching up fast.

Twenty two per cent of children between the ages of five and 12 are obese. Obviously the answer must be that we're getting fatter.

Years ago, children ran in woods, played in parks or threw down four coats in a field and made a football pitch. They would then play football or hurling for hours on end. As Barney Garry used to say where I grew up, in Dungimmon: "You'd hear the thump of a ball across the fields and you'd be gone to join in." Somebody had a football. It was magnetic. It was magic.

It was a time of pure joy, fun and excitement. Now children sit at home and play video games by themselves or maybe with the child next door ... while still sitting in their own homes.

We were born to run, hunt and gather but now we sit in our caves eating lots of cheap, fast, sugar-filled processed foods watching flickering screens.

Where do healthy bodies fit into our education system?

We are at the bottom of the European league for physical education in primary schools. The recommended time for PE in Irish primary schools is an amazing, astonishing one-hour per week. Compare our PE time of 37 hours per year with that of France, which devotes 108 hours per year to PE.

In years to come, can you imagine the cost of this madness in terms of heart disease, obesity and diabetes, on the country's health system?

The bias towards academic education at the cost of physical education makes no sense at all. Have they never heard that a healthy body makes a healthy mind? "Anima sana in corpore sano."

We need to begin to motivate ourselves to take regular exercise and eat nutritious food. One by one we can motivate each other. We also need to put the structures in place to enable us to take exercise or change the structures that are already there. There's no point in putting a 6' 5" man in a three feet square cage and then tell him to go for a run, have a swim and take lots of exercise. There is a built-in bias against exercise in the structure, the cage.

Nor is there any point in bemoaning children's obesity when we have powerful anti-exercise structures in place in our schools and in our homes.

We have to create the structures and the space where these children can exercise, flourish and grow — and not just academically, but physically as well. We need to educate the whole person: body, mind and spirit.

I remember one day when Fionn, our second eldest was in primary school. I dropped by the school with something he had forgotten. Lunch or a book or something. I found him sitting on the wall in the process of being punished. His crime. He had been caught running in the schoolyard. It had something to do with some draconian insurance law.

Compare Fionn's experience with this one from a school in Scotland. As soon as the children at St Ninian's primary school in Stirling hear the words 'daily mile,' they down their pencils and head out of the classroom to start running laps around the school field.

For three-and-a-half years, all pupils at St Ninian's primary have walked or run a mile each day. They do so at random times during the day, apparently happily, and despite the rise in childhood obesity across the United Kingdom, none of the children at the school are overweight.

Elaine Wyllie, head teacher of St Ninian's, said: "I get at least two emails a day from other schools and local authorities asking how we do it. The thought of children across the country running every day because of something we've done is phenomenal."

It makes sense, doesn't it?

"It's a common sense approach to children's fitness, which is free and easy. The most important thing is that the children really enjoy it. Otherwise you couldn't sustain it. They come back in bright-eyed and rosy-cheeked, how children used to look. It's joyous to see," said Wyllie.

Obesity is the plague of our times.

Ireland's then Minister for Health Leo Varadkar said recently. "Let me say at the outset: overweight and obesity are a major and a serious personal and public health issue. It is of great concern to me that a quarter of three-year-olds are overweight or obese. Obesity affects all sections of society in Ireland. There is no other disease or medical condition that affects so many people in Ireland... It is estimated that overweight and obesity levels have doubled within the last 20 years and according to the latest projections from the World Health Organisation (WHO) the situation is likely to get worse. The cost of obesity to the Irish Health Services is estimated to be €1.13 billion. As well as the financial cost, there is also personal and societal cost.

People's self-esteem is generally lower; children may be bullied and their mental health is affected. People with chronic diseases are likely to retire early, have poorer health or die early. In terms of loss of productivity, it is a burden on industry."

Each one of us needs to take personal action. A walk. A jog. A run. A swim. Even 10 minutes a day. Then we need the communal team project. We need to set up running clubs, walking clubs or swimming clubs or join a football, hurling or rugby club.

But most of all we need the political will to change the minds of the powers-that-be who run our education system and demand that they give more time to PE in our schools and get us off the disgraceful bottom rung of the European league of PE in schools.

Then maybe there's a real chance that our children that instead of getting fatter, our children will get fitter.

RED PLATFORM: Sit down at a desk all day. Silently, slowly and steadily increase levels of obesity.

GREEN PLATFORM: Build in a daily mile and watch the children get fit and smile.

15

Bouncing Back
To A New You

O NE of the toughest times in anyone's life is when he or she gets an injury. A very good friend had just completed six workouts in a new gym. He felt fantastic.

He was running home in the rain when he tripped and smashed the side of his head against the footpath. The impact shattered both of his jaws. He somehow managed to walk home with blood pumping from his mouth.

After losing a lot of blood and spending long hours in the waiting rooms of two different hospitals he finally had an operation to set his broken jaws.

He's had two plates inserted for life on both sides of his face and a wisdom tooth extracted to help realign his teeth. In one moment his exercise regime and indeed his life faced a fairly large transformation.

How do you bounce back from something like that?

You can either be a rubber ball and bounce back up, or be an egg and go splat.

You're only defeated when you don't get back on your feet. The only failure is staying down. Failure is the fuel to get it right next time. There is no such thing as failure, only feedback. Only those who give up are defeated. Everyone else is victorious.

A man called W. Mitchell inspired my friend in his predicament. In 1971 Mitchell had a horrific motorbike accident in San Francisco when a laundry truck made a sudden turn in front of him. The cap flew off the bike's petrol tank, spewing petrol all over him and he became "a human bonfire."

It burned 65 per cent of his body. His face and hands were badly scarred and his fingers were horrifically burned. In fact he lost most of them.

What did he do? Did he go into "woe is me" mode? Far from it. He bounced back and instead of a riding a motorbike, he became a pilot and learned to fly an airplane.

Then in 1975 he crashed on take off in a small plane he was piloting and injured his spinal cord, leaving him paralysed from the waist down.

Once again he bounced back, and he now travels the world in his wheelchair giving motivational speeches. He insists that in life it's not what happens that matters, but how you respond to what happens.

"What I focus on in life is what I get," he says.

"If I concentrate on what's bad, what's wrong, how inadequate I am and on what I can't do — isn't that what I'm going to get every time?

But when I think about how powerful I am, and what I have left to contribute, and how I can make a difference in this life, isn't that what I am going to get back? You see I recognise that it's not what happens to you; it's what you do about it that really matters."

When bad things happen to good people, they don't ask: "Why me, what did I do to deserve this?"

Their Green Platform response formula is: Acceptance + Positive Action Now (PAN). Of the 100 things I can do, what is the one positive thing I can do now that will make a difference?

Often we cannot control what happens, but we are totally in control of how we respond to what happens.

Circumstances do not make the person; they reveal the person. We are not responsible for other people's actions. But we are 100 per cent responsible for our reactions.

A young woman in the US told me recently about her friend who had given up smoking. Then she went back to smoking. Here's what the smoking woman said to the young woman: "My boyfriend left me and he made me go back on the cigarettes."

The young woman replied: "No, he didn't. It was totally your choice to go back on the cigarettes. Your choice only and only your choice."

To which her friend replied: "Yes, but I never saw it like that. While I was blaming him I didn't realise that all the time I had a choice and I was making my own choices. You're right. I made the choice to start smoking again. Now I am going to make the choice to give them up."

The power to choose is that great hidden power that we so often forget when we're in blaming mode.

We all get knocks in life; at home, in the workplace and in whatever sport or fitness regime we pursue. Really though, these are great opportunities disguised as impossible situations. In every misfortune lurks good fortune. You can do things you never thought you could do. There are no limitations in what you can do except the limitations of your own mind. In training courses I always ask people to look for three gifts in every so-called disaster. Interestingly enough, they always find them.

Success is not measured by what you accomplish, but by the setbacks you have encountered, and the courage with which you have maintained the struggle against overwhelming odds. It's all about your growth, character building and your development as a human being.

"Before I was paralysed," Mitchell says, "there were 10,000 things I could do. Now there are only 9,000. I can either focus on the 1,000 I have lost, or on the 9,000 I have left."

The key thing is to become aware of where you focus your thoughts and your feelings. Then the powerful question: "What do I do now with the 9,000 things I have left?"

My very good friend has recovered. He, too, is discovering the 9,000 things that he can still do and he's inspiring us all, every day in every way.

RED PLATFORM: Fall and go splat like an egg. Stay down. Focus on what's wrong, how inadequate you are and what you can't do.

GREEN PLATFORM: Fall and bounce back like a rubber ball. Focus on how powerful you are, what you can contribute and how you can make a difference.

16

Making The Best
Of What You Have

THEY say that there are those who make excuses and then there are those who make things happen.

That thought struck me after I encountered a man recently who told me he had given up exercise. He had an excuse to go along with it. "I'm too old for all that now," he said sadly.

He'd made a decision to fade out, not to burn out. I told him a story that thankfully changed his mind, and his body. And he's now back exercising and enjoying every moment of it.

You see, most of us live two lives. The first is the life we are living now where we are not that fit and not that healthy. The second is the unlived life within us. That's the life we could live if we were fit and healthy... but we keep it inside as a kind of pipedream.

Between these two lives stands the first of the 3-Rs of Success and Failure, namely 'Resistance'.

The Three 'Rs' are:
1. Resistance
2. Resourcefulness
3. Relationships

1. Resistance

Let's take a look at the first 'R' — Resistance. Have you ever joined a gym in January, gone for a week and then got so busy in your own mind that you could perfectly reason why you couldn't go anymore?

Or have you ever brought home a treadmill and let it gather dust in a spare room? What about going on a diet or a course of yoga, and then letting it slip after the initial enthusiasm wore off? Are you a writer who doesn't write, a painter who doesn't paint, an entrepreneur who never starts a new venture?

If so, then you know what resistance is. You're not alone. Many good men and women have been defeated by this first 'R'.

Resistance is about the self-sabotaging demons within us that cause so much self-belittling. It's the voice in our heads that forces us to doubt, fear and remain inactive during times when action is all that's required.

2. Resourcefulness

To take action let's look at the second 'R' — Resourcefulness. On November 18, 1995, the violinist Itzhak Perlman performed at the Lincoln Centre in New York City. He had polio as a child and walks with crutches.

The audience waited patiently as he made his way slowly across the stage to his chair, sat down, put his crutches on the floor, removed the braces from his legs, settled himself in his characteristic pose, one foot tucked back, the other pushed forward, bent down to pick up his violin, gripped it with his chin and nodded to the conductor to indicate that he was ready.

It was a familiar ritual for Perlman fans, the genius making light of his disability before his sublime music transcended everything.

But this time was different. Just as he finished the first few bars one of the strings on his violin broke. You could hear it snap. It went off like gunfire across the room. There was no mistaking what the sound meant... he now had a disabled violin.

It was obvious — he had to get another violin or restring his instrument.

He didn't.

He closed his eyes for a moment, and then signalled to the conductor to begin again. The audience was spellbound. Everyone thought it was impossible to play a symphonic work with just three strings. But that night Perlman refused to know that.

What actually happened was that he encountered the first 'R,' Resistance and immediately, he moved on to the second 'R', Resourcefulness.

He started to play again with passion, power and purity. You could see him modulating, changing and recomposing the piece in his head. At one point he sounded like he was de-tuning the strings to get sounds from them they had never made before.

When he finished there was an awed silence ... and then the audience rose as one.

The music critic, Jack Riemer recalls that amazing moment in 1995: "We were all on our feet screaming and cheering — doing everything we could to show him we appreciated what he had done.

"He smiled, wiped the sweat from his brow, raised his bow to quiet us, and then he said, not boastfully, but in a quiet, pensive reverent tone: 'You know sometimes it is the artist's task to find out how much music he can still make with what he has left.'"

3. Relationship

His relationship with the audience, the third 'R' made his resourcefulness possible.

My friend who thought he was too old to exercise found his three 'Rs' in Itzhak's story. He considers himself no longer 'retired,' but 'refired'.

Life is not happening to him. He's happening to life. He's not making excuses any more. He's making waves.

RED PLATFORM: Throw in the towel. Give up. Blame the broken strings. Make excuses.

GREEN PLATFORM: Be creative. Make it happen. Get curious. Be innovative with what you have left.

17

When Your 'Why' Powers Your 'How'

LAST year my friend Steve Bourne, from Stamford in England, decided he was going to run the London marathon. What motivated him to run over 26.2 miles around London? He explained that he had three major mental motivations that drove him on.

1. Purpose and Meaning

The first thing he said was putting "purpose or meaning" into his run. Not just to his own health and well-being but he also wanted to make a difference to thousands of children who were not able to run. So he picked a charity and decided he was going to raise funds through sponsorship with every step he would run.

His chosen charity in England was 'Get Kids Going' which was set up in 1997 with Sebastian Coe as its president. The charity raises funds that are used for equipment and support to give disabled children and young people up to the age of 26 the chance to take part — and even compete — in a wide variety of sports.

There are 200,000 youngsters who benefit from this charity in some way and some will have aspirations to compete at the level of Baroness Tanni Grey-Thompson, winning 11 gold medals in Paralympic wheelchair athletics in three consecutive Olympic Games.

Steve raised around £5,000 for his charity. In an email he said: "I would like to take the opportunity to share with you the experience of one of the most amazing days of my life.

"This year's London Marathon surpassed every expectation I could ever have had and even put the previous time in the shade, with crowds thronging the 26.2 miles and the noise and support unimaginable. Every runner and every charity represented must put this amongst their best days ever."

His £5,000 contribution will purchase "specially adapted wheelchairs that will make a massive difference to many children in many ways similar to a horse in Para Equestrian sport. It is really a great equaliser."

2. Positive Uplifting Encouragement

His second mental motivation came along every step of the marathon from the enthusiastic encouragement and support of the spectators who lined the route.

"Whatever you read in the papers or see on television simply does not do justice to the noise, the encouragement and cheering that the crowds provided to all us runners," said Steve.

"There's no doubt that some of my success and that of others was due to those spectators carrying us along the route. Having my name in big print on my T-shirt meant that I got extra encouragement."

3. A Personal Best — A Stretch Goal

His third mental motivation was to run the race in under 3 hours 30 minutes. That was his personal realistic but stretching goal. His finishing time, 3 hours 25 minutes and 14 seconds, meant he knocked almost five minutes off his personal goal time.

Steve's three personal motivational triggers cross over to any life or work challenge.

Do you have a powerful reason or 'why' for your upcoming challenge? Do you have a positive supportive team? Do you have a personal-best stretch goal?

RED PLATFORM: "There's no way I could ever run a marathon or achieve this huge life challenge."

GREEN PLATFORM: "I can not only run a marathon and achieve a personal best, but I can also help disabled children achieve their dreams. It's how I live my life."

18

Response Ability

W HO is really responsible for your personal health? If it is to be, it is up to ... ?"

Your doctor? Your husband? Your wife? Your children? Your parents? Your team manager? Your sister? Your brother? Your grandfather? Your grandmother?

No. You, and only you, are responsible for your own health and lifestyle. Perhaps the most important decision any person can make is the decision to take personal responsibility for their life.

Remember Pavlov and his dog? Every time Pavlov fed his pet juicy red meat, he'd ring a bell. After some time, all Pavlov had to do was ring the bell and the dog would salivate, drool and dribble.

Am I any different? Am I a bunch of predictable reflexes being triggered by people and events into predictable responses, or can I creatively and proactively choose my response? Am I a passive object of history or am I a creative subject of history?

I'm either in responsibility mode or I'm in blaming mode. When I'm in blaming mode, I'm a reactor. But don't we also pay a huge price for being reactors?

Alex Ferguson was a great Manchester United manager. I heard him giving an interview one time about a player who got a red card. He said: "The player who provokes or instigates the incident rarely gets a red card. The player who reacts, the reactor always gets the red card."

What Alex added was that the player who chooses his or her response when provoked in the heat of the moment is then free not to react, but to respond differently and really punish the perpetrator on the scoreboard where it matters.

This proactive response cannot happen when a player is sitting in the dressing room after an early shower thinking about a recently acquired red card and blaming the referee.

Did you ever watch or listen to children. Very early they lock on to this blaming mode. It's like an inbuilt gene chip.

"He started it."

"It wasn't me."

"It's all his/her fault."

Back to personal responsibility. It is you who have to live in your skin. This body you have is the only place you will ever live. You'll never live anywhere else. Your moment of choice is your moment of truth. It's the testing point of your character and competence. Your destiny is not a matter of chance. It's a matter of choice. When you make a choice you create the future. Decisions shape destiny. It is you alone who can choose to take the positive steps to bring well-being into your life.

I often talk to smokers and ask them: "Why don't you stop smoking?"

"Oh, you've got to die some way," they reply, more often than not with a cough.

They're avoiding taking responsibility for their lives. They're wasting away years and quality of life by continuing to smoke.

Fitness is a great goal in life yet only about one in 10 of us are doing enough about it. The resting heart rate is 60. Training between the 60 and 70 zone (long slow runs) improves the ability of your heart to pump blood and improve the muscles' ability to utilise oxygen. The body becomes more efficient at feeding the working muscles, and learns to metabolise fat as a source of fuel.

So how much longer will you choose to live a life of mediocrity, remaining unfit, out of shape and never achieving your goals? You have the power to change every aspect of your life.

Today.

You can change it all if you want. You can be the person you want to be — but only if you want it badly enough. So read the books, do the research, ride the bike, take the long walk, join the gym or do that job you've been postponing for so long. Go for it and don't stop until you reach your own health, fitness or work goals. Response-ability. You have the ability to choose your response, to make today your masterpiece and to make your life wonderful.

RED PLATFORM: I react to what happens and blame other people, events and situations for all that's wrong with my life. Life happens to me. It's all their fault.

GREEN PLATFORM: I proactively choose my response. I happen to life. I have personal response-ability. I'm totally responsible for how I choose to respond to what happens to me.

19

Finding Your Own True Grit

C AN you get fit and healthy without putting the work in? Can it be done without sweat? Is there a machine that will get you fit while you sit on the couch?

A man explained his thinking to me recently: "I have a routine every day I go through before my run. I come up with about 20 excuses not to go for my run. Not now. Maybe later. I have more important and urgent things to do now. Then I convince myself not to go for my run. Tomorrow will be better. That's my routine every day."

A real case of the urgent taking over from the important. Exercise is not urgent, but it is important. My friend illustrated how things that matter least get in the way of things that matter most.

One time I was invited to a beautiful graduation ceremony in Bailieborough Community School in Co Cavan. What struck me was that despite the fact that the students had achieved great sporting and academic achievements in the past year, there were no first prizes or second prizes or runners up.

Nobody was a nobody. Everybody was a somebody.

Everyone in the graduating class was made to feel special. The principal, Ms Martha Lievens, spoke about the simple launching pad to success in life: "Hard work with purpose and meaning in the service of others," she said. "Working hard at what you love and making your community and the world a better place."

Ms Lievens was on to something when she spoke about consistent hard work. Real fitness mastery can be a pain. Every year, 1,200 students from all over America come to the United States Military Academy at West Point, New York, to take the four-year course. But before they even see a classroom they go through seven weeks of what's officially called Cadet Basic Training, also known as the "Beast Barracks."

By the time the summer ends, one in 20 of these talented, dedicated young adults drops out. The academy brought some of the top researchers in the country to study the magical ingredient that took some students all the way to mastery and success while others simply dropped out?

What was it?

The best predictor of success, the researchers found, was the prospective cadets' rating on a non-cognitive, non-physical trait known at 'grit.' In another study the West Point 'grit' researchers found that grittiness rather than IQ or standardised test scores is the most accurate predictor of college grades.

They defined it as "Perseverance and passion for long-term goals." That's what they call it in West Point.

In Cavan they call it "Hard work with a purpose."

True grit.

This emphasis on perseverance and passion for long-term goals is in line with what political scientist Dr Edward Banfield of Harvard University wrote in a book in 1970 entitled *The Unheavenly City*.

He started off convinced that the answer to this question would be found in factors such as family background, education, intelligence, influential contacts, or some other concrete factor. What he finally discovered was that the major reason for success in life was a particular attitude of mind and that this was a "long time perspective."

Mastery can be a pain but again it's a good pain. Many characteristics that we once believed to be innate talent are actually the result of hard work. Mastery in sports, music or business always involves huge effort. Very often it means excruciating, painful, all-consuming persistent struggle and stamina.

If you don't believe this, ask Gerry Duffy to tell you about how he won the 2011 UK Deca Enduroman Ironman distance challenge, an event called: "The toughest 10-day endurance challenge in the world."

He certainly worked hard during the contest itself and he also put in the long hours of training and preparation. Sociologist Daniel F. Chambliss called this "the mundanity of excellence."

If you want to get fit and healthy it may just involve a bit of hard work or true grit. Smooth seas do not make skilful sailors. You cannot discover new oceans and lands unless you lose sight of the shore. Courage is not the absence of fear. It's doing what you're afraid to do in spite of the fear. You don't have to be great to get started but you have to get started to be great. Your true grit will make you great.

RED PLATFORM: Short term goals with no staying power. No real reason to persevere. Gutless. Clueless. Gritless. Must be great first and then start.

GREEN PLATFORM: Perseverance and passion for long-term goals. Hard smart work underpinned by a powerful purpose. Real true effort, stamina and grit. Start first and let greatness follow.

20

Regret Nothing

I N the film *On the Waterfront*, Marlon Brando as Terry says: "I coulda been a contender. I coulda been somebody ..."

Terry's one major regret was that he never fulfilled his boxing potential. Flying back from the US recently, I was sitting beside a woman in her sixties. She told me that she'd always wanted to see the world, but she confided that her husband "wouldn't let her".

Then she got this vision of the end of her life and what she called "her deathbed bag of regrets." So she decided to cut loose and see the world. Her husband agreed just so long as he didn't have to come on the journey with her. She was now living her dream.

It's a huge thing to die without regrets. A life fully lived is one that has discovered, usually through trial and error, what works and what doesn't. We then have a better sense of what's valuable and enduring, and what isn't.

An Australian nurse called Bronnie Ware worked several years in palliative care and routinely spent the last three to twelve weeks of her patients' lives with them. She listened to their dying stories and recorded them in a blog called 'Inspiration and Chai,' which she later compiled into a book. According to her, these were their five greatest dying regrets:

1. A Life True To Themselves
People wished they'd had the courage to live a life true to themselves, not the life others expected of them. This was the single most common regret in Ware's study.

2. Not Doing What They Loved

They wished they hadn't worked so hard at things they didn't love. This was about their work/life balance. No dying person has ever said: "My one regret is that I didn't spend more time at the office." Workaholics often sacrifice so much for so little. Especially quality time with their families.

3. Using The Voice They Were Born With

They would like to have had the courage to express their feelings and to use the voice they were born with to speak up when it was important. Speaking honestly either raises a healthy relationship to a higher level or eliminates an unhealthy one. Either way, you win.

4. Friends

They felt they should have made a bigger effort to stay in touch with their friends. Old friends are irreplaceable. Even golden friendships fade with inattention or neglect.

5. Allowing Happiness

They regretted not having allowed themselves to be happier. It's sad how many people only realise at the end of their lives that happiness is an inside job, an attitude and not a particular set of circumstances. Worry and regret can poison a life and diminish the only time you have to be happy right here, right now. For it's always the present moment, the 'now' that's the doorway to happiness.

When you come into this life you have one body. Your daily challenge is to keep it fit and healthy. You can't trade it in for a new and better model. This is it. Life is not a rehearsal. It is the real thing. As the poet Mary Oliver said: "Tell me what is it you plan to do with your one wild and precious life?"

No 'couldas,' or 'shouldas' like Terry. Be a contender now in the game of life. And then at the end of your life you can sing like Edith Piaf: "Non, je ne regrette rien ...!"

RED PLATFORM: Living a lie to yourself, being a pale second-rate imitation of somebody else. Working at a job you don't like. Going where you are merely tolerated.

GREEN PLATFORM: Being true to yourself, being happy doing what you love. Spending time with friends. Going where you are celebrated. "Non, je ne regrette rien …!"

21

Detach From The Outcome

IT was one of those beautiful days in the beginning of June over in England in the early morning (exam weather, I call it) when the grass was at its freshest, the trees were a resplendent kaleidoscope of different shades of green against a clear blue sky. My friend Alric was out playing golf with some of his friends who are actually golf professionals.

They were in a different golfing class, but almost instantly he slid down the slippery slope of comparison. Here's what he told those golfing pros in an email later that evening: "Guys, I guess I should say 'thank you' for totally embarrassing me on the golf course today. It is an absolute pleasure to see a sport such as golf played at such a high standard at close hand. In future... whenever I play you I will play my own game and not try to compete with you two as it gets me nowhere (but you know I'll never take any shots off you.)

"An observation: I have only known you both a year or so but I have to say when you are relaxed in your games, you play at such an incredibly high and different standard. It's very noticeable to me and to others. It also shows in your scoring."

In that paragraph he nailed the greatest sporting challenge of all time. To be "relaxed in your game," as my friend put it when there is a big prize at stake. These golfers play in the British Open and the top tournaments.

Their key mental challenge is this: "Can they bring this focus, relaxation and fun to the Open?"

The mental enemy is attachment to outcome.

The Chinese philosopher Zhuangzi (300 BC) explained the same idea with reference to the art of target shooting: "When an archer is shooting for nothing he has all his skill. If he shoots for a brass buckle he is already nervous. If he shoots for a prize of gold he goes blind or sees two targets and he is out of his mind.

His skill has not changed. But the prize divides him. He cares now about winning. He thinks more of winning than of shooting and the need to win drains him of power."

His attachment to the outcome caused him to lose the present, the now, and the moment.

Process and performance are lost in outcome addiction. The future fear-fuelled focus destroys the now. Fear and doubt replaces freedom and fun. Then the action in the now withers and shrivels and loses its free-flowing power.

I remember one time a manager had to give a presentation to GAA officials. His outcome or goal: To get a player off a red card. The red-carded player was really the victim in the particular circumstances. The manager had prepared very well. Video footage. The lot.

"Do you think I'll get him off this red card?" he said.

"It's really none of your business," I replied.

"What do you mean it's none of my business," he said. "I've travelled all the way to Dublin for this presentation and you tell me it's none of my business. Then you tell me, 'what is my business?'"

"Your business is to give this presentation your absolute best. That's all you can control. Whether or not he gets off the red card is the GAA's business, God's business, somebody else's business, but certainly not your business."

"Is that what you mean by detachment from outcome? Controlling only the controllables?"

"That's exactly it," I replied. "Detachment from outcome. You have to have an outcome first to detach from it, but then you put all your energy into the present moment action, into your presentation that's geared towards achieving that ultimate outcome. That's really all you can control."

Imagine if you had a 30-inch putt to win the Open. How nervous would you feel? Now imagine this same putt with thousands standing around the green and millions watching on TV. Doug Sanders has been immortalised for the putt that never dropped. He missed it. When he was asked what happened he is supposed to have said: "I was thinking about my victory speech."

The journey is there to be enjoyed, not endured. Like some lines from the Greek poet Constantine P. Cavafy's famous journey to Ithaka:

"When you set out for Ithaka,
Ask that your way may be long, full of adventure and full of instruction.

Have Ithaka always in your mind ...
But don't in the least hurry the journey.

Better it last for years, so that when you reach the island you are old and rich with all you have gained on the way and not expecting Ithaka to give you wealth.

Ithaka gave you a splendid journey.
Without her you would not have set out."

That's the purpose of a destination. This is at the core of my friend's insight into the minds of those professional golfers: "When you are relaxed in your games, you play at such an incredible high and different standard."

It's the paradox: When you are detached from the outcome, you achieve the outcome. That GAA manager gave an outstanding presentation. The player got the red card rescinded. He achieved his outcome. He told me he thoroughly enjoyed making the presentation once he detached from the outcome. That was how he achieved his outcome.

So by all means have a great dream, a goal or an outcome. Then detach from it. Put all your energy into the process. Better to travel well than to arrive. Then, like the golfers: "When you are relaxed in your games, you will play at such an incredibly high and different standard." Ithaka will give you, too, a splendid journey.

RED PLATFORM: Attachment to outcome. Grim determination. Not present in the moment or in your performance.

GREEN PLATFORM: Detached from outcome. Relaxed and focused on your performance in the present moment.

22

You Can Decide
To Be The Difference

MANY years ago when God was young I worked in the slums of the Philippines as a Columban missionary priest where I witnessed the brutal levels of poverty, hunger and injustice in our world.

In my last 90 days there I buried 65 children under two years old who died from hunger or hunger-related diseases. Their challenge was not lifestyle, it was survival.

When I came back to Ireland, I helped set up the Philippines Human Development Fund to support hen projects, sewing projects, pig projects and other long-term sustainable projects like the hugely successful micro-financing Grameen Banks with Columban Fr Sean Connaughton.

Over the past number of years the fund is supporting Preda, a Foundation set up by Columban Fr Shay Cullen to care for children he rescues from brothels and jails, and for the homeless ones from the back streets and alleys of Manila and other towns.

I am writing this in Thailand on a work-tour through Asia. Last week I was in the Philippines. On the journey out I had our son Fionn with me. He was volunteering for three weeks in the Preda Centre. First, Columban Fr Mickey Martin took him around the slums of Manila and I can tell you it was a real eye-opener for him.

He was amazed at how the poor people continued to hammer boards around their little shacks during the typhoon wind and rains.

"I saw three families living in an area smaller than our bathroom at home," he told me.

We saw so many tricycles and their riders peddling around the streets carrying anything from one to five passengers in their sidecars. We saw one rider as lean and fit as a Tour de France cyclist peddling up a hill with a very fat man in the sidecar. It symbolised the global health and fitness crisis in the world today.

I took the bus back from Olongapo to Manila when I dropped Fionn off at Preda. It was a five and a half hour journey through lashing rain as we meandered our way through flooded roads. Manila really does a different kind of traffic gridlock. There was wifi on the bus, which worked some of the time. I got a quick update on world news.

A Malaysian jet had been shot down over Ukraine. As I tried to absorb that tragedy, news came through that Israel had invaded the Gaza Strip. There were more savage executions in Iraq, not to mention kidnapped girls in Nigeria.

War and rumours of war. Death and destruction falling from the sky. Conflict, scandals, crises and turmoil.

Based on the news, the world is in trouble. People are dying. We seem to be violent creatures with endlessly inventive ways to destroy each other. We managed to murder 100 million of our fellow citizens on this earth in the last century and we're getting a good start in this new century.

Fionn wrote a reflection after his immersion experience in the slums and the jails of the Philippines. He opened it with the following sentence: "When I first told people I was going off to the Philippines to volunteer, their first question was 'Am I going to get paid?'

"I was first introduced to the extreme poverty in the Philippines by my dad, Declan Coyle, who was a former Columban Missionary. He worked here for many years. He told me stories about the work he ventured into which got me initially interested in this mysterious world of the Philippines.

"But to me these stories that my Dad told me were nothing more than stories that I could not relate to being a teenager from Ireland where my biggest worry each day was what the Internet speed would be like ..."

Fionn finished his eight-page reflection with the following sentence: "And to all my friends wondering, 'Am I going to get paid?' Yes, I am paid — in six figures, S-M-I-L-E-S.'"

Fionn got an insight into the other world of real news. His reflection reminded me of that famous Independent newspaper in London that Bono guest-edited in 2007. The cover all in red, designed by Damien Hirst, simply said "NO NEWS TODAY!" and in very small letters at the bottom: "Just 6,500 Africans died today as a result of a preventable, treatable disease."

Each one of us has a life to live. It is ours, and only ours. No one can live it for us, and we cannot live anyone else's life for them. It is up to us to find, build and live the best life we can. We cannot change the world, but we can change ourselves by being the best we can possibly be.

Then we can take action, make a contribution and make a difference instead of doing nothing because we think our contribution is so small that it will make no difference.

RED PLATFORM: Do nothing because I can only do a little. Indifference, apathy and overwhelm. Curse the darkness.

GREEN PLATFORM: Do something. Anything. Be the difference. Forget numbers. Help one person, the person nearest to you. Light a candle.

23

Life's A Cycle – And You Have The Pedals

THE other night my neighbour Hugh was telling me about a Leitrim man, Colin Regan, who stayed on in New York for a few days after Leitrim won the first round of the championship there a few seasons ago. He had the most amazing experience. He had never really seen New York, so he hired a bicycle and took off to explore every corner of the island of Manhattan from Harlem to the Lower East Side, from Soho to the Meatpacking district and all along the Hudson River.

He met all kinds of amazing people along the way and from his bicycle he got a totally different experience of New York and got great exercise in the process.

Years ago growing up in Dungimmon in County Cavan we didn't have spinning classes, or gyms or a school bus but every morning we rode our bicycles three or four miles to school and home again in the evening. Lifting bales of hay and feeding cows, pigs, sheep and horses were our gym workouts. We did our daily abs exercises at a time when we didn't know what abs were.

We didn't think about exercising or how good it was for our health. We didn't know that cycling, like regular exercise, increases aerobic fitness, reduces the risk of cardiovascular disease and lowers cholesterol. Nor did we know that it helps tone up calves, thighs and hips and can burn off up to 700 calories per hour. Studies have even shown those who cycle to work have a significantly lower mortality rate.

We knew none of that. Ninety-nine per cent of the students rode bicycles to our school. We even had a big bicycle shed along the wall in the yard. The most common excuse for being late for school was: "The chain came off my bike, Sir." Then the blackened oil covered hands would be held up for display. Sometimes this excuse was actually the truth.

The number of children riding bikes to school here now hovers between one and two per cent. When you take a scan across Europe, this is an incredibly low figure. When it comes to secondary schools, there are more girls driving cars to school than there are riding bicycles.

Compare this with Germany, where 14 per cent of children ride bicycles to school or Holland, where 49 per cent of children cycle to school. All of this is against a background where our children are now amongst the unhealthiest in Europe.

These children have a great chance of developing serious health problems, like high cholesterol, diabetes, breathing problems, and musculoskeletal problems — not to mention low self-esteem and depression. A panel of doctors and nutritionists addressed the Irish parliament, the Oireachtas, some time ago and described our obesity situation among children as a "pandemic."

Let's say we do nothing and we don't provide safe cycling lanes to schools where exercise will become once again a by-product of getting an education. Then the trend will continue and by 2030 almost half the adults in Ireland will be obese.

If we want different results, we need to make different decisions. We need to do different things. Do you park your car as near as possible to the supermarket door or do you park it in the farthest away spot to get in the longest walk?

Exercise is a matter of life ... and death. So inculcate its importance into your children. If you're going on holiday build exercise into your plans and make it fun for all the family. It worked for Leitrim man Colin Regan in the Big Apple and it will work for you.

RED PLATFORM: Sit into the car and get a lift to school or work.

GREEN PLATFORM: Get a bicycle and cycle or walk instead.

24

From Couch To Camino

"Maybe it's the simplicity of the life on the Camino and the closeness to nature that makes one conscious of deeper realities and I hope, as a result, I have learned to be a better person, or at least I will try to be."
An English pilgrim, 1998

A PERSON I know well completed a walk on the Camino de Santiago and told me that he felt absolutely fantastic after finishing it.

The Camino is all about living lightly and simply on this earth. People carry a backpack and carry all they need for the journey in it. In 2010, some 272,130 pilgrims made the trip.

About 10 years ago a friend from Dundalk walked it and was full of the same kind of excitement as he talked about not just the physical fitness, but also the unexpected bonus of a profound spiritual transformation.

The next time I came across the Camino was when I read Paulo Coelho's life story. Paulo is now one of the world's bestselling authors. He was inspired to make the 500-mile plus pilgrimage to Santiago de Compostela.

Coelho wrote *The Pilgrimage* that year — 1986. This was a turning point in his life. On the way, he too had a spiritual awakening. "I was very happy in the things I was doing. I was doing something that gave me food and water... I was working, I had a person whom I loved, I had money, but I was not fulfilling my dream. My dream was, and still is, to be a writer."

Coelho left his lucrative career as a songwriter to write full-time.

The following year he wrote *The Alchemist,* which sold over 65 million copies, becoming one of the best selling books in history.

The insight to follow his dream or what he calls his "personal legend," transformed his life and the lives of millions of his readers. Walking in the fresh Spanish mountain air, he downloaded his inner blueprint for personal magnificence.

My third encounter with the Camino was Martin Sheen's movie about the pilgrimage called 'The Way' that he made with his son.

So why do the Camino? Let me give you nine reasons:

1. Simple Pleasures of Life

Enjoying one of the most simple pleasures of life: walking. Back to the basics. Savouring every step of the journey. Walking and more walking. You'll never come back from a holiday in better shape.

2. History and Sacred Tradition

Along the Camino you will pass cities, towns and villages of all sizes with their stunning churches, monuments and historic landmarks. Pilgrims have used the trail for centuries so it's steeped in history and sacred tradition.

3. Amazing Landscapes

You will see some amazing landscapes from snow-capped mountains to magnificent valleys and a farming lifestyle that will remind you of the 1950s.

4. Right Pace

You can pick out a stretch each day that suits you, and do just the stages that fit into your schedule and your pace.

5. Amazing People

You'll meet some amazing people from all over the world along the way.

6. Great Guilt Free Food

Simple but fabulous food. Each route has its own flavours, traditional dishes and specialities. You know no matter how rich it is — you'll burn it off.

7. Bonding Time

It can be a great bonding time for family and friends whether you are walking or cycling.

8. "Buen Camino"

The warm "Buen Camino" ("Have a good Way or Walk") blessings and greetings from so many people along the way.

9. From Mental Misery To Gratitude

Most people arrive weary and weighed down with loads of mental luggage. Like an overloaded airplane that can't take off, they find that they carry an extra backpack filled with their trials, tribulations and troubles.

On the Camino, they leave that backpack behind somewhere along the way and only think and carry and care about what's important, really important. Instead of the backpack of trials, tribulations and troubles, they finish with a new backpack full of gratitude.

Of course, there are reasons why you mightn't be able to walk the Camino, as times may be tight and family circumstances often mean it is out of the question.

I was thinking about this when I got a call from another friend. He told me about someone he knew who was getting treatment for cancer. This man came to Bray and walked the Cliff Walk all the way to Greystones.

It's a beautiful walk with stunning views and despite his condition, he felt as if he had been given a mental and physical transformation by just enjoying nature — looking down on the seagulls against the blue backdrop of the sea, hearing the sounds of the waves lapping along the shore and feeling the fresh salty sea-weedy ocean breezes on his face.

It dawned on me then that we all have a Camino Walk on our doorstep, whether we live in Wicklow, Waterford, Kerry, Kildare or Donegal. There is always a forest walk, a hill climb or a beautiful beach that can imbue you with its own personal transformational energy.

If you are one of those people who have been meaning to do something this year, but have yet to get around to it, then here's a challenge for you for the coming weekend.

Phone a few friends or agree with some family members that you are going to circle a two-hour time slot in your Saturday or Sunday for your 'Camino Time.' No 'ifs,' 'buts' or 'maybes.' Nail it down. Make it a personal priority and just do it.

You don't know what you'll discover, but one thing for sure is that you will feel a hundred times better than if you stay in bed all morning or lounge around in front of a television set all day.

Perhaps Andrea Smith summed up the real deep inner feeling that you get on the Camino in one of her reports back to Irish Independent readers about her pilgrim journey called 'Couch to Camino." In one column she said:

"For someone like me who lives in my head and rarely gets physical, it was kind of invigorating to be idly walking in the gorgeous mountains, looking at nature and trees and gorgeous views around every corner with not very much else cluttering up my mind. The sun began to shine and I felt amazing.

A weird thing happened as I walked along and maybe the peace got to my head a little, but I began to feel really grateful for my life. Like I felt really thankful that I still have my lovely parents, when so many of my friends have lost theirs, and that all my troubles are little ones."

Maybe like Paulo and Andrea, as you set off on your own Camino journey you may find something more than just a walk or even end up following your dream — your own 'personal legend.'

Who knows, you too could end up full of gratitude as you download your own inner blueprint for personal magnificence.

RED PLATFORM: Not fulfilling your dream. Putting in the time. Getting through the day. Living in your head, slightly to one side.

GREEN PLATFORM: A "journey in." Walking in nature, reconnecting with your inner light, your inner wisdom and your inspiring dream. Feeling really grateful for your life as you follow your dream. Discovering your own personal legend.

25

Decisions Shape Destiny

MORE than half a century ago the country was electrified by the visit of President John F. Kennedy to Ireland, and in 2013 we welcomed the Kennedy clan back home for various 50th anniversary 'Gathering' events.

June 11, 1963 may not be a widely recognised date these days, but it is probably the single most important date in civil rights history in the United States and also John F. Kennedy's finest moment. That day he made a momentous decision. He surprised his staff by calling the three television networks and personally requesting airtime at 8.00 pm.

Meanwhile down in Alabama, Gov. George Wallace in an effort to block the integration of Afro-Americans into the University of Alabama, made his futile 'Stand in the schoolhouse door'.

Kennedy asked every American that regardless of where they lived to stop and examine their consciences. He eloquently linked the fate of Afro-American citizenship to the larger question of national identity and citizenship. "America for all its hopes and all its boasts will not be fully free until all its citizens are free," he said.

On July 2, 1964, almost a year after Kennedy's assassination, Lyndon Johnson got a strong civil rights bill through Congress. The bill was born the day John F. Kennedy made a decision. The *New York Times* called this decision on June 11, 1963: "Kennedy's finest moment."

In terms of your personal life, what is the decision that you would say is creating your finest moment? Have you made it? Or have you yet to make it?

Decisions shape destiny. Choice is power. Choice is change. One tree can start a forest. One candle can wipe out darkness. One hand can lift a soul. One hope can lift our spirits. One smile can lift a friendship. One word can frame a goal. One laugh can conquer gloom.

One choice can change your life.

We are the creative force in our own lives, and through our decisions rather than our conditions and circumstances we can accomplish great goals. But it all comes down to making a decision and following through on that decision with action. Stay committed to your decisions, but stay flexible in your approach to achieving them.

Like President Kennedy, when you make a decision you too can change your future history and shape your destiny.

Recently I met a friend I hadn't seen for many years. He was a very jovial but obese man. He was always threatening to start exercising and dieting. He used to close his eyes, raise his chin, let out a big sad sigh, make a kind of sucking noise through his teeth and say to me every time: "Next week when I get a few things sorted."

When I met him recently he had changed into a lean, mean, exercising machine. He oozed health, vitality, vigour and strength. He was a new man.

"What happened?" I asked.

"Well," he said, "it all began when I went to the doctor. She sent me for a full check-up. I finally did for myself what I've been doing for my car for years. I got my personal body NCT (National Car Test).

I failed.

At every level I was heading for an early appointment with the human scrapheap. They told me I had to change my lifestyle or die, to change my diet and start a serious exercise regime. They also told me that it was entirely up to me.

I made a decision and stuck with it. Then the next time I went for the check-up, I passed my test. It all came down to making that one decision … the best decision I ever made in my life, not only for me, but for my wife and children."

I met a man three weeks ago who told me he had decided to give up smoking for good. He was still smoking yesterday. His decision lacked action.

To decide means "to cut off" any other possibility of not doing what you say you'll do. You'll do what you say you'll do long after the inspiring mood that moved you to make the decision in the first place has long passed and evaporated. You'll still do it.

They called the decision he once made on that June day in 1963 "President Kennedy's finest moment." So ask not what your body can do for you; rather ask, what can you do for your body? What decision can you make to get and maintain a fit and healthy body?

Can you make that kind of decision in terms of your health and fitness in a manner that you will forever recall as your finest moment?

RED PLATFORM: Always intending to do something. Never getting around to doing it. Never doing today what you can put off until tomorrow.

GREEN PLATFORM: Making that decision and doing it now. The one life changing choice. Your finest moment. Never putting off until tomorrow what you can do today.

26

Creating What Doesn't Exist

MY friend was on a great health and fitness run for some time, but with the advent of the hot weather and some fairly severe bouts of hay fever he "eased off a bit," as he put it.

"I need motivation again," he said. "Can you help me kick-start my mind again, and I'll take it from there? Once I get the head right I know my body will follow."

"Okay," I told him, "start off by saying to yourself, 'I think I can.' It's the first step to achieving your fitness goals and getting back on track. Just keep saying to yourself, 'I think I can.' As you repeat that phrase your mind will want to fight back. It might say, 'You can't. It's too hard. Go back to bed.'

That's okay. Just keep saying it. Push yourself to feel like you really can. When you keep saying that you think you can, then you start to believe that maybe, just maybe, you actually can.

But you need to go one step further and really believe you can. Saying 'I think I can' is a good start but on its own the phrase is just too weak. Your subconscious will be quite happy having you 'thinking' you can so long as you don't translate that into action. It will settle down into that old comfort zone of actually knowing what to do but not doing what you know."

However, to achieve your health goals and to create the change and confidence you need, you have to go from "I think I can," to "I know I can," or even the famous Obama mantra, "Yes, we can." The difference between "I think I can," and "I know I can," is a belief.

The difference in terms of results is massive.

"I think I can" offers hope. "I know I can" states a belief. Something almost magical happens when you move from a "hoping" to a "knowing". It's the most electrifying and empowering of all transformations.

Belief comes before performance. To achieve performance, to achieve potential — you just need to alter your belief.

Your 'knowing' and your corresponding confidence is always based on your level of competence. It's profoundly reality based. Can you ride a bicycle? Do you have a "hoping" or a "knowing" that you can ride a bicycle?

It's your belief and your inner knowing that your subconscious and your inner creative powers pick up on. They create your life based on what you believe. This 'knowing' is embedded in your muscle memory.

That's why when you believe you can, you will. When you believe you can't, you won't.

When you create a strong belief that says you can — then you will. That means no wavering. It also means not having any doubts. Get rid of those doubts by getting rid of the negative thoughts that destroy and sabotage your success.

Nothing will cripple your success like negative thinking. So start believing that you can and your belief will enable you to bring about what you think about.

Banish the doubts.

As the author of *Zorba the Greek*, Nikos Kazantzakis says: "When you passionately believe in that which doesn't exist, you create it. And that which we call non-existent, has not been sufficiently desired." Passion and belief are essential for creation.

"Yes, you can." Forget about the past failures. You can and will achieve your goals and get back on track. Ignore the failures and remember your successes. Magnify those successes. Attention amplifies everything.

Make those past successes bigger and brighter. Feel those great feelings again. Then you don't just begin to think you can, you believe you can. You have a 'knowing,' and in no time at all you are back on track achieving your health and fitness goals.

Does all this work? Well, my friend is back in the gym, back on his bicycle and once again on track to his health and fitness goals. Once his positive belief kicked in, he was up and running. It works in fitness but it also works in life.

Try it and see!

RED PLATFORM: Hoping you can achieve your goals. An anaemic hoping founded and grounded in fear and doubt.

GREEN PLATFORM: Knowing you can achieve and exceed your goals. Your confidence based on your competence.

27

Is Discipline Your Missing Ingredient?

'DISCIPLINE," said the woman, "that's my problem. I just can't get anything going. I keep falling off the exercise wagon as it were. And my diet is similar. There's a name for people like me, but I can't remember it."

"Is the name 'recidivist'?" I asked.

"That's it."

I knew the word because I had a friend who used to keep calling himself a 'recidivist', and I had to look up the meaning. It is the act of a person repeating an undesirable behaviour or relapsing back into an old bad habit.

So I explained to her how I viewed her challenge in terms of discipline.

In its original sense, discipline is systematic instruction intended to train a person in a craft or other activity or to follow a particular code of conduct.

Discipline has over the years got a bad name because of its connection to punishment. It's linked back to the centuries old "spare the rod and spoil the child". The words that a school principal was, "a strict disciplinarian" never brought joy to a young person's heart at school.

In its original sense, discipline is systematic instruction intended to train a person, sometimes literally called a 'disciple', in a craft or other activity, or to follow a particular code of conduct.

But because of the bad press discipline has received over the years, many people want to be free of discipline to do what they like and live as they please.

At first glance it looks like freedom but if you take the train off the tracks, it's free but it can't go anywhere.

Take the steering wheel out of your car, and now nobody's controlling the car, but it's absolutely useless.

The harsh reality is that until sailors discipline themselves to be obedient to the compass, they will have to stay within sight of the shore. But once they have the discipline to follow the compass, they can sail the seven seas without fear.

Discipline is indeed the missing ingredient that will make the difference in your life. Self-discipline, when you become your own "disciple" and train yourself is actually a huge form of freedom.

Freedom from laziness and lethargy. Freedom from weakness, low self-esteem, fear, obesity, diabetes and doubt.

There is another kind of discipline we sometimes forget. That is the discipline to rest, recover and recreate. It's the discipline to take holidays, mini-breaks, or even power-naps to replenish our energy, our excitement and our enthusiasm for what we are doing.

Otherwise we can get worn down by routine, over-stressed by work, burned out, or stuck in a rut — and the only difference between a rut and a grave is depth.

Burning brightly should not mean burning out.

A lecturer in the following story illustrates the importance of the discipline to handle stress, rest and recovery.

Explaining stress management to an audience, he raised a glass of water and asked: "How heavy is this glass of water?" Answers called out ranged from 20g to 500g.

The lecturer replied: "The absolute weight doesn't matter. It depends on how long you try to hold it. If I hold it for a minute, that's not a problem.

If I hold it for an hour, I'll have an ache in my right arm.

If I hold it for a day, you'll have to call an ambulance.

In each case, it's the same weight, but the longer I hold it, the heavier it becomes."

He continued: "It's the same with stress. If we carry our burdens all the time, sooner or later, as the burden becomes increasingly heavy, we won't be able to keep it going. As with the glass of water, you have to put it down for a while and rest before holding it again. When we're refreshed, we can carry on with the burden."

Whatever burdens you're carrying now, leave them down for a moment if you can. Don't pick them up again until you've rested a while. Can you discipline yourself to do that?

A pint container can't hold a quart. If it holds a pint, it's doing all that can be expected of it.

So there are the two kinds of discipline. They are both about freedom. The first is the freedom to take consistent exercise and stick to a nutritious diet or complete a task at work, and the second is to take refreshing breaks at regular intervals.

With these disciplines, when you become your own coach and disciple, the chances of you slip-sliding back into becoming a "recidivist" will gradually disappear. You'll discover a new you and a better and greater quality of life.

RED PLATFORM: No discipline like a train without tracks, like a car without a steering wheel or a sailor without a compass. Indifferent. Apathetic. Sluggish. Or burnout from compulsive obsessive non-stop working.

GREEN PLATFORM: The discipline to balance both working hard and then resting, re-creating and recovering. Burning brightly without burning out.

28

Success Comes In Cans

IF you always do what you've always done you'll always get what you've always got.

Albert Einstein was pretty much on the ball when he said: "Insanity is doing the same thing over and over and then expecting different results."

In other words, don't work harder at what's not working in your life. If it's not working, change it. And if that's not working, change that too.

The first car Henry Ford built was the famous Model T. He said when he asked people if he could he build 100 cars a day on an assembly line they all gave him the same answer: "No, Henry, it can't be done."

Ford used to say that whether you believe you can or you believe you can't do something, either way you are probably right. He passionately believed that he could build 100 cars on an assembly line, and when you passionately believe in what doesn't exist, you create it.

Every time someone told him: "You can't," he silently repeated, "I can."

He was right. What he conceived and believed he achieved.

His "I can" became reality on August 12, 1908 when he built the famous Ford Model T car. When they asked Henry, "Where did you get the 'T' from?", he replied, "I just took the 't' out of can't."

When there is something you believe you can't do, could you, too, start taking the 't' out of your can't? If you believe you can —

you can. Again, your goal must be grounded in reality. Realistic, but stretching like Henry Ford's goal.

A teacher in Cork told me one time that he got his students to list all the realistic but stretching things they felt they couldn't do under the heading "I can't."

Then he gathered up all their lists and put them into a shoebox. They then went out to the garden, dug a hole, and buried the shoebox in the earth. They had a funeral for their "can'ts."

Next he got them to write out all those things that they said they "can't" do by switching them to a new list starting off "I can …"

The following week, they all set off walking up a local mountain where they planned to have a picnic at the top. At one stage, one of the girls got tired and said: "I can't finish this trek up the mountain." Then they all said to her: "You buried that 'can't' back in the school garden, come on, you can finish the walk up the mountain."

He told me that she laughed and said: "I forgot; of course I can." She then climbed without any apparent problem to the top. Where the mind goes, the body follows.

In sport, as in life, if you break the cycle and you don't always do what you've always done by sometimes bringing in the element of surprise, you can create an enormous advantage for yourself. But if you keep doing the 'surprise' thing over and over, then you'll fall back into a predictable rut.

Tennis player Michael Chang is in the record books as the youngest winner at 17 of a Grand Slam title, but his French Open triumph in 1989 is largely remembered for one extraordinary game-changing moment against the top ranked player in the world at the time, Ivan Lendl.

Injured and exhausted near the end of the match, Chang broke two of the most basic commandments of winning tennis. He refused to do what he'd always done. First, in a sport where powerful overhead serving is usually the key to winning, Chang served underhand, and the confused Lendl's return went into the net.

Second, on match-point, facing Lendl's 120+ mph serve, Chang again refused to do what he'd always done, instead he moved closer to the net and stood at the line of the server's box.

The bewildered Lendl double-faulted, and this led to one of the most memorable upsets in tennis history.

By challenging the conventional wisdom on these previously sacred aspects of the game, doing different things to get a different result — a different way of serving and returning serves — Chang radically changed his strategy, surprised his opponent and raised his standing in the world of tennis.

As you prepare to do some exercise or indeed work in the coming week, ask yourself: "How can I use the element of surprise to break the rules of always doing what I've always done in order to make a breakthrough?"

What are you going to stop doing?

What are you going to start doing?

What are you going to do more of?

What are you going to do less of?

If you believe you can do different and better things, you will achieve different and better results. You can do it.

Success really does come in "cans!"

RED PLATFORM: You believe you can't. Always doing what you've always done. Always getting the same results.

GREEN PLATFORM: You believe you can. Belief comes before performance. Doing new and different things to get different results.

29

Laughter – Your Best Medicine

ON my way to the US, an airline stewardess offered me a national newspaper. The heading on the front page caught my eye: "All Stressed Out".

"We're entering the dawn of the super-stress era," said Ann Mack, former global director of trend spotting at JWT, an ad agency that picked "super-stress" as one of the year's most highly charged trends. "Since it's become a cost issue and serious medical concern, you'll see more efforts to prevent or reduce it."

According to the American Psychological Association, some seven in 10 Americans said they regularly suffer physical symptoms due to stress, and two in every three say they regularly experience psychological symptoms because of it.

The top three causes of stress are related to money, work and the economy. "We're just not very good at dealing with stress," says Dr David W. Ballard, the group's assistant executive director for organizational excellence. We all experience stress. There is good stress and bad stress. The good stress can help motivate some of us to become world champions, but harmful stress can drive others to despair. When people talk of stress, they are normally talking of bad stress — the invisible disease.

The three kinds of stress that cause a reaction in the body are:

1. Chemical
Caffeine, alcohol, nicotine or sugar.

2. Physical
Physical inactivity or over-activity, lack of sleep or dehydration.

3. Emotional
Fear, anger, guilt, sorrow, jealousy, hurt and anxiety.

The effects are additive. For example, one sip of coffee may not cause a stress reaction but one sip of coffee, plus one puff of a cigarette, plus one heated argument, plus inadequate sleep, plus a day of sitting at a computer can cause a physiological change in the body's chemistry. It all adds up.

So what can we do about stress? Here are three things:

1. Exercise & Water
Take exercise and lots of it. Vary it. Run, walk, swim, jog, cycle or do yoga or Pilates and drink lots and lots of water. Then rest and recover.

2. Meditation
We live in a kind of shallow, fast breathing Attention Deficit Hyperactivity Disorder (ADHD) culture. Daily meditation is a great antidote to this lifestyle.

"You can't buy un-stress just like you can't buy love," says anthropologist Robbie Blinkoff, managing partner of Context-Based Research Group in Baltimore, USA. "Unstressing is easy and inexpensive. Sit still for 10 minutes every day and breathe deeply, breath slowly and follow your breath. It will do wonders."

Alternative-medicine advocate Deepak Chopra says: "Simple meditation can be the best way to de-stress and to chill out."

How do you meditate? Sit down. Relax. Breathe deeply. Simply follow your breath. Breathe slowly, breathe deeply and simply follow the breath. Any thought, or feeling ... just acknowledge them, put them aside and follow your breath. Back to the breath. That's all. Soon you'll feel the inner peace.

There are a number of scientific studies that show the benefits of meditation:

• Blood pressure comes down.

• Stress is alleviated.

• There is increased brain wave coherence that improves attention span, creativity, learning ability and memory retrieval and the immune system is boosted.

3. Change The Way You Look At Things

Studies have shown that it is not reality that causes us stress but rather our perception or our story about reality. People are not disturbed by things but rather by the views they take of things, the stories or interpretations they make up in their minds about things. These, however, we can control.

What one person sees as a problem, the other sees as an opportunity. We don't need new landscapes, but we do need new eyes to see the landscapes that are already there. Change the way you look at things and the things you look at change. Are we looking at life with eyes of misery or with eyes of joy?

"Turn the other cheek" is just a symbolic way of getting a different view of reality. Beauty is definitely in the eye of the beholder. As the English poet William Blake says: "The eye altering alters all."

Stress is very similar to the strings of a violin. If the strings are too loose, they will not play properly. If they are too tight, they will snap. It's the same with the human body.

We have to get the stress balance right.

Stress is like the wind. Like a yacht sailing on the high seas we can ignore the wind, fight it, or channel it positively to achieve our goals or sail to our destination.

For me, nothing eliminates stress like a good laugh with good friends by the shores of Lough Sheelin. I spent a day there recently at John (my nephew) and Maggie's wedding. Mixing with old friends, meeting new ones and seeing old faces and places were all a real tonic for the body, mind and spirit. Laughter is indeed the best medicine to de-stress.

RED PLATFORM: All work and no play. Sitting, smoking, eating and drinking to excess.

GREEN PLATFORM: Balanced work and play. Exercise, meditation, seeing with the "altering" eyes of joy and having great conversations and fun with friends.

30

That Still Small Voice – Your Inner Tuition

SELF-BELIEF is the foundation of greatness. The pathway to waking up to your greatness comes from listening to your intuition, that 'still small voice' inside that wants you to be the best that you can be.

It's your inner-tuition, your intuition, or your gut feeling prompting you like an inner coach or mentor (but not an inner critic) telling you that you must be what you can be. To be the best that you can be. It's like an inner guidance system.

When film director Robert Altman received his Oscar, he told the audience: "The job of the director is to create the space where the actors can become more than they've ever been and more than they've ever dreamed of being."

There is a director inside every one of us called 'the still, small voice'. Like its Hollywood counterpart, this unseen hand behind the camera is constantly directing us — but it doesn't bark out orders.

"To create the space" is to create the silence where you can hear that "still small voice" whispering, nudging, and prompting you to be "more than you've ever dreamed of being" for your family, your team or your community.

Listen to it with the ears of your heart. Listening not just to the words, but also to what's beneath the words, to the music of what's really happening.

This intuitive inner voice keeps urging you to march to the

music that you hear, to connect to your purpose, to do what makes your heart sing ... and not to die with your music still inside.

Of course, your brash, logical linear left brain then cuts in and barks: "Don't take risks. You might disappoint all those who have a different view of what you should be doing." The brain has a ferocious habit of getting in your way. In the East, they talk about achieving your dharma — your true purpose and living 'on purpose.'

The purpose of an acorn is to become a magnificent oak tree, not a tulip. The oak tree is what's in its DNA. It must be what it can be as you must be what you can be.

A caterpillar's purpose is to become a beautiful butterfly, not a shaggy dog. Like the caterpillar, you have a blueprint for personal magnificence deep within you. All you have to do is download it. It's sending you signs and signals.

But this does not mean that you will achieve your goals without struggle and effort, nor does it mean that you will even get quiet enough to listen to it. The butterfly's dharma unfolds by a natural, organic process of allowing, not forcing.

What's the secret power of allowing what is your best self to emerge naturally? Why not forcing?

Once a little boy was playing outdoors and found a caterpillar. He carefully picked it up and took it home to show his mother. He asked his mother if he could keep it, and she said he could if he would take good care of it.

The little boy got a large jar from his mother and put plants to eat, and a stick to climb on, in the jar. Every day he watched the caterpillar and brought it new plants to eat.

One day the caterpillar climbed up the stick and started acting strangely. The boy worriedly called his mother who came and understood that the caterpillar was creating a cocoon. The mother explained to the boy how the caterpillar was going to go through a metamorphosis and would become a butterfly.

The little boy was thrilled to hear about the changes his

caterpillar would go through. He watched every day, waiting for the butterfly to emerge. One day it happened, a small hole appeared in the cocoon and the butterfly started to struggle to come out.

At first the boy was excited, but soon he became concerned. The butterfly was struggling so hard to get out! It looked like it couldn't break free! It looked desperate! It looked like it was making no progress!

The boy was so concerned he decided to help.

He ran to get the scissors. He snipped the cocoon to make the hole bigger and the butterfly quickly emerged!

As the butterfly came out the boy was surprised. It had a swollen body and small, shrivelled wings. He continued to watch the butterfly expecting that, at any moment, the wings would dry out, enlarge and expand to support the swollen body. He knew that in time the body would shrink and the butterfly's wings would expand.

But neither happened. The butterfly spent the rest of its life crawling around with a swollen body and shrivelled wings. It never was able to fly ... because the boy's action was forced action, not natural, organic, inspired action.

As the boy tried to figure out what had gone wrong his mother took him to talk to a scientist from a local college. He learned that the butterfly was supposed to struggle. In fact, the butterfly's struggle to push its way through the tiny opening of the cocoon pushes the fluid out of its body and into its wings.

Without the struggle, the butterfly would never, ever fly.

The boy's good intentions hurt the butterfly.

There's a difference between struggling and forcing.

In fact, it's the struggle, the effort, the getting off the couch that develops your ability to fly ... but at your own time and at your own pace. Not when somebody is hitting you over the head with a stick or cutting the couch up with a big scissors from under you.

Struggle, effort and challenges matter. As American football

Coach Vince Lombardi said: "Leaders aren't born, they are made. They are made by hard effort, which is the price which all of us must pay to achieve any goal which is worthwhile."

'The Sound of Silence' is perhaps one of the most beautiful songs of all time. It is deeply poetic and meaningful. It describes our struggle to truly communicate with one another. Most of the time we only really communicate on a superficial level and therefore do not understand one another. A lot of talking without listening and a lot of listening without really hearing. Never hearing the feelings hidden behind the words.

We live in a world of texting, computer games and television. It's often hard to get the silence to hear that 'still small voice' whispering: "Now is the time." Whispering: "Seize the day." Whispering: "Create that space to be the best that you can be, more than you've ever dreamed of being so that you can contribute more to others and build a better world." That still small voice is so accurate, powerful and transformational as it guides you along your path to greatness. It's the true north on your inner compass.

RED PLATFORM: Busy, stressed, filling in time with television, texting and computer games. Blocking the download of personal magnificence. Smothering the still small voice.

GREEN PLATFORM: The sound of silence. Quiet time. Listening to the still, small voice inside. Feeling the inner nudges. Downloading and living your personal magnificence.

31

A Day To Seize The Time

THE late Irish poet Seamus Heaney was a positive man who had a great bit of 'get up and go' about him. In his poem *Station Island* he imagines James Joyce giving us advice: "Let go, let fly, forget. You've listened long enough. Now strike your note."

He is calling on us to 'seize the day' and make life happen. *Carpe diem!*

Do you seize the day, or does the day seize you? Do you get up and get your exercise in early or do you keep putting it off until later? Instead of letting go, and letting fly do you sit and stay put? Choosing the couch instead of taking off for your early morning swim, run or bicycle ride? You know what it's like if you leave your exercise to later in the day. You get caught up in the thick of thin, trivial rubbishy tasks and you end up just too busy to exercise.

I remember years ago seeing the film *Dead Poets Society*. The late Robin Williams played the English teacher John Keating. Keating takes a group of regimented, uptight and spiritually impotent students at a rigid boarding school and inspires them to make their lives extraordinary. He wanted them to make their lives spectacular. He challenged them to "let go, let fly", and strike their own notes.

Before Keating came, like Oprah Winfrey, they were clueless of what it was like to be their real selves instead of being pale second-rate imitations of somebody else.

Oprah says: "I had no idea that being your authentic self could make me as rich as I've become. If I had, I'd have done it a lot earlier."

One of the biggest, toughest and hardest challenges in this life is to be yourself, your true self, fully yourself, authentic, valid and real, living your own story, drinking from your own rich well of experiences and speaking with your own voice when everybody is trying so hard all the time to make you be like everyone else.

If Oprah had simply been her true, valid and authentic self earlier in her life, she would then have been listening to the beat of her own drum. This is what American author and poet Henry David Thoreau urges us all to do: "If a man does not keep pace with his companions, perhaps it is because he hears a different drummer. Let him step to the music which he hears, however measured or far away."

Is there anything as bad as keeping pace with somebody else's drummer like those singers on a TV talent show whose natural joyful pathway through life is perhaps nursing, but definitely not singing?

Keating took his students down to the lobby of the school where a trophy case displays the pictures of past students. "Look at these pictures, boys," Keating directed the students. "These young men whom you behold had the same fire in their eyes that you do. They planned to take the world by storm and make something magnificent of their lives. That was 70 years ago. Now they are all pushing up daisies. How many of them really lived out their dreams? Did they do what they set out to accomplish?"

Then Mr Keating leaned into the cluster of students and whispered audibly: "Carpe diem. Seize the day."

Did any one of these students in the pictures connect to their life's purpose? Did they do what made their hearts sing? Or did they die with their music still in them?

Today, let's make our lives extraordinary. Let's make our lives spectacular. Let's make our lives magnificent.

Let's make today our masterpiece by starting and seizing the day. Let's strike our own note. At our own pace. At our own time. Running to the drumbeat of our own inner music.

RED PLATFORM: Not living your dreams. Not accomplishing much. Never ready to strike your own note, let go and take off. Living to the beat of somebody else's drum. Dying with your music still in you. Unplayed. Stillborn.

GREEN PLATFORM: Carpe diem! Seizing the day. Striking your own note. Listening to the beat of your own drum. Doing what makes your heart sing. Making your life extraordinary, spectacular and magnificent — a masterpiece.

32

Turning Off Your Negative Voices

L IKE any marathon, the Dublin Marathons are a huge occasion for so many people from all walks of life. In the weeks leading up to these events, you'll see ordinary people out all over the place getting in their training runs.

Early mornings. Late evenings. People out running.

Every one of them has a purpose, a reason or a meaning fuelling their training runs, running for a good cause, helping the sick, the vulnerable and those who cannot run or simply activating that 'reward' part of the brain that kicks in when we accomplish some great and challenging goal.

Before a recent marathon a friend of mine who has been training for the previous few months to run his first marathon came to chat about the race. He had fears, worries and anxieties. The normal outside negativity had penetrated his mind. It was firmly planted inside.

"What's the problem?" I asked.

"Fear and doubt," he said.

"But, look," I said, "have you any idea of all the positive support you will get from the people on the footpaths cheering you on and encouraging you?"

"No," he said, "but my enemy is on the inside. It's that voice in my head, that negative little man that keeps telling me I won't be able to finish. When I get to 15 or 18 miles, my mind is invaded by that famous posse of negative thoughts. I begin to doubt myself.

"It's been happening in training. These negative thoughts in my head seem to drain my energy. The positive voices on the footpaths are really great, but it's the negative voices within my head around the footpaths of my mind that are drowning the other voices out. How do I stop them?"

I told him about something my friend Gerry Duffy, the famous Deca Ironman champion, mentioned to me some time ago. When Gerry didn't hit a target he'd set for himself, he was very disappointed. Then one thing struck him. He remembered when he was injured for a long time and couldn't run. In his book *Tick, Tock, Ten*, he disclosed how one sentence changed it all.

He said: "I don't have to run or take part in races. I don't *have to* run." Instead, full of gratitude and appreciation he said: "I *get to* run." The difference between 'have to' and 'get to' makes all the difference.

His feelings totally altered when he changed his inner vibrations from the low energy of disappointment to the higher energy of gratitude and appreciation.

So back to my doubting friend. I simply asked him to start off a run by appreciating and being thankful for the trees, the flowers, the singing birds in the fresh air and all the people he encountered on his run.

I then told him a story about a bunch of tiny frogs who once arranged a running competition. The goal was to reach the top of a very high tower. A big crowd had gathered around the tower to see the race and cheer on the contestants.

The race began. No one in the crowd really believed that the tiny frogs would reach the top of the tower. You heard negative statements such as:

"Oh, it's way too difficult."

"They will never make it."

"Not a chance that they will succeed. The tower is too high!"

The tiny frogs began collapsing. One by one, except for one group which continued climbing higher and higher.

The crowd continued to yell: "It is too difficult. No one will make it. Give up now."

After a while, all but one tiny frog had given up. He just wouldn't give up and eventually he reached the top.

Then all of the other tiny frogs naturally wanted to know how this one frog managed to do it?

A local reporter from the 'Green Frog Times' asked the tiny frog how the one who succeeded had found the strength to reach the goal while all the others failed?

It turned out that the winning frog couldn't hear a word from those spectating Energy Vampires roaring at him that it couldn't be done. The winning frog was in fact deaf. He explained afterwards that he really thought they were cheering him on, supporting him and encouraging him to reach the top.

Now back to my friend, the doubting, fearful runner. Appreciation and gratitude are working and they have silenced the negative voices within him. Just like the frog, whenever they do return, he pretends he's can't hear them. Now he simply won't listen to those negative voices.

In the same way that an entire ocean of water cannot sink a ship unless it gets inside the ship, similarly the negativity of the world could not put him down unless he allowed it to get inside him. All he had to do was to batten down the inner hatches of his mind.

Once he aligned the voices in his head to echo and vibrate with the positive energy from the spectators on the footpaths, everything changed. When he realised that he didn't have to run, but that he got to run, it made all the difference. Instead of tuning in to the negative voices, he began to appreciate and be thankful for the trees, the flowers and the people he encountered on his run. He was now filling up on the fuel of gratitude, appreciation and wonder.

He discovered that just as light and darkness cannot co-exist, and worry and action cannot co-exist, neither can gratitude and negativity.

RED PLATFORM: Listening and responding to all those inner and outer negative voices — planting seeds of fear, doubt and failure.

GREEN PLATFORM: Listening only to the positive uplifting inner and outer encouraging voices — planting seeds of confidence, self-belief and success.

33

Finding Your Type
On The Enneagram

ONE of the greatest breakthroughs in the world of training, coaching and mentoring in the past 30 years is the discovery of the nine different energies or personality types known as the Enneagram.

Years ago we thought we could do a time management course, or a motivation course with the idea that one size fits all. Not true. We have nine utterly different ways of managing time. We have nine totally different ways of being motivated. We have nine radically different ways of influencing, communicating and negotiating; and nine different ways of running, swimming or working.

There are nine types for nine different people powered with nine different energies. So which one are you?

TYPE 1 — Perfectionists or Reformers
They pay great attention to detail and are precise, responsible and hard working. They demand high quality and standards of themselves and others. Preparing for a race they may postpone taking part until they feel they are prepared properly. They will carefully choose to sponsor the 'right' charity.

TYPE 2 — Helpers or Givers
They prioritise relationships and helping others. They'll work for a great and worthwhile charity where they can really contribute

and help. They need to take time off from helping others to boost themselves. They need to understand that self-care and compassion for oneself is not being selfish.

TYPE 3 — The Achievers

Their attention is centered on being successful. They're very focused on goal achieving in the most efficient and effective way. For their life, they'll put a plan in place and follow it rigorously. Their goal is to achieve a personal best. They're natural born winners. Normally they have a fairly full trophy cabinet. They'll also link up with what they believe to be the most deserving charity where the money will be used in the most effective and efficient way to achieve the greatest good.

TYPE 4 — The Creative Artists, the Romantics

They're special, with individual creative insights. They're sensitive, intuitive, expressive, artistic and dramatic. They'll most likely work in a very special type of job. They won't have 'ordinary' running gear. It'll be special. They'll stand out. They'll be dressed up like a Disney character or something like that. They're very sensitive to people suffering from depression or who are prone to suicide and the charities they support will reflect these causes.

TYPE 5 — The Observers

They're logical and intelligent and enjoy gathering information and ordering data. Excellent thinkers and strategists they'll work around a carefully coded and coloured spreadsheet. They'll use things like apps to give them precise feedback on how they're doing in training — mileage, times and calories burned. Gatherers of information, they're fascinated by all this informational feedback. They'll carefully research the best, most deserving charity.

TYPE 6 — Sceptics, Supporters and Troubleshooters

They have questioning minds. They like to be prepared and they easily see pitfalls as well as possibilities. But they're also loyal and dependable. They prepare diligently and look around the corner for possible obstacles or ways that things might fail. They love manuals and will read all the manuals on training and they'll probably write a training manual or blog as well. Once a charity earns their trust, they'll remain loyal to it forever.

TYPE 7 — Optimists and Visionaries
Positive thinkers who see different ways to enjoy life and work. Where other people see problems, they see opportunities. They'll turn the race into a fun run, and will definitely throw the best party afterwards. Everyone will have fun running for their own charity.

TYPE 8 — Leaders and Challengers
They're direct, assertive and commanding, and they just get things done. They know what they want to accomplish in life and they have the willpower to make it happen. They view serious problems simply as challenges to be met or obstacles to be overcome. Forceful and direct, they'll make a pile of money for their charity.

TYPE 9 — The Peacemakers and Mediators
They put people at ease and resolve conflict. They are big-picture thinkers and once they write something down they do it. They are supportive, inclusive and work easily with everyone. They want to live in an atmosphere of peace and harmony. They'll choose one charity and stick with it.

While each of us has all of these nine energies within us, there's one predominant, stronger or leading one. So which one is yours?

Before I discovered the Enneagram nine types, I thought there were two kinds of people in the world: People like me and people who desperately wanted to be or should be like me. (Most failed relationships and marriages are based on this premise.)

The person sitting next to you has a totally, utterly and radically different way of viewing the world to you. A different lens. Not better or worse, not right or wrong, just different.

Have a look around at home, in your work or in your fitness regime and have some fun seeing the different types. Ultimately it's all about acknowledging, respecting and celebrating these differences. All the types are rubbing shoulder with you every day and each one of them has its own unique gift, talent or signature strength. Let us enjoy our work and exercise journeys through our nine different Enneagram energy landscapes.

RED PLATFORM: We're all the same. To be is to be like me. There are two kinds of people: people like me, and people who want to be like me. "My way or the highway."

GREEN PLATFORM: Nine totally different people with nine totally different gifts, energies and talents. Recognising, respecting and celebrating each one of them.

34

Never Fear — Freedom Is Near

MY friend who was full of fear and doubt some time ago when he was training for the Dublin marathon has been making progress. More and more he's enjoying the early morning runs, the sounds of the birds, the dawn views of the trees, the flowers and the mist in the valley.

He told me the other day: "I'm gradually losing the fear and the doubt. I'm casting them out, but then even on the best of mornings the fear comes creeping back in again."

So I went through the original mental routine with him.

"There are only two major drivers in our lives. Fear and love. We are born with love but fear is something that we learn.

Fear is really False Evidence Appearing Real.

There are two ways of looking at F-E-A-R:

1. Forget Everything And Run
   Or
2. Face Everything And Rise

Fear is merely an invitation to creativity and freedom.

Now, while a little bit of fear is useful to keep us from driving on the wrong side of the road, the majority of our fears actually arise from false evidence appearing real. Courage is not the absence of fear; it is feeling the (generally false) fear and doing it anyway. It's showing up fear to be the imposter that it is. Fear persists because the Ego, the false self, feeds on fear. Fear is the fuel of the Ego. Once you wake up and become aware, the Ego and its feeder, fear, disappear like a shadow in sunshine.

"I know," my friend said, "that I should be more grateful for the fact that I can run, but I should be doing more training. I should be further ahead with my training programme."

Now there's another word you need to avoid — 'should.'

You'll notice that you think thoughts like this all the time. 'Should' catapults us into arguing with reality and whenever we argue with reality we will lose, but only 100 per cent of the time.

As in:

"I should be thinner."

"I shouldn't be so tired all the time."

"My partner should be more sensitive and attentive."

You get the idea.

These thoughts are ways of wanting reality to be different or other than what it is. A lot of the stress in life is caused by this constant 'should-ing' and arguing with 'what is.'

No matter how blessed a life may be with health, wealth, family, close friends, opportunities to learn and grow and a chance to give back, the number one pattern that diminishes, and, in some cases, completely destroys people's lives on that poisonous Red Platform is negative 'should-based' rigid expectations.

That's it. Isn't that the catch?

If you really want to be stressed, all you have to do is expect life and all the people in it, to think, behave, speak, and act the way you have predetermined they 'should.'

The best formula for a great positive Green Platform life of peace, joy and happiness is to swap your expectations for appreciation and expectancy.

Expectations on the Red Platform are hard, cruel and rigid. Savagely tough taskmasters shoehorning, manipulating and forcing life. Appointing people and things in a manner that sets up disappointments. Things just don't turn out the way they 'should'.

Expectancy on the other hand is warm, kind and flexible. Expectancy brings about inspired action where you are one with life and full of appreciation.

Gratitude is the key.

The moment you focus on and feel gratitude, your whole world transforms. You know how it feels when people 'expect' you to give them something, it takes away the gift of spontaneous surprise and the joy you're able to feel from your giving.

By contrast, when you appreciate whatever life or people bring you, you are choosing to guarantee openness and invite in to your life the joy that young children have ... full of expectancy ... before we spoil them and create the unrealistic expectations that life and people all exist to meet their desires and needs.

So much anger, frustration, rage, hurt, depression, and sadness comes from a rigid Red Platform 'expecting' people to be loving, generous, courteous, compassionate, proactive, present, supportive and caring. They are as they are. Then you end up that famous favourite Red Platform teenage mantra: "It's not fair."

So the first commandment for the 'shoulda,' 'coulda,' 'woulda' people might be: "Thou shalt not 'should."

If you argue with reality with your arsenal of negative 'shoulds' you will lose every time. We cannot undo or rewrite the past. As the Iranian poet Omar Khayyam put it some 1,000 years ago: "The moving finger writes; and having writ moves on: Nor all thy piety nor wit shall lure it back to cancel half a line, or all thy tears wash out a word of it."

It's over. It is as it is. Done and dusted.

My friend argued: "But if I simply accept reality then I will become passive and nothing will change. I'll just become indifferent, apathetic."

He's right. If you just bring acceptance on its own to reality, it can easily degenerate into indifference or apathy. You accept reality, and then you take positive action by focusing on the one thing you can do to improve it.

The Green Platform formula for this is: Acceptance plus Positive Action Now (PAN). "Of these 100 things, what one positive thing can I do now to improve the situation?"

Which of these statements makes more sense?

1. "I wish I hadn't lost all that money, I should have been more careful!"

2. "What one thing can I do now to create more income?"

Accepting 'what is' doesn't mean you settle for the way things are, it just means you give up all the resistance and inner struggle by stopping all that 'should-ing' and wishing things were different. This will free up your energy to take positive action now.

Just by being more appreciative and more grateful, you will be amazed how much your life changes.

It's not just my friend. Last week I was giving myself every reason why I shouldn't go for a run when I met a woman out on the street in a wheelchair. She smiled and said: "Isn't it a beautiful day?"

I replied that it was, but in truth I hadn't even noticed. Within minutes of returning home I was in my gear and out for a run. The woman in the wheelchair had told me it was a day to smell the roses. She was right ... and I did. I didn't 'have to' run. It was a beautiful day and I 'got to' run with gratitude.

RED PLATFORM: Argue with reality. Locked into the negative past. Lots of 'Shouldn't' negative expectations, and fear-fuelled inaction. Resentment that things are the way they are. Expectations.

GREEN PLATFORM: Acceptance, "It Is As It Is" + Positive Action Now (PAN)." Of the 100 things, "what one positive thing can I do now?" Appreciation and gratitude. Expectancy.

35

Rest Your Way To A Smarter 'You' In Work

EVERY now and then someone contacts me who is desperate for a bit of motivational help or guidance.

Like the man who wrote me this email: "I need some motivational help. I'm a kind of an all-or-nothing person. When I'm training and exercising I just keep telling myself that it's mind over matter. I just go and I go and I go. But then I get overwhelmed. I'm burned out and I feel like giving up altogether. Can you help me not only to get back on track but also to stay on track?"

We had a chat over the phone. First I told him to look at the recent trends in Ireland. We are not only eating too much but we are also drinking far too much. Seventy-five per cent of all alcohol consumed in Ireland is part of binge-drinking sessions and 1.3 million of us are problem drinkers. Alcohol-related problems cost the country an estimated €3.7 billion in 2007. And between 2004 and 2011, 4,606 people died directly, or indirectly, from illegal drug use.

I'm writing this from China and it struck me how we need to look at things differently in Ireland to get different results. Here, too, they are beginning to face the challenges of obesity and diabetes from overweight. It's a sad by-product of their increasing wealth.

My challenge was to get my emailer to return to regular exercise and this time to stick with it over the long term. I told him the following story.

Once there were a group of men, a young hot-blooded man and a number of older men, cutting down trees in a forest. The young man was very hard-working and continued to work through his breaks and complained that the old men were holding up the job as they took several breaks during the day to eat, drink water and chat.

As time went by, this young man noticed that even though he worked through breaks and hardly ever took a rest, those older men were chopping many more trees than he was. He decided to work harder and harder. Still the results were the same.

A few days later, one of the old men invited him for a drink during their breaks. He refused and said he had no extra time to waste talking to them. Then the old man smiled and said: "It is just a waste of effort to keep chopping trees without re-sharpening your axe. Sooner or later you will give up or be totally exhausted because you have spent too much energy."

Suddenly the young man realised that during break times while those old men were chatting, they were also re-sharpening their axes. That's how they could chop faster than him and yet spend less time working.

The old man said: "What we need is efficiency by making use of our skill and ability intelligently. Only then can we have more time to do other things."

First you breathe in. Then you breathe out. You can't breathe out all the time. By taking a break from your exercise you not only feel fresher but you also think and work better. Taking a break does not mean that you stop taking exercise, but it does give you the time to rest, recover and rediscover your freshness.

People who are rested and feel good about themselves produce incredible results. When you feel good you are not only energised but also calm, enthusiastic, confident, optimistic and passionate.

We feel better and perform better when these four core energy needs are met:

• Sufficient rest, including the opportunity for intermittent renewal during the workday.

• Feeling valued and appreciated.

• Having the freedom to focus in an absorbed way on our highest priorities.

• Feeling connected to a mission or a cause greater than ourselves.

Is that what you need? A time out to sharpen your axe so that you can get those other three energy needs met as well?

RED PLATFORM: Keep on chopping trees until your axe wears down to the wooden handle.

GREEN PLATFORM: Sharpen your axe. Rest, recover and rediscover your freshness to focus on what matters most.

36

Moderation Matters

THERE'S one thing for sure in your life. Twelve months from now you will be either better or worse. You won't be the same. Should you line up a year of exercise or will you overdo exercise in the same way that we overdo eating or drinking?

It's probably not news to you that we just don't exercise enough. Most of us don't meet the recommended amount of weekly physical activity despite research that shows exercise can be just as effective as drugs in some cases to treat diseases such as diabetes.

So why don't we prescribe exercise in specific doses, like the chemist does in a prescription? To do that, we need to know exactly how much exercise produces how much benefit. Is there an upper limit? At which point do the helpful effects either start dropping off or begin to do more harm than good?

That's what Paul T. Williams, a staff scientist at Lawrence Berkeley National Laboratory, and his colleagues wanted to know, and they found out in a report published in Mayo Clinic Proceedings.

He started off with a group of heart attack survivors. As the data continued to emerge, it appeared that, like with any other prescription, exercise could be dangerous in high doses.

Those who had heart attacks and ran more than 30 miles a week or spent more than six hours in vigorous activity weekly were at an increased risk, up to twice as much, of dying from a heart event.

"I certainly expected a point of diminishing return, but I wasn't expecting to see the increase in mortality," says Williams.

In contrast, those who exercised moderately, which is to say, more than the admittedly low recommended minimum but not as much as the extremely active, lowered their risk of heart-related death by 63 per cent compared to those exercising the least.

"I would say the gains of being active are substantial," says Williams, "but up to a certain point." Williams says that the results only apply to a relatively small group of people who have a history of heart disease and who exercise at high levels, but he's currently studying the same thing in the general population to see if similar trends are at work.

The data could form the foundation for a chemist-like prescription-based approach to exercise, as researchers become more familiar with how much exercise can influence factors that affect our health.

"For now," added Williams, "the message is that at least for heart attack survivors, more is better, but only up to a point."

According to a recent study published in the *Journal of the American College of Cardiology*, running five minutes per day can increase a person's life by about three years.

Researchers found that people who ran less than an hour per week also saw an increase in lifespan, not just a decrease in risk of premature death.

The study took place over the course of 15 years, testing participants ranging in age from 18 to 100.

According to that research, individuals who exhibit consistent but moderate exercise patterns are likely to live the longest.

"What we need are more people doing moderate exercise every day and not running heroic distances. You can get 70 per cent to 80 per cent of the benefit of exercise from doing it 15 to 30 minutes a day," says by Dr James O'Keefe, a cardiologist at the Mid America Heart Institute of St. Luke's Hospital in Kansas City, Missouri.

For someone who doesn't love exercise but is looking to significantly benefit his or her heart, the ideal amount is about 30 minutes a day at least three days a week.

I suppose it comes back to what our mothers used to say to us: "Everything in moderation."

If you make a commitment to take consistent moderate exercise over the next 12 months, you will have a better quality of life and an increased lifespan.

RED PLATFORM: Bite off more than you can chew. You're not fit. You run 15 miles every day. Breaks are for wimps.

GREEN PLATFORM: Eighty per cent of the benefits of exercise come from about 30 minutes a day.

37

Shine A Light
On What Is Right

'WHAT'S right with you?" Have you ever been asked that question? I'll bet not. But try the opposite one. "What's wrong with you?"

Those two questions inevitably evoke two totally different responses. One will motivate you. The other will demotivate you. One question will contribute to your energy and the other one will contaminate it.

Shamu is the largest killer whale in the world and that's the question: "What's right with you?" that has turned him into a peak performer. While there's some controversy over the future of Seaworld in San Diego at the moment, Dave Yardely, Shamu's trainer, has learned a huge amount about peak performance at any level from working closely with this killer animal.

A huge gasp goes through the crowd of over 3,000 spectators, as they are thrilled and astonished by the performance of the leaping killer whales. Dave has trained Shamu to jump, do summersaults and all kinds of tricks. How does he get a killer whale to hit peak performance so consistently?

"The secret is to catch him doing things right," he says.

"It's also very important to catch him doing things better and to praise progress immediately and specifically."

This incredible show didn't happen overnight. Shamu taught Dave patience. First of all he wouldn't do anything until he trusted Dave. Trust was the first cement in this amazing relationship of success.

At the beginning, Dave would jump into the pool and play with him and convince him he meant no harm. Shamu had to be convinced of Dave's good intentions. At Seaworld the trainers make every effort to persuade the animals to see them as friends. Then they make everything in training into a game. Just like great education, learning and laughter go together.

When you are positive in the present moment — that turns on all the learning centres of the brain. (Harvard Study, Shawn Achor, American author, 'The Happiness Advantage.')

Dave kept including easy lessons into the routines so that the whales could learn almost without effort. Whales are no different to people in this regard. They'll show the trainers when they don't like how you're treating them and they'll show you when they like what you're doing.

To build and keep the trust and friendship, Dave and the trainers keep accentuating the positive and eliminating the negative. Energy flows where attention goes. The more attention you pay to a behaviour, the more it will be repeated. Attention amplifies everything.

The trainers don't pay attention to what the whales do wrong, but instead give lots of attention to what they do right.

"What we focus on is getting them to do things right. That's the key," Dave says. They then reward right behaviour with a fish or a pat on the snout.

It's all about energy management. "If you don't want to encourage poor behaviour, don't spend a lot of time on it," he says. Performances follow focus.

He insists that the most harmful habit in animal education is the human habit of mentally limiting animals. Animals can sense expectations with astonishing accuracy. They can 'live down' or 'live up' to expectations just like humans do. The killer whales have taught Dave always to expect the impossible.

So based on the lessons that Dave learned, how can you achieve peak performance?

Trust
Build friendship and trust

Shine A Light On What Is Right
Shine a light on what is right. Keep hammering home the positive. Catch people doing something right or even just a bit better and praise that specifically and immediately.

After Mistakes, Redirect
When mistakes occur, learn the lessons and then ignore the mistakes. Release the mistakes and let them go. Instead get people do something else to redirect or re-channel their energy so that they're doing something, anything right or even better. Then you can praise what's right or praise and reward progress specifically and immediately in a way that's genuine and sincere.

Great managers see people's brilliance long before the people see it themselves. Then they draw it out of them. We learn to walk by remembering how we walked. Not by videoing, replaying and remembering how we fell.

Instead of asking your work colleagues: "What's wrong with you?" pose the much more intriguing: "What's right with you today?" question. "Let's look at and focus on all the things you've done right first. Now what are the things you would like to improve?"

You can say to a boxer: "Your jab is too slow," or you can say" "Here's how we can get your jab three times faster?"

Which of these two comments will give you your greatest return on your training time? Isn't it the same if you're helping your child with his or her homework?

By shining your light on what's right, you'll see an incredible difference in mood, self-belief and performance.

RED PLATFORM: Command and control. Catch people doing things wrong. Focus on the falls, mistakes and failures. "What's wrong with you?"

GREEN PLATFORM: Friendship and trust. Catch people doing things right. Praise and reward progress. Learn from mistakes. Shine a light on what is right. "What's right with you?"

38

Eleven Rules
To A Better You

THE young man came to me. He just wanted to talk. To chat about what he called "the things that really matter". He was, he said, "stressed out". But he didn't seem to be doing anything much to stress him out. As he put it, he was "just ticking over." He was drifting, aimless, and goalless.

"What do you do most of the time?" I asked.

"Play video games, but I just feel empty all the time. I want to change my life and I need some help. Can you help me?"

Most fathers spend a lifetime saving their sons from the problems that made men out of them and I'd say the same is true for most mothers and their daughters. They save them from the problems that made real women out of them. We give our children everything in life except perhaps the ability to handle adversity, to bounce back from setbacks, to turn stumbling blocks into stepping-stones.

We continued to chat. This particular young lad was definitely of the opinion that the world owed him a living. He was blaming other people, events and situations for his own problems. His constant phrase was: "It's not fair."

I shared with him my version of 'The 11 Rules of Life' based on a book by Charles Sykes called *Dumbing Down Our Kids*.

Those rejigged 11 Rules of Life are:

1. Not Fair

Life is not fair. Get used to it. The average teenager uses the phrase

"It's not fair" 8.6 times a day. Expect difficult. This is no surprise; it is not unfair or unusual. Life is complicated. Get good at it. No matter how much you blame others, it will never change you.

2. Self-Esteem

The real world won't care much about your self-esteem. It will expect you to accomplish something before you actually feel good about yourself. This may come as a shock.

3. Life Lessons

Sorry, you won't make €30,000 a year right out of secondary school. You may even have to wear a uniform that doesn't have a label. The key is to understand that challenges are how we learn and grow. Life is about the lessons we learn. Expect interesting situations. Taking them in your stride builds your confidence. Never fear trouble. Just learn to triumph over it. Be resilient. Learn to bounce back. It's not about falling but it's all about how quickly you get back up again.

4. Learning Opportunities and Solutions

If you think your teacher is tough, wait until you get a boss. When you mess things up, he or she's not going to ask you how you feel about it. View difficulties as challenges or learning opportunities rather than as problems. How we talk about our difficulties makes a huge difference. Words matter. Identify your problems, but give your power and energy to solutions.

5. Texting Through The Weekend

Flipping hamburgers is not beneath your dignity. Your grandparents had a different word for burger flipping. They called it opportunity. They weren't embarrassed making the minimum wage either. They would have been embarrassed to sit around texting all through the weekend.

6. Conscientious

It's not your parents' fault. If you make a mess of things, you are responsible. This is the flip side of "It's my life," and "You're not the boss of me," and other eloquent proclamations of your generation. Learn from every experience. Learn from difficulties, make changes, and move on. Never repeat the same life-lesson.

Attitudes of optimism, enthusiasm and persistence are essential. Conscientious is not a very sexy word but it is essential for success in marriage or in work. It means that in a marriage I actually put out the rubbish and I put the dishes in the dishwasher. In work it means that when I say I'll do something I'll actually do it.

7. Saving The Rain Forest

Before you were born your parents weren't as boring as they are now. They got that way from paying your bills, cleaning up your room and listening to you tell them how idealistic you are. And by the way, before you save the rain forest from the blood-sucking parasites of your parents' generation, try tidying your bedroom, delousing your closet or try mowing the lawn.

8. Effort Matters

Your school may have done away with winners and losers, but life hasn't. Effort still matters. Hard work to achieve goals and deliver results is what happens in the real world.

9. Show Up Every Day

Life is not divided into semesters, and you don't get summers off. At work, they expect you to show up every day at work. While we're at it, very few jobs are interested in fostering your self-expression or helping you find yourself.

10. Leave The Coffee Shop

Television is not real life. Your life is not a sitcom. Your problems will not all be solved in 30 minutes, minus the commercials time. In real life, people actually have to leave the coffee shop to go to jobs.

11. Nerds

Be nice to nerds. You may end up working for one.

Only one person will help you achieve your potential.

You.

If not you, who?

"Drifting, aimless and goalless" is not a formula for success in the real world.

RED PLATFORM: A life of video games. Drifting. Aimless. Goalless.

GREEN PLATFORM: Dreaming a great dream and paying the price in effort, hard work and resilience to make your dream come true.

39

Let Positivity
Change Your Life

HOW many of us go through life like this friend of mine: "I keep getting negative thoughts in my head just about everything and they're so strong they spread like weeds."

She was a young athlete so I asked her what her major running challenges were. She immediately responded: "The self-belief and confidence to enjoy what I am doing."

The presence of negative thoughts in our minds is something we can do something about — but first of all we need to be aware that they are there. Otherwise, as my young friend was saying, they can take over your life by telling you that you are not capable of doing what you have planned. They are really Automatic Negative Thoughts (ANTs).

After a while, you not only believe those thoughts, you obey them. Every time you have an Obama-like: "Yes, we can" moment and think you can do something, just as you start to think that... then those ANTs, those automatic negative thoughts try to force you to give up. Then you give up and say: "What's the point?"

The good news is that you can turn things around. "So, is getting rid of those automatic negative thoughts your top priority?" I asked her.

"Absolutely," she said.

"Those thoughts that say you can't or you're not good enough need to be changed and replaced," I told her.

Instead of ANTs we can actually fill our minds with Positive Automatic Thoughts (PATs).

However, when you try to get rid of them your mind will fight back. That's because these negative thoughts and beliefs are planted in your subconscious and it, in turn, controls 96 per cent of how you live your life.

You can't just reach in and pluck them out like weeds. Instead, you have to re-direct and influence your subconscious. Give it new thoughts, new images and new beliefs to follow.

The transfiguration of this negativity is one of our continuing tasks, as negativity keeps us outside in the cold and away from our own love, nourishment and warmth. Eventually, these ANTs, all this negativity can become the greatest force for our renewal, creativity and growth. Each one of us has this task every moment of every day.

There are two approaches here.

The first is the Western militaristic approach: "Eliminate the negative. Zap those ANTs. Take them out. Rat-tat-tat machine gun them out of your head."

The second is much more powerful.

It's the Oriental approach that sees all these ANTs, all this negativity and uses it like a good gardener uses compost — to grow beautiful plants and flowers.

Negativity is always a clarion call for compassionate awareness and out of that awareness comes a fresh commitment to renewal, creativity and growth.

I would recommend that you take a gentle approach and every time you catch yourself having a negative thought, change it by simply replacing it.

Our life moves primarily in the direction of what we think about and talk about.

If we spend a good part of our day complaining about what's not working, we'll actually start generating a lot more of what's not working. A mind filled with judgment, anger and blame has trained the brain to favour those neurocortical pathways.

Instead of complaining about what's not working, let's be creative about what's positive and what is working. A mind filled with peace, joy and positivity has trained the brain to favour those different pathways.

The really good news is that you cannot hold a negative thought and a positive thought at the same time. You simply cannot have a picture of an elephant and a picture of a ballerina at the same time. It's either one or the other.

Next give your subconscious some support, like reasons why you can do something instead of reasons why you can't. Reasons come first. Purpose has power. Answers come second.

For example if you catch yourself having those Red Platform negative thoughts that say: "I won't do well at this. I'm not good enough," just replace them with Green Platform positive thoughts like: "I'll give this my best shot and see where it takes me."

Then give yourself reasons why you can achieve your goals. When you believe without a doubt that you can, that's when real change happens ... and quickly at that.

Your thoughts and beliefs create your life. Generally whatever you think about and believe you will see manifested in your day-to-day living. Your subconscious obediently follows your thoughts and beliefs as instructions or commands. It's your obedient slave. Your every thought is received as a command.

You can achieve your goals. You can banish negativity. You can dream and shoot higher than you think you can. Forget about being better than others. Just aim to be a better person today than you were yesterday.

You are a powerful person. Much more powerful than you realise.

'Normal' living is truly a travesty of your potential. No more settling for less. No more thinking you're not good enough. No more merely wishing and hoping. No more saying: "I can't, I'm not good enough, I don't know." No more negative thoughts. No more negativity, doubts and fears. What you put up with, you end up with.

So as of today stop settling for less. Today you stop giving up. Today you turn things around. Today you get rid of those negative beliefs. Today you live life to the limit.

Live with passion, joy and gratitude on the Green Platform where you are supporting yourself with positivity all around you. Whatever you want to do, do it now. Don't wait. See how it will work for you once you make up your mind to banish those ANTs and replace them with PATs. Then celebrate your success. Give yourself a symbolic 'PAT' on the back.

RED PLATFORM: Never good enough. Lots of ANTs limiting your potential and blocking your growth and development.

GREEN PLATFORM: Living life to the limit with passion, joy and gratitude. Always replacing those ANTs with PATs.

40

Sitting Is The New Smoking

I HAD an interesting chat with a doctor recently. As usual the topic got around to health, exercise and fitness. I said to him: "Imagine you're on your deathbed. After all your experiences with human bodies, hearts, minds and souls during your lifetime, what are the three last sentences based on your experiences and the lessons you have learned that you would like to say to people before you die? Just three sentences. Now they must be short."

Without missing a beat, he instantly replied: "Firstly, elevate your heart rate because prolonged sitting poisons your body. Secondly, wash your hands. Thirdly, be kind to people."

"Why is it so important to elevate your heart rate on a regular basis?" I asked him. "Interesting that you put that first."

"When people tell me about their arthritis, migraine or lack of energy, I always ask them this simple question: 'How many times a week do you elevate your heart rate to 70 per cent of its maximum?'"

Your blood vessels, the arteries and the veins, are a bit over 60,000 miles long. When you elevate your heart rate it pumps blood at an accelerated pace through your body's incredibly complicated system of veins and arteries.

This accelerated flow of blood through your body helps to provide increased oxygen to your cells and also helps to keep your veins and arteries clear of plaque that builds up gradually.

It's like the plumbing in your house. After years of use, a drain can easily get clogged up with calcium, lime, sludge or other gunky materials. If the pipes are too clogged they close up and shut down the flow of water. A plumber will then have to come out and clear the sludge from the clogged pipes.

Your body's veins and arteries can also get clogged up and as a result you'll have bad health problems. Sitting is really the silent killer, sitting is the new smoking," he said.

"If you sit a lot on the sofa, in the car or at a desk — then you're in trouble. If that's your lifestyle, then don't complain to me when health issues such as obesity, diabetes, heart problems, migraines and a lack of energy suddenly appear in your life. In many cases they are the result of the prolonged sitting lifestyle you have chosen."

One recent study compared adults who spent less than two hours a day in front of the TV or other screen-based entertainment with those who logged more than four hours a day of recreational screen time. Those with greater screen time had:

• Nearly 50 per cent increased risk of death from any cause

• About a 125 per cent increased risk of events associated with cardiovascular disease, such as chest pain (angina) or heart attack.

The solution seems to be less sitting and more moving overall. You might start by simply standing rather than sitting whenever you have the chance. For example — stand while talking on the phone or eating lunch.

If you work at a desk for long periods of time, try a standing desk, or improvise with a high table or counter.

Better still, think about ways to walk while you work. Walk laps with your colleagues rather than gathering in a conference room for meetings.

The impact of movement, even leisurely movement, can be profound. You'll burn more calories leading to weight loss and increased energy.

Even better, the muscle activity needed for standing and other movement seems to trigger important processes related to the breakdown of fats and sugars within the body.

When you sit, these processes stall and grind to a halt as your health risks increase. Then when you stand or actively move, you kick the processes back into action. Change your sedentary lifestyle today and reap the rewards of improved health. Sitting really is the new smoking. Elevate your heart rate. When you're kind to yourself in this manner, you find it easier then to be kind to others.

RED PLATFORM: Sitting all day. Couch potato. "Sitting = The New Smoking." Just as poisonous in the long run. Dirty hands full of germs. Little kindness at any level.

GREEN PLATFORM: Elevate your heart rate. Wash your hands. Be kind to yourself and to others.

41

Massive Mental Strength

WHAT the mind can conceive and believe, it generally can achieve. Whether it is business, sport or just trying to get a bit fitter, once you conquer what you have to do in your head, the rest will follow.

The mental approach is the tipping point.

Before the rugby world cup won by England in 2003, their manager, Clive Woodward, said he was convinced that the fittest team would not win the tournament, nor the strongest, but rather the team that had massive mental strength would.

He was right, of course, because his England team were a little over the hill by that time, had lost a yard or two around the pitch, but each member believed totally in himself and the group dynamic. Their confidence was based on their competence. They won the cup.

There are really only two things that drive us, fear or freedom. We are either weakened by fear or we are strengthened by freedom. England knew how to press the freedom button and ended up as champions.

The name of the fear driver is the Ego, and in our day-to-day living it consistently exposes whatever mental weakness we have. It finds its home on The Red Platform.

The Ego's favourite story is,

"You're not good enough."

"The others are better."

"You are not near ready for this challenge."

Going to bed, the Ego says: "You didn't get enough done."

Waking up in the morning, the Ego rants on: "You didn't get enough sleep."

Nothing is ever enough for the Ego. The Ego will conjure up all kinds of false assumptions as evidence that you're really not up to the task at hand.

Now the scene is set for the other weapon in the Ego's arsenal — doubt. Once you begin to doubt yourself, the Ego smiles. Job done. It smirks: "That's what life's really all about — fear and doubt. Deep down you know you're rotten to the core and you'll never amount to anything."

It stalks your mind by reminding you of your own shortcomings. It loves to fuel your thoughts with fears as you contemplate your next challenge, be it a new position, a change at home or a sport you are involved in.

However, the Ego, too, has a vulnerable spot that all of the mystic masters of the world have unearthed. Like Dracula's inability to live in the light, the Ego can't live when you are awake, aware, alert and living fully in the present.

You can dismantle the Ego's power with one simple step called 'awareness.'

That's how you search for and activate the hero, which is the real you, inside yourself and living all the time on The Green Platform.

You go the Triple-A route. You become awake, aware and alert. Once you fully commit to what you are doing, the shadow of doubt disappears. Your dream becomes your destiny because you are sure that this is what you want to achieve. This awareness prevents you from being browbeaten by the belittling Ego voice inside your head.

If we all put as much energy into visualising our achievements as we do into focusing on our failures, we would be happier, healthier and a much more satisfied people.

The Kentucky Wildcats became the National Basketball Champions in the US against the odds in 2012. Their spiritual leader is their legendary coach John Calipari, known in Kentucky as 'Coach Cal.'

I remember doing a mental-strength session with his team. I spoke for maybe 45 minutes. Coach Cal thanked me sincerely and then summarised the session with one 10-word sentence: "You heard the man: fear and doubt, cast 'em out."

He hit the nail on the head, because when you drain those two negative vampires of fear and doubt out of your life, all that's left is the transforming power of confidence and self-belief.

So bring that feeling of confidence, self-belief and optimism to what you are doing, whether you want to gain promotion in your job, run a personal best in a 10k or go back into education.

You will see and feel a difference straight away. What you conceive and believe, you will achieve.

RED PLATFORM: Fear and doubt. You're not good enough.

GREEN PLATFORM: Self-belief and confidence based on your competence. Dream it and do it. Conceive it. Believe it. Achieve it. "Fear and doubt — cast them out."

42

Partner Power

SHAKESPEARE was on to something when he declared through Hamlet that nothing was "good or bad but thinking makes it so." As Milton said, the mind "can make a heav'n of hell, a hell of heav'n."

Let's say you want to get up in the morning and go for a run. The thought of going for a run — that's good. So you set the alarm for 6 o'clock. At that moment you're thinking: "This is good for my health, good for my mental energy, good for my body and good for my job." You're thinking all the right positive thoughts.

However, it's a different a number of hours later when the alarm goes off. There you are in a cocoon of sheets, a duvet and a pillow. You're so relaxed and cosy. You're thinking, if you got another hour in this warm and comfortable cocoon and reset the alarm for 7 o'clock it would set you up for the day. You convince yourself. So you sleep on for another hour. Heavenly bliss, your mind tells you. And you know that when that alarm goes off, you'll have come up with yet another excuse to stay wrapped up for another few minutes.

Setting a goal and achieving it are two different things. The challenge with any goal is to keep our commitment to it — to do what we say we'll do long after the mood that we set the goal in is gone. If you don't get up, no one will know it, but you've just set up a neurological pattern in your brain that gives you more reasons not to do something every time you give in.

If you get up at six and keep your promise to yourself, you're beating a different pathway through the jungle of your brain. You do it one more day and it becomes easier. You do it another day and you're on your way to making it a habit.

It only takes between 21 and 28 days to form a lifetime habit. Less than a month to form a great life path which can only be of benefit to you.

First we make our patterns or our habits and then our habit or patterns make us. Private personal victories always precede public victories. As the famous mountaineer and explorer Edmund Hillary said about Mount Everest: "It's not the mountain we conquer, but ourselves".

Former English middle-distance athlete Roger Bannister was the first man to run a sub four-minute mile in 1954. He didn't just turn up and do it. He failed time and again before achieving the milestone. His desire to be the first man to dip under four minutes stemmed from his failure to do well at the 1952 Olympics. He created a new habit. The limit that people said couldn't be broken became the major sporting goal in his life. It helped that an Australian, John Landy, was trying to break the same barrier, so the two pushed one another as partners in adversity. They knew what they wanted to do.

It's not 'knowing what to do' that matters — it's 'doing what we know.' The single biggest challenge facing CEOs is not goal setting but rather goal-achieving.

Implementation.

It's the same with all of us when it comes to pushing ourselves.

Research has shown that implementation of goals more than doubles when a person has an 'accountability partner.'

If I know I have a friend, an 'accountability partner,' waiting for me at the top of the road at 6.15 a.m., then there's no way I'm going to let him or her down when the alarm goes off at six. I'm up, into my gear and running shoes, down to the kitchen for a few glasses of water and out the door.

That's partner power.

Years ago my brother Vincent, ran a lot of marathons and put in the training miles with his friend Donal. Some evenings he wouldn't feel like going out to Malahide to run. Then the call would come from Donal. "I'll be waiting for you." And he would go. Some other evening Donal wouldn't feel like going, but Vincent would say: "I'll wait until you get here." Then Donal had no choice but to turn up.

As part of our Andec management and team building training, we have what we call a 'GPPP', a Green Platform Partnership Programme. Two people meet once a week on a Friday for a 15-minute reflection and hold themselves positively accountable for having a positive attitude and staying on The Green Platform during the week. They also reflect on their goal implementation process. In terms of goal achievement it's been incredibly successful.

In general, on your own, the implementation of your goal hovers around 40 per cent. But with a Green Platform Partner who will encourage you and support you, your implementation zooms up to 95 per cent. Who wouldn't want an astonishing 55 per cent increase in goal implementation?

Get a Green Platform Accountability Partner and more than double your chances of starting and sticking to what you've always wanted to achieve on the exercise, running, cycling, swimming, walking or job fronts.

The famous runner and author Dr George Sheehan, who ran faster marathons at 64 than he did at 24, was once asked on television what was the toughest part of a run for him. He replied: "The hardest part of a run has always been putting on my running shoes. Always there's been that tiny inner voice saying that I'd be better off going to bed for an hour."

The doyen of Irish broadcasters, Gay Byrne, once said that he never ever went out for a walk in the evening or a ride on the bicycle and regretted it when he came home. My neighbour Hugh says the same thing. He always feels better after a walk to the Bray seafront and back.

Since we cannot change reality, let us change the eyes with which we see reality. People are not disturbed by things but by the views, the interpretations or the meanings they make up in their heads about things.

The bottom line is that if you don't like something, change it — and if you can't change it, change the way you think about it. A run or a walk or a job is neutral. Neither good nor bad. But the way you think about it makes it so. We don't need new landscapes. We just need new eyes for the landscapes that are already there. It's not what we look at but what we see that matters.

Could it be that all you need is a real good Green Platform Partner to flip your 'thinking' and give you a real positive boost to launch you on your path to greatness? The only thing you will feel is better.

RED PLATFORM: Knowing what to do but not doing it. Going it alone without a positive supportive Green Platform Accountability Partner. Viewing lens — the eyes of misery.

GREEN PLATFORM: Knowing what to do and just doing it, with the encouragement of a Green Platform Partner. Viewing lens — the eyes of joy.

43

'Ronan, You're Great'

RONAN TYNAN holds 14 world records from competing as a Paralympian. As a 20-year-old he lost his two legs but within a year, he was making serious waves as an athlete. He represented Ireland in the 1984 and 1988 summer Paralympics winning four golds, two silvers and one bronze medal.

Between 1981 and 1984, he won 18 gold medals from various competitions.

In the following years, he gained admission to the National College of Physical Education in Limerick on the road to becoming a surgeon.

Then he became famous internationally as a tenor. Clearly it was not only his aptitude but also his attitude that determined his altitude at all these levels.

He sang for US American presidents at their inaugurations. I heard him singing 'Danny Boy' to an audience of 3,000 in Lexington, where he brought the house down.

Ronan has an amazing voice and he uses it to send feelings to his audiences. From his success you also know he uses it at two levels. The first is to sing beautiful songs, but the other is to spur himself on with that other voice — that quiet inner voice inside his head. He claims it all came down to those three words his father kept saying to him despite all the obstacles, setbacks and stumbling blocks he's faced in his life.

Those three magical words that his father always said to him after every effort, no matter how small, were: "Ronan, you're great."

And no matter how difficult things were, no matter how

challenging, no matter how tough things got — these three words echoed in his head over and over again: "Ronan, you're great."

So what is your voice saying?

Is it telling you that you'll never amount to much, that you are not enough, that you're worthless or is it, like Mr Tynan's, telling you that you are in fact great?

Is that inner voice contributing to your energy and well-being or contaminating it? If it's uplifting and constructive, then the chances are you're already enjoying the thrill of achieving your dreams — whatever they are.

We have on average 50,000 thoughts a day. But they keep floating around in a disorderly fashion unless we prioritise them.

Writing down goals helps enormously. It you think, it ink it.

Once we put what we want at the top of the list, our subconscious can take over and get to work making it happen.

The best image about the role of your subconscious and how it operates is that of an unquestioning slave. It will give you total obedience. Like the Genie popping out of Aladdin's Lamp saying: "Your every thought is my command."

It responds to your thoughts and the voice inside your head. It will move mountains to carry out what they are telling you to do.

Another image for the subconscious is that of land. The farmer plants and the land returns what's been planted. If the farmer plants weeds, the land will return weeds. If the farmer plants potatoes, the land will return potatoes. The land (your subconscious) doesn't care. It will return whatever is planted. You either plant positive, constructive, uplifting thoughts or negative destructive, belittling thoughts. Your subconscious (the land) doesn't care. It will return what you plant.

Which is why when someone commits totally to something realistic but stretching, strange things happen. You leave self-sabotage behind and the poison thought of saying that you can't do something is no longer a thought you allow in your head.

We live in a world that is full of negativity. You only have to turn on the radio or watch the news on television. That's why it is now more important than ever to become aware of the power you have within to change yourself — and maybe those around you too with your new reality.

The greatest poison in any family, any workplace or any sporting team is the inventory of Negative Belittling Remarks (NBRs) that many people in Ireland use to put others "in their place".

"He's no use at leading a team" or "she's very limited when it comes to taking responsibility." We almost seem to glory in knocking back colleagues. The voice inside our head does the same job on us: "You're no good at that."

On the other hand, the greatest tonics we find in life are contained in what we call Positive Affirming Remarks (PARs) where we praise people for how well they do something in a way that is genuine, specific and sincere. We catch them doing something right or just better than before. We give them a new sense of worth by using our voice and our encounter with them in a positive way.

Remember Ronan's inner voice that came from his Dad's empowering words — "Ronan, you're great." Imagine having that voice drummed into your mind, heart and soul all your life. Could it have something to do with all those world records and all his other life successes?

Your inner voice can become your inner coach bringing out the best in you, and not your inner critic bringing out the worst in you. Make sure that your inner voice is your best friend, not your worst enemy.

Remember, if you have no enemy on the inside, the enemy on the outside doesn't matter.

Ronan lost his legs and could have felt like a victim for the rest of his life. Instead, he picked himself up to soar to success as a surgeon, an athlete and also as a world-famous singer.

Switch your inner voice on to his channel and just take off down the road to your own achievements.

Ronan, you truly are great and you continue to inspire us all.

RED PLATFORM: "You're useless. You're no good. You're the world's worst. You'll never amount to anything."

GREEN PLATFORM: "Ronan, you're great." Sincere and genuine praise always pays.

44

Tiger's Turnaround

IT'S funny how we treat every problem that arises in our daily lives almost with surprise — as if setbacks shouldn't happen to us. We play the role of the victim well and consequently never really get a handle on how to take problems in our stride.

If we decide we want to go back into education and do a degree or get an extra qualification and then we find that we might have to write a four-page letter explaining why we should be considered for that course, we use the excuse: "I've no chance anyway," and end up not doing it.

So we use up all our energy peddling these negative stories and we back them up with more negative questions. "What's wrong with me?" Imagine all the belittling answers that question will evoke. We're only paving the road for failure by allowing one little setback to equal total defeat.

How often have you told yourself in such a situation that what you're trying to do is beyond you because you're too old or too tired or just too lacking in exams results?

Make any of these statements and you have justified why you'll never progress your education.

Imagine if you flipped that thinking on its head and said: "Every time I do something to improve my goals, I expect something to happen which on the face of it is an obstacle. But I'll take it in my stride and move on. In fact, I'll use it to strengthen my resolve in order to make my goals more achievable."

Now there's a groundbreaking approach to bring to every part of your life.

Tiger Woods was a golfing prodigy. From an early age his dad, Earl, taught him to expect trouble somewhere in every round he played. So when the US star player found himself in deep rough or behind a tree or buried in a bunker, he would use it not to curse his luck, but rather to search for an excellent response.

In other words, Tiger was programmed to feel that what would normally be looked on as an obstacle or potential disaster by his golfing peers would be seen as an opportunity to shine by him. He used to say to himself: "How will I hit this shot so brilliantly that it will forever go down in the annals of golf?"

What an empowering question to carry around in his head. I know Tiger has had his own personal and playing problems since, but with that sort of positivity burnt in his inner software, it's not too hard to see why he has won so many majors, 14 so far, ranking only second at this stage of his career to the legendary Jack Nicklaus.

Tiger saw such moments not as obstacles but opportunities, not stumbling blocks or tombstones but stepping-stones.

He was taught to consider that every problem he would face is there for one reason, to make him a better golfer. The true test of a champion is the ability to overcome obstacles and not to let what you cannot do interfere with what you can do.

Challenges are what make life interesting. Overcoming them is what makes life meaningful. If you believe in yourself you will discover that there's something inside you that's greater than any obstacle.

Even in life, Tiger brought that willingness to adapt bad situations like the break-up of his marriage to his thinking.

"It's not what we achieve in life that matters, it's what we overcome," he said as he explained how he hoped to cope after he publicly admitted it was over.

I think Tiger's real strength is that he understands the importance of the stories he tells himself every day and the questions he asks about every situation he's in.

That's the challenge for us right now in our lives. Our own capacity to tell stories is just about our profoundest gift in our lives. We are all reporters who put headlines up in our minds and these basically decide whether we enjoy our day or not.

It's the same with your ambition to go on to further education or change your career in midstream. It can and will happen if you decide that's what you want to do regardless of what obstacles might be put in front of you. You're not what you have done. You're what you have overcome.

Every time you find a Tiger bunker in your life, there's a shot you can play that will not just keep you on track but will also uplift you. The real loser is you if you allow an obstacle to put you off course. The real winner is you if you use it to spur yourself on to great things. The more obstacles you overcome, the better you become. An obstacle can define you, destroy you or strengthen you.

When you look at life that way, the decision you make the next time you find yourself facing a problem or a setback should come much easier. "How will you hit your shot out of that life bunker so well that it will give you pride, satisfaction and inspiration for years to come?"

US artist and author Mary Anne Radmacher sums up your ability to continually bounce back over and over again when she says: "Courage does not always roar. Sometimes courage is the quiet voice at the end of the day saying: 'I will try again tomorrow.'"

RED PLATFORM: "What a disastrous shot! It's just not my day. What's wrong with me today? I'm useless and that proves it. I'm giving up."

GREEN PLATFORM: "How will I hit this shot from the bunker of my life so magnificently that it will forever go down in my personal history as one of my greatest moments?" Or the quiet voice: "I will try again tomorrow."

45

Purpose Gives
You Power

I N the year 1970 in the United States, two billion tablets were consumed. Thirty-seven years later, in 2007, that number had skyrocketed to 113 billion per year — a rise in a bad habit that generally tinkers with the symptoms of disease without ever getting to the root causes.

In the United States, spending for prescription drugs was $234.1 billion in 2008. That was more than double what had been spent in 1999.

It's not just bad habits with tablets; we in Ireland have gone down the wrong road too with our excessive eating and drinking. The renowned Dr Patrick Wall of University College Dublin calls it "globesity." He is so right. Obesity is a global challenge.

The simple fact is that a bit of regular exercise could put a stop to most of our ills. We have the greatest pharmaceutical plant on the planet available to us in our own bodies, provided we get them fit and healthy. A good walk or run, cycle or swim can release the endorphins in our bodies and increase the seratonin levels to make us feel good naturally.

We all know what to do to flourish, to live a happy and fulfilled life and to have a fit and healthy body. We're fooling ourselves if we say we don't know. Of course we do. The cure is within. We just need to rouse ourselves out of such a poor way of accepting conventional wisdom and replacing it with more decisiveness in our lives.

It's about a little more commitment. It's about breaking limiting beliefs and doing what we keep saying we want to do — learning a language or doing an extracurricular course.

When the Moors landed on the south coast of Spain, their commander Tariq ibn Ziyad asked them if they were ready to fight the Spanish no matter what they had to do.

"Absolutely," they assured him, "we're 100 per cent committed. "Alright," he said, "just to make sure, let's burn our boats because then there's no going back."

About a thousand years earlier, the world's greatest empire builder, Alexander the Great, burned his boats upon arrival on the shores of Persia. By burning his boats, Alexander committed his men to victory over the Persians, whose great numbers far outnumbered the Greeks.

Another such incident was in 1519 AD, during the Spanish conquest of Mexico. Hernán Cortés, the Spanish commander, scuttled his ships so that his men would have to conquer or die.

Total commitment for us is deciding that we too are not going back. Not putting it on the long finger, not saying that we should do something but we'll wait until next year. Next year never comes for that person. You have to cut off any other possibility of not doing what you decide to do. You have to burn those boats of fears, doubts and limiting beliefs.

Your subconscious is not a logical part of your inner software. It doesn't matter how many reasons you give it or how many decisions you make in your conscious mind. The two parts, your conscious mind and your subconscious mind, speak different languages.

Your subconscious speaks the language of images, pictures and emotions.

So if you want to follow through on your decision to achieve a goal, you need a powerful story filled with images of what you want to achieve, and then you need to activate those powerful feelings of success, achievement and happiness that accompany the inner pictures. Only then will you have your conscious and subconscious minds aligned.

If you want to learn a new language see yourself having great conversations in that language with the people of that country.

The subconscious laps all that stuff up — pictures, images and emotion and will make you more likely to align your conscious and subconscious to achieve your goal.

What story are you telling yourself? Is it laden with reasons why you should not do something or is it action-fuelled with emotional images of the goals and dreams you want your story to achieve?

The great German philosopher Friedrich Nietzsche said: "Give me a 'why' and I'll go through any 'how'." This 'why' is what sustained Viktor Frankl and helped him survive the concentration camps. His 'whys' were that he would see his beautiful young wife again after the war, and he visualised himself on stages around the world telling people that these horrendous atrocities must never happen again. Those 'whys' sustained him and enabled him to survive. They killed his wife, but he didn't know that at the time.

About 80 per cent of the energy to achieve any goal comes out of our 'why' — our reason, our purpose.

Purpose gives power.

Reasons come first.

Get your inspiring 'why'.

If you procrastinate or put something off until later, then you'll find that worry will always takes the place of action. will persist. Worry is putting attention on what you don't want. What you *resist* will *persist*. Worry is like praying for something that you don't want to happen.

Worries love procrastination and non-action and we often boast in an inverse way about how we are "terrible worriers" as if that were something to be proud of. The reality is that worry is negative and does nothing for us or those who live closest to us — our family, friends and work colleagues.

The bottom line here is that worry is actually a call to action, because it wants you to rock in the cradle of inaction, apathy and indifference.

Just as light and darkness cannot co-exist, and gratitude and negativity cannot remain on the same platform, neither can worry and action share the same platform.

So take action. Be decisive. Do something, anything about the thing you worry about and worry will disappear. As Albert Einstein said: "Nothing happens until something moves."

So what worries have you in your head as you read this? Pause for a second and think.

Only put into your imagination what you want to create and attract into your life. Only give life and voice and energy to what you actually want, not to what you don't want to create and attract and manifest in your life. Don't download into your mind everything that could go wrong on the Red Platform. Only download everything that could got right on the Green Platform.

Control the controllables in your life and let the rest sit. Cast out the 'fluff' stuff and control what is in your hands to control.

Take positive action by remembering your 'why,' your reason or your purpose and then keep focused on the benefits awaiting you and others. Keep your eye on the prize, and detach from it. This will inspire you to keep on taking present moment action.

Keep your thoughts on what you want, not on what you don't want. Be positive by imagining how you'll feel when you change your story and start living it.

Two billion pills to 113 billion is far too big a jump in 37 years. 111 billion of an increase. Something is seriously wrong here.

So find your own personal purpose or 'why' to take exercise and activate the inner pharmaceutical plant. Eat nurtritious food. Take action. Unleash that feel-good seratonin chemical. Let the happiness dopamine rip through your system. As a friend said to me recently: "I love that feeling after I go for a run when all those 'endolphins' start swimming and jumping around my body."

I thought that he provides a much better image than "endorphins" and certainly a much better image than sitting on a sofa eating pills, tackling symptoms and camouflaging the root causes of our unhealthy lifestyle.

RED PLATFORM: Consuming 113 billion pills per year. Tinkering with symptoms. Camouflaging root causes. Sticking Band-Aids on a tumour.

GREEN PLATFORM: Burning the boats of indecision and taking exercise to activate your inner pharmaceutical plant unleashing all those natural feel-good chemicals like serotonin, dopamine and 'happy' endorphins. Tackling the root causes. Removing the tumour.

46

Being The Greatest
You Can Be

A RGUABLY the best affirmation of a positive Self-Image of all
time came from Cassius Clay (aka Muhammad Ali) when he
declared long before he became heavyweight champion of the
world: "I am the greatest."

While some might see this as arrogant, for Ali it was vital at a
time when he was being thrown out of restaurants and drapery
shops because of the colour of his skin.

In that context, it was more than an idle boast. It was a
declaration of defiance to the world that he was somebody great.

The idea came from his grandmother, who told him to say these
words over and over, emphasising that if he believed them,
eventually others would too.

The strongest force in the human personality is the need to
remain consistent with how we view ourselves — our Self-Image.
It is like a thermostat. It is a powerful internal mechanism that the
subconscious uses to self-correct upwards, or downwards, until
you find that level with which you are comfortable.

While Ali used it all his life to tune up and raise up his inner Self-
Image, most of us have it as an agent of sabotage to self-correct down.

Very rarely will you do something that is not in line with the
mental image that you have of yourself, your inner picture of
yourself. The way you set your goals, choose your values or react
to life is never determined by who you are, but by who and what
you think you are — your Self-Image.

When you leave school for better or worse you will have a story about yourself branded on your soul in the same way that a farmer will brand a bullock. Generally it's with you for life, and usually it's the Ego's story that you are not good enough.

Not beautiful enough.

Not handsome enough.

Not thin enough.

Not intelligent enough.

Not young enough.

Not old enough.

No matter what way you slice it or dice it you are not 'enough.'

The truth is that not only are you 'enough,' but in fact you are perfect. You have a unique gift and a talent that no one else has and all you have to do is to embrace it, cherish it, cut loose and unleash it in the service of humanity to build a better world.

You will throw away any level of success that does not match your Self-Image. The first man I know who really discovered the incredible power of a positive Self-Image was a man called Maxwell Maltz. He was an American cosmetic surgeon, and he wrote a book on the power of Self-Image called 'Psycho-Cybernetics.' His life changing moment came when he finished cosmetic surgery on a lady's nose and face. It was a fantastic job. He was so proud of his work. She looked stunningly beautiful. Then when the lady looked in the mirror, she said that one sentence that changed his life: "But I still feel ugly on the inside."

Then he knew for sure that real beauty is on the inside and he gave up plastic surgery and started his work on inner cosmetic surgery — changing the Self-Image.

If an egg is broken from the outside, life ends. If an egg is broken from the inside, life begins. All real and lasting change happens from the inside and works its way out.

Your Self-Image is your dominant partner in life. It's a case of: "The you that you see is the you you'll be," and it is with you all day, every day, for better or for worse.

A negative Self-Image says: "That's just me. It's the way I am."

This is where Ali comes in. His inner partner was a positive Self-Image that said over and over: "I can choose who I am."

Ali went one step further though by saying everything in the present tense. "I am the greatest."

There was no doubt that it might take a few years or a few more fights. No, he was certain of who he was.

You will never be different from what your Self-Image says you are. If you change your Self-Image to think of yourself as you want to become in a manner that's realistic but stretching for you, then you will automatically self-correct up and become the new person.

There are three keys to developing a new and powerful Self-Image that will serve you well:

1. Visualisation

The first key to installing a new Self-Image comes from your power to visualise: "The you that you see is the you that you'll be." Turn on your VCR. 'Visualisation Creates Reality.'

2. PowerTalk

The second key is PowerTalk or affirmations — to affirm this new image with positive present-tense statements beginning with "I am." Go from zero to hero with your positive powerful "I ams."

"I am" is the start of all Self-Image change beliefs. How many times do we use the power of poison "I ams" against ourselves?

If you look at "I am" in your life as a party that you are having in your house where you send out invitations to a lot of people, then whatever comes after your "I am" is on your invitation list. They will receive your gilt edged invitation and they will come. "Build your 'I am' and they will come."

Here's some Red Platform "I am" invitation examples where you are inviting what you don't really want into your life:

"I am unattractive." (Ugliness comes looking for you.)

"I am unlucky." (You're inviting disappointments.)

"I am so clumsy." (Clumsiness comes looking for you.)

"I am always tired." (Fatigue will find you.)

"I am so overweight." (Calories with catch up with you.)

"I am so old." (Wrinkles will come looking for you.)

Whatever follows "I am" will eventually find you.

You're inviting these "I ams" into your life. They're receiving your invitations to your house party, and you're opening your door and giving them permission to come into your life.

The good news is that you can choose what follows your "I am." You can choose your guest list. You can choose who you want to invite into your life.

Instead choose to follow your "I ams" with all that you want in your life. Send out some new invitations. Take control of your guest list. Step over to the Green Platform and send out positive "I am" invitations that focus on what you really want in your life and only what you want.

"I am healthy." (Health starts tracking you down.)

"I am energetic." (Energy comes looking for you.)

"I am creative." (Creativity starts heading your way.)

"I am happy." (You're inviting happiness into your life.)

"I am confident." (Confidence comes to you.)

"I am motivated." (Motivation zooms towards you.)

"I am disciplined." (You're inviting discipline into your life.)

Change your mental guest list. Send out new invitations to a new set of positive guests.

Go from saying, "I am no good at anything," to saying with feeling, "I am really enjoying this job, this walk or this swim."

Observe the kind of "I ams" that are coming out of your mouth? Only you can control and choose the ones that are coming out of your mouth. Words have creative power. Words are like seeds. When you speak you give life and power and energy to what you are saying. Pay attention to all those things you are inviting into your life. Why ever would you think or give voice or energy to inviting into your life what you don't want in your life?

When you see yourself not as who you are, but as who you can become, you stimulate incredible growth, incredible change and incredible energy for your future Self-Image.

That's why the single biggest challenge with anyone is to get them to see and affirm themselves as successful in a manner that is realistic but stretching for them — to discover their new Self-Image and self-correct up to that with the help of those powerful "I ams."

How can you be it unless you see it, affirm and say it? The you you see and the you you say with your "I ams" really is the you you'll be.

3. Power Questions

The third key is to start asking yourself PowerQuestions.

"How can I be the best that I can be?"

"How can I be the change I want to see in my family or my team?"

"How can I turn this around and enjoy the process?"

The Self-Image is the key not just to the human personality but also to changing human behaviour. Change the Self-Image and you change the personality and the behaviour. Self-Image sets the boundaries of individual accomplishment.

Psychologist Dr Joyce Brothers really nails the power of a positive Self-Image when she says: "An individual's Self-Image is the core of his or her personality. It affects every aspect of human behavior: the ability to learn, the capacity to grow and change. A strong, positive Self-Image is the best possible preparation for success in life."

Muhammad Ali's mission now is to help every man, woman and child to be the greatest they can be. He wants to pass on his grandmother's wisdom about the power of a positive Self-Image that radically changed his life and the lives of millions of the poor around the world who benefit from his Muhammad Ali Fund.

He couldn't leave us a better legacy.

RED PLATFORM: I am no good. I am the world's worst. That's just me. It's the way I am. I can't help how I feel. I'll never be good enough. Poison "I ams." Horrific "I am" guest list of things you really don't want in your life.

GREEN PLATFORM: I am the greatest and I will help everyone I can to be the greatest that they can be. I am the change I want to see in the world. Positive powerful "I ams." Superb guest list containing all the things you want in your life.

47

Mind Your Most Powerful Motivator

IF you want to achieve any of your goals make sure to stand guard at the door of your mind.

Think of your mind as a cup of coffee. If your worst enemy came and put a spoon of sugar into your coffee, no problem. But if your best friend put in a spoon of strychnine in your coffee, you're a dead man or a dead woman. Since thoughts have a habit of becoming things, we have to watch our thoughts. Are they positive power thoughts or poison negative thoughts? Thoughts shape our reality. Thoughts control our lives. Thoughts are powerful. Thoughts become actions. Actions become habits. Habits shape our character and determine our destiny. Thoughts determine destiny.

So who's putting what into your coffee? Watch your coffee and watch it like a hawk.

Stand guard at the door of your mind.

Feed and strengthen your mind with only positive thoughts, positive images and pictures of only what you want. Watch out for the poison negativity and the body-weakening toxic thoughts. All those things you don't want.

Stand guard at the door of your mind.

Well, the good news is that we already have an inbuilt guard at that door. We've all heard of or watched the movie *The Bodyguard* but did you ever think that a great blockbuster in our lives might be our 'Mindguard?'

Believe it or not we all have one, but mostly in our day-to-day rushing around, we don't recognise that fact.

The fancy name for it is our Reticular Activating System (RAS). It comes from the Latin (retica), meaning a net to catch things in.

What is your RAS?

Basically, it's a small network of neurons at the back of your brain about the size of your thumb, which acts as a filter on your thoughts. It takes in and then sorts the eight million stimuli coming at you from your surroundings and decides whether they are important or not.

Your mind is as busy a spot as Dublin Airport at the height of the summer's rush. There is a whirlwind of activity going on and unless you had your RAS as your 'Gatekeeper,' you wouldn't know what to let through or what to filter out.

So, of those eight million pieces of information coming at you, what will get through? Your Mindguard or Gatekeeper RAS has a habit of only letting in only top priorities. It is critically important to get anything you want to manifest in your life on to that top priority list so that they can gain entry.

Like what?

Anything that matches your current Self-Image (your inner picture or image of yourself) or your visualised emotionalised written goals come in near the top.

Such functions as sights, sounds, smells and feelings come at us from our surroundings at any given time. For instance, a mother sleeping at night does not hear cars passing or music from loud neighbours next door, but a tiny cry from her baby's room and suddenly she is wide awake. That picture or image of her crying baby gets straight in and cuts through all the surrounding clutter. Her Gatekeeper RAS lets that significant and important sound in.

A mother will go to pick up her child in a kindergarten and of the 150 children laughing, playing and screaming she will instantly hear and pick out her own child. Her Gatekeeper RAS lets that unique sound in.

You buy a red car. You think it's the only one in the country. Then you immediately begin to spot other similar red cars. They were there all the time but your Gatekeeper RAS is only now letting them in. You say: "I've never noticed them before." They were blocked out in the same way that the spam filter on your computer blocks out the unwanted emails.

Now we're getting to the important bit. Your Gatekeeper RAS thinks in pictures, not words. That's why a daily visualisation of what you want is picked up on your Gatekeeper RAS's radar and helps it to start prioritising information for you.

As a result, your Gatekeeper RAS will start to pay attention to anything that might help you achieve your goals.

It then activates a forensic pursuit of the clues you feed it. If you have a negative Self-Image then it will welcome all the negative toxic evidence to support that negative image. It will activate a similar forensic pursuit of positive powerful uplifting evidence to support a positive Self-Image.

This is where you need to have a positive and visualised list that ensures such a positive attitude passes into your overall system. Feed your mind only pictures and images of what you want. Only put into your imagination what you want to create and attract into your life. Don't give life or voice or energy to what you don't want to create and attract into your life.

That's why visualising yourself having lost 10 pounds in weight will translate into such action if you know how to curry favour with your Gatekeeper RAS. Your Gatekeeper RAS can be your biggest supporter once you get it to work with you rather than against you. It can be your greatest supporter or your greatest saboteur.

It's the reason writing down a clear goal works, while half aspiring to a vague or wooly one — but neither writing it down nor visualising it — means that that inertia will rule. It's not a clear focused picture. Your Gatekeeper RAS will block it and label it 'spam.' It remains buried in the incoming clutter. If you think it, ink it.

However, if you make a very clear picture in your imagination of the end result, a picture of your goal so clear you can almost touch it, one you can really feel, and then turn that goal into PowerTalk with positive, present tense affirmations or incantations or auto-suggestions of your goal in its already achieved state like:

"I am grateful and happy to have a fit and healthy body."

"I am confident, positive, strong and secure."

"Every day in every way I am getting better and better."

"I am now really enjoying this new course."

Once you have this clear picture of your goal, your Gatekeeper RAS will kick into action and you will be surprised at how things fall into place to help you. You will find that you attract the people, the resources and the opportunities to achieve your life or fitness goal.

You'll pick up the right magazine, the right book, or you'll meet the right inspiring friend or you'll get a complementary pass to the right gym.

You'll be in the right place at the right time, meeting the right person attracting the right outcome.

What you practice, you become. Repetition is the mother of skill. If all you did was to tell your dog your goals every day, with your alert Gatekeeper RAS, they'd be more likely to happen.

As the Swiss psychologist Carl Jung said: "Until you make the unconscious conscious, it will direct your life and you will call it fate."

Once you become aware of the power you can have to control your mind, achieving your goals becomes easier. The hard part is knowing how to set them up properly.

So for the coming week watch and see who's putting what into your coffee? Is it a spoon of poison or is it a spoon of healthy honey? Watch your coffee and watch it like a hawk.

Stand guard at the door of your mind.

Just remember to direct the top priority things in your life to the top of your list and your Gatekeeper RAS and your 'Mindguard' will scan their entry tickets and wave them in for immediate implementation and 'decisive action now' attention.

RED PLATFORM: Sleepy 'Mindguard.' Welcoming and entertaining poison negative thoughts. Vague, wooly, fuzzy abstract goals. Waves on through all that stuff you don't want in your life.

GREEN PLATFORM: Alert 'Mindguard' welcoming positive uplifting thoughts and images. Clear, specific, measurable written goals. Seeing them accomplished beforehand and tapping into that great feeling now.

48

Where Attention Grows, Energy Flows

IF I am dreading the thought of doing something I will find an excuse not to do it. However, if I transfer my attention to seeing myself do something big like graduating with a degree and how I will feel then, I change the whole focus.

How?

By putting your attention on the result and how you will feel then. By developing that process, you will find a new source of energy. It's almost like feeling the feel-good benefits beforehand of something you have yet to complete. Because you are now thinking in a certain way, then there is a greater chance that you will get up and achieve you've set out to achieve.

Most of the energy to achieve even that ordinary daily goal comes from the reason you give yourself — the powerful 'why.' All of this goes back to the role the subconscious plays in our lives.

Recent research by Bruce Lipton says that the subconscious controls 96 per cent of our actions but unfortunately for us, most of it is for personal sabotage purposes.

Like most things, even the powerful subconscious has its own weakness — it doesn't know how to process negatives.

For example, if I say to you: "Don't think of a white rabbit"... Bang, the white rabbit is there in your mind.

A mother will say to a child: "Be careful, don't drop that," and sure enough the child will drop it. The problem is that the child listened.

If a child is climbing out on the branch of a tree, what do you say?

"Don't fall." No.

"Hold on tightly." Put attention on the picture or image of what you want to happen.

That's because the subconscious takes in pictures and the emotions connected with those pictures but it won't process negatives. Your mind is logical, but your subconscious is not. It will zero in on the image you feed into it — ignoring the 'don'ts,' the 'nots' or the 'instead ofs'.

It takes time and practice to flip this inner mind switch. All it needs is a change of emphasis by you on the language you feed into your subconscious.

When we say: "Where attention goes, energy flows", we are talking about putting attention on the images or pictures that we are feeding into our subconscious.

Years ago in an All-Ireland semi-final, it was a draw, and there was a 21-yard free in front of the goals in the last few minutes — a chance for the team to make it into the final.

Sometime later I asked the player who took the free what was the last thing he thought of before he kicked the free. "Well," he replied, "I said to myself that if I kick this wide, I may never go back home." And where did he kick it? Yes, wide. Where attention goes, energy really flows.

Republic of Ireland player David O'Leary was asked what was the last thing that went through his mind before he took the famous penalty against Romania that got Ireland to the World Cup quarter-finals in Italia 1990. He said: "I could only think of the place in the net I was going to put it and keep my mind focused on that." He scored the goal.

Perfect. Picture and follow-through.

Have you ever listened to golfers? "Be careful, whatever you do don't hit it into the water!"

Whack, water.

"Don't hit it into the bunker whatever you do!"

Whack, bunker.

"Don't hit the tree!"

Whack, tree.

I remember author and motivator Tony Robbins one time talking about learning to drive a racing car. When it went into a skid, the instructor kept saying: "Think open track." One time when he went spinning towards the wall, the instructor literally took Tony's head in his hands and pointed it towards the open track.

How many times have you seen cars wrapped around telephone or electricity poles? They become magnetic. "I mustn't hit the pole!" Then whack, pole.

The subconscious will always move to the brighter picture. You are controlling the satellite feed of those pictures. You are the one beaming in the pictures to your subconscious.

So, if you are going to do something where do you put your attention? On how hard that something is? No — focus on the rewards, the good feelings afterwards. The benefits. Put your attention only on what you want.

If you are doing your driving test, you can put attention on what you don't want. "I'm very nervous. I'm going to fail."

Or you can simply flip that switch and put attention on what you want.

"I feel very excited. I going to give this my best shot and in a relaxed and focused manner and I'm going to enjoy this test drive. I'll do that and see where it takes me."

RED PLATFORM: Clear vivid images and pictures of what I don't want with lots of 'Nots,' 'Don'ts' and 'Instead ofs.' Don't fall. Worries help this process enormously. Clearly see the shot going wide.

GREEN PLATFORM: Clear vivid pictures of what I want and only what I want. Hold on tightly. Clearly see the shot going into the corner of the net.

49

Create Your Own Law Of Attraction

THE Chinese have a saying: "Life is like an echo, whatever you give out comes back to you." The great English physicist, Isaac Newton, put it another way when he said: "To every action there is an equal and opposite reaction."

When I was growing up in Dungimmon my mother used to say to us: "What goes around comes around," and another of her favourites was: "What's for you won't pass you by."

From these examples, we can see that life is indeed simple. It is made up of only two kinds of things. Positive things and negative things. Wherever you go or whatever you want to achieve, the one thing you will always bring with you is your mind. And your mind is a magnet. What we've learned from the world of quantum physics is that like thoughts attract like thoughts, positive or negative.

Your thoughts attract their equivalent, a vibrational match. Think good, positive, uplifting things and you will attract similar feelings. Think bad, negative thoughts and you'll attract more of the same. This is more popularly known as the Law of Attraction. It is probably the most powerful law in the universe. Just like gravity, it is always in motion, always active. Simply put, the Law of Attraction means that you will attract into your life whatever you focus on with emotion and feeling.

Emotion is the key word here. It's the powerful feelings that kick in the magnetism or vibrational match.

Whatever you give your intense emotional attention and energy to will come back to you. Your emotion will set the universe in motion to bring a similar vibrational match back into your life.

The Law of Attraction is what holds every star in the universe in place and forms every atom and molecule. The force of attraction of the sun holds the planets in our solar system, keeping them from spinning off into space. It can be seen in all of nature from a flower attracting a bee or a seed attracting nutrients. It is the force that draws people together when they fall in love and it operates through all the animals on the earth, the fish in the sea and birds in the air.

Since your emotion sets the universe in motion, the real tragedy is that most of us send out more negative emotional signals about the things we don't want rather than those we want.

The old story of the glass half-full or half-empty has an even deeper meaning. Or remember Langbridge's poem about prisoners: "Two men look out through the same bars; one sees the mud, and one the stars."

Guess whose happiness levels kept getting better? Guess whose misery levels kept getting worse?

How you use your mind and your self-talk is critical. What we are talking about here is control of your life and how you feel in your life. The key is to control what you are attracting into your life. We are either creating our life unconsciously by default or consciously by design.

Are you in design mode or default mode?

Realise that if you are in default mode, you are the unconscious creator of your life. You are in the passenger seat of a car.

Cars have driver seats and passenger seats. Passengers have no power or control over what happens in the car. It's the driver who has all the power and control. When you are in default mode you are the unconscious creator of your life, you are in the passenger seat.

But when you are in design mode, you are the conscious creator of your life. You are the driver. You have the steering wheel at your command. When you proactively take control of your thoughts, you take that steering wheel and start to live your life by design.

I was talking to a friend recently who was challenged by some other friends to run up a mountain. Halfway up, he got tired. He was frustrated, exhausted. He gave me examples of the thoughts that were going through his head. He was in default mode and this was on full negative beam.

He was creating his life unconsciously by default. But he found himself getting more and more tired. His energy followed his thoughts, emotions and inner stories. His energy drained as he was putting his attention by default, on the negative, or on what he really didn't want in his life.

Then one of his friends said: "Come on, it's mind over matter. Think positively. Focus on how you'll feel at the top of the hill and focus now on the next step."

My friend's mind shift was immediate. He said that it was like throwing a switch in his mind. He pulled the hatch and released all the negative thoughts. He ran up the hill like a gazelle and he kept getting stronger. From then on he could only see himself getting to the top.

He stopped being 'driven' by his mind; he took over control and jumped into the driver's seat of his mind. To just let life happen to you is irresponsible. To create your own day is your human right. Then your positive 'likes' will attract more positive 'likes.'

Think of it this way. It is a lot like transmitting and receiving radio waves. Your frequency has to match the frequency of what you want to receive. You cannot tune your radio to 98.5 on your FM dial and expect to get a station broadcasting at 88.8 frequency.

You are a human transmission tower and you are transmitting your frequency with your thoughts and corresponding emotions. You are sending out that magnetic signal that is attracting similar things back to you.

Most of us are complaining and thinking about what we don't want and then keep wondering why it keeps turning up in our lives over and over again.

If you tune into a radio station day after day that plays music you hate, do you sit there complaining about the music and focusing on how much you wish you were listening to something different or do you change the channel?

You change the channel! You control the dial to change the channel. You are the driver in design mode.

If you are feeling excited, enthusiastic, passionate, happy, joyful, appreciative or full of energy you are sending out positive energy, positive vibrations and you'll get more of this positive energy back into your life.

On the other hand if you're feeling bored, anxious, stressed out, angry or resentful you are sending out negative vibrations and it's fairly likely you'll get a load of that negative energy back into your life.

You are a powerful magnet attracting more of what you think about and feel at any moment in time. You literally attract the things, people, ideas and circumstances that vibrate and resonate at the same energy frequency as yours. The stronger and more intense your thoughts and emotions are the greater the magnetic pull becomes. You may not attract what you want in your life but you will always attract what you are.

The key part of the Law of Attraction is the second part of the word — 'action'. If you sit on the sofa all day visualising a new dress saying: "Universe, manifest a new dress for me now," you'll sit there a long time before it appears.

The key to the Law of Attraction is that whatever vision is the clearest, the most vivid and the most specific — and is shot through with powerful emotion, wins.

So have a Massive Action Plan (MAP). Make a list of tasks and prioritise them. Pull the hatch on the negative thoughts. Then listen to your intuition and take inspired action. Choose actions that bring joy to others and watch that good energy return to you one hundredfold.

RED PLATFORM: Vibrational Match: Negativity attracting more negativity. Misery attracting more misery. Anger attracting more anger.

GREEN PLATFORM: Vibrational Match: Positivity attracting more positivity. Joy and love attracting more joy and love. Freedom attracting more freedom.

50

Ignite The Fire Inside

"When You Are Inspired By Some Great Purpose ...
Some Extraordinary Project.
All Your Thoughts Break Their Bonds ...
Your Mind Transcends Limitations ...
Your Consciousness Expands in Every Direction ...
And You Find Yourself In A New and A Great and A Wonderful
World.
Dormant Forces, Faculties and Talents Come Alive ...
And You Discover Yourself To Be A Greater Person By Far Than You
Ever Dreamed Yourself To Be."
Patanjeli 200-25 B.C.

I SPOKE to a truly inspiring woman last year who told me that she got sick and tired of being sick and tired of being overweight. She was about 42 pounds overweight and she decided to do something about it. She got a clear picture, an inspiring vision of her ideal weight and having a really fit and healthy body. This was her inner vision or her own "personal magnificence." Like Patanjeli says, she got "inspired".

She went on a very good fitness and diet programme and now she feels fantastic again, 42lbs lighter and wearing clothes she'd only dreamed of fitting into before. When you see yourself not only as you are but also as you can become, you stimulate incredible growth, incredible change. This woman now is so proud of those before and after pictures. Well, really, just the 'after,' picture. She is now living in Patanjeli's "new, and a great and a wonderful world." She has discovered herself to be "a greater person by far than she ever dreamed herself to be."

The key word from Patanjeli and this woman's story is "inspired." His first words here are: "When you are inspired." Now we live in the information age, but he didn't say, "informed." He didn't say: "When you are informed" by some great purpose, some extraordinary project.

To achieve a worthwhile goal, information won't do it for us. We need inspiration, and inspiration is an emotional or spiritual thing. To in-spire. To put 'spirit' into. Martin Luther King didn't have a strategic plan. He had an inspiring dream.

Why won't information do it?

Look at people who smoke. The label on the packet says 'smoking kills,' but the person who reads it will say, almost in their next breath: "Excuse me, I must go outside for a cigarette." They know the information that one in two smokers will die from a terrible lung disease, but still they smoke and die in instalments. One cigarette at a time.

We need inspiration. We need to be inspired. You cannot motivate people by lighting fires under them, you need to light fires inside them.

To be inspired you need an inspiring vision, "some great purpose, some extraordinary project."

Or maybe the driving force is to find something that you are aiming to become. They say that without a vision, people die. We all need a vision, a dream or a fiercely important, big, outrageous and audacious goal in our lives.

As Steve Jobs said: "If you are working on something exciting that you really care about, you don't have to be pushed. The vision pulls you."

We have the current reality. That's our lives here and now. Then we have a vision, a goal or an outcome. The gap between our vision and our current reality is what gives us energy. The clearer the goal, the more energy we generate. If I have a clear, mental picture of my goal or my vision or the ideal me, then I generate enormous energy to make change happen. If I have a vague, wooly, watery goal, then I generate little energy. So the first thing we need to get fit and healthy bodies is an inspiring goal. The goal could be to run a marathon, to lose 40lbs in the coming year, or to swim 50 lengths of the pool without stopping or to achieve that challenging work goal.

As always, every best dream or vision has to be realistic, yet stretching, for you. Michelangelo said: "The greater danger for most of us lies not in setting our aim too high and falling short; but in setting our aim too low, and achieving our mark."

So, have a dream of the ideal you. Let that dream inspire you to take positive action to make your dream come true. Build that burning desire. Light that inner flame. Then, one step at a time, set out on your great adventure where you are your own hero or heroine, slaying the dragons of obesity, lack of fitness or procrastination.

T.S. Eliot was right when he said: "It's never too late to be the person you might have been."

The woman I mentioned above is the living embodiment of that quote. She went the 'inspired route' and is now an inspiration to all who interact with her. She is indeed a greater person by far than she ever dreamed herself to be.

RED PLATFORM: Information.

GREEN PLATFORM: Inspiration.

51

Your Most Valuable
Currency — Your Thoughts

I RECENTLY met a young woman alive with possibility and full of potential. A world of untapped creativity within her. However her mind was full of negativity. She was facing a big exam and she felt really overwhelmed. She had hit a massive roadblock. With her beautiful head hanging and her eyes on the floor she said: "I'm useless. I'm no good. I'm a failure. When I see how good the others are, I get depressed."

I told her that her mind was like a garden or a shopping mall.

"Like a garden?" she wondered.

"You sow weeds, you harvest weeds. You sow vegetables or flowers, you harvest vegetables or flowers. You sow negative thoughts, you reap and harvest negative actions, failures and poor performances."

"Your mind is like a shopping mall?"

"A shopping mall?"

"You come into this world with a currency to spend, say €10 million. That precious currency comes in the form of your thoughts. Yours to spend however you like. To spend on what you love and want to create and attract in your life on the one hand or to spend on what you don't love and don't want to create and attract into your life on the other hand."

So you go into this shop. There are sofas there all covered in vomit and rats running in and out through them.

You say: 'How much are those sofas?'

'€100,000 each.'

'Ugh, that's disgusting. They're hideous. I'll take 10. Send them home. Here's my address.'

Then you go into another shop. Here there are lamps all over the place covered in dust and dirt with maggots crawling all over them.

'How much are the lamps?'

'€50,000 each."

'That's disgusting,' you say, 'I'll take 20 of them.'

And you pay out your precious currency to get more and more of what you don't want.

Meanwhile, there is a shop across the mall that has everything you want but you won't go in there. Why do you spend your money on what you don't want? Then you wonder: "Why is this happening to me?"

I then reminded her of what she said to me. Her own exact words.

"I'm useless. I'm no good. I'm a failure. When I see how good the others are, I get depressed!"

I asked her why was she spending the precious currency of her thoughts that are there available to her to purchase all that she wants in her life to purchase instead all the things she doesn't want in her life.

"'The greatest currency in this life is the positive effect you have on yourself and on others. Start spending your currency wisely only on what you want to have in your life."

Thoughts become things. So you need to flip the switch, cross the mall, change your shop and only think and talk about what you want. There is a shop across the way that has everything you want but you are refusing to go into it."

When our son Alexander was in Crumlin Children's Hospital some time ago he was in an 'isolation room.' There was a big sign, 'Isolation' on the door. People could not just come in and out willy-nilly for fear of contamination. They had to wear protective clothing.

We should have these isolation signs on these negative shops that only sell mind viruses chock-a-block with poison perceptions.

Feed and strengthen your mind with only positive powerful thoughts. Watch out for those poison and the body-weakening toxic thought shops. Avoid them simply by entering the powerful body-strengthening energising thought shops.

Comparisons are odious. We only compare ourselves negatively to someone else. By all means model the best parts on someone else, but don't ever compare. I asked her to flip her inner mental switch and go shopping across the mall for all the things she really wanted in her life by thinking and saying to herself:

"I am confident of achieving all my goals and dreams."

"I am able to use failure as feedback to learn great life lessons and grow as a person."

"I am unique and special. I have a once-off special talent to be used in the service of others."

I left her with this little slightly rejigged poem from the 19th century by Walther D. Wintle:

"If you think you are beaten, you are;
If you think you dare not, you don't.
If you'd like to win, but you think you can't,
It is almost a cinch that you won't.
If you think you'll lose, you're lost;
For out of the world we find
Success begins with a person's will
It's all in the state of mind.
If you think you're outclassed, you are.
You've got to think high to rise.
You've got to be sure of yourself before
You can ever win the prize.
Life's battles don't always go
To the stronger or faster woman or man;
But sooner or later the woman or man
Who wins are the ones who think they can."

She passed her examination. She now plants only positive thoughts in the garden of her mind. She uses the precious currency of her thoughts in the shops that sell only what she wants to create and attract into her life. She has become a very positive, confident and happy young woman.

Delighted with her progress, she asked me: "How could something so powerful, so transformational and so life-changing happen by simply flipping my thoughts switch and crossing that imaginary mall?" She found that powerful switch. She crossed the mall. It transformed her life. It will transform yours too. Spend the precious currency of your thoughts only on what you want in your life.

RED PLATFORM: Spend the precious currency of your thoughts on everything you don't want.

GREEN PLATFORM: Spend the precious currency of your thoughts only on what you want.

52

Who Are The Positive Wizards In Your Life?

"Sometimes our light goes out but is blown again into flame by an encounter with another human being. Each of us owes the deepest thanks to those who have rekindled this inner light."
Dr Albert Schweitzer, Nobel Prize winner who served in Africa

AS I said previously, I love the Dublin Marathon because the people on the footpaths along the route are light givers. They just keep on rekindling the runners' inner lights. They have nothing but encouragement for every single runner and walker.

Those positive affirming remarks from the footpaths are what sport is all about. Contrast the Dublin Marathon with an under 12-football match and listen to the adults bellowing out negative belittling remarks from the sideline. Inner light-quenchers. It's contagious. Watch it spread. Then watch the young players as their inner athletes shrink and shrivel by the minute while their energy drains away.

Dr Schweitzer says: "Sometimes our light goes out," but more often than not our inner light does not go out by itself, rather it is other people who quench it whenever we allow them to flick our inner switch.

Look back on your life and see who were those people who quenched your inner flickering flame of self-belief and who were the ones who gently rekindled your inner light and belief in yourself?

Who were the positive wizards, the dream enablers and the light kindlers in your life and who were the negative wizards, the dream killers and light quenchers in your life?

One man I know made a list of 73 negative dream-quenchers in his life on a journey back from the States. When I ask people on courses who were the positive wizards and who were the negative wizards in their lives, the most popular answer for the negative wizards is a parent or a teacher.

When I ask them for the positive wizards, the same pair come up — a parent and a teacher.

The greatest poison in any team or family is the person with the Inner Light Extinguisher full of Negative Belittling Remarks (NBRs) spray. The put-downs. The dream-killers. The light-quenchers. The toxic mind and spirit poisoners. They live on The Red Platform and we call them Energy Vampires.

Isn't it interesting that in the English language we are so familiar with the word, "belittling."

"Oh, come on now, that was a very belittling remark."

Do we hear the word to "bebig?"

"Oh, wasn't that a wonderful bebigging remark."

We don't even have the word "bebig".

"Ah go away out of that. You're an awful bebigger. You only see what's wonderful in people and you seem to always bring out the best in them."

The perpetrators of these NBRs hide behind the lie that they are "only telling the truth." They brag that they tell it as it is.

So many great people have suffered the brunt of NBRs that were far, far from the truth. I remember reading an article about the great Irish soccer player Paul McGrath where he described his life in the Birds' Nest orphanage in Dún Laoghaire. He encountered some negative wizards there.

"Generally you were made to feel odd and unloved. There was a routine comment made in moments of temper that you were 'only here because nobody else wants you'. You were constantly being put down."

Lucky for Paul that he also met many positive wizards who rekindled his inner light so that he could deliver so many magical performances on the soccer fields of the world.

Socrates succeeded despite being called "an immoral corrupter of youth."

Professor Sir John Gurdon won the 2012 Nobel Prize for medicine or physiology. He went to Eton College in England where his parents were told that it would be "a sheer waste of time" for him to pursue a career in science.

Lucky for medicine that John and his parents decided on the Mary Anne Radmacher approach, which believes that "Criticism and pettiness may knock, but the lock is on my side of the door."

So many great people in life became great in spite of the negative light-quenching wizards who knocked them down. They discovered the lock on their side of the door.

Ludwig van Beethoven became a huge musical influence despite his teacher telling him: "You're a hopeless composer."

Walt Disney created movie magic for millions of children despite being fired from a newspaper after his editor told him: "You lack ideas."

Leo Tolstoy, author of *War And Peace*, succeeded despite flunking out of college and hearing the poisonous put-down: "You're both unable and unwilling to learn."

Thomas Edison brought us all into the light despite being told: "You're too stupid to learn anything."

Enrico Caruso the famous opera singer succeeded despite his teacher's remark: "You have no voice at all and you cannot sing."

The sculptor Auguste Rodin succeeded despite his father's nasty comment: "I have an idiot for a son."

Albert Einstein, who later entered the orb of intellectual greats in his own lifetime, was once told: "You're mentally slow, unsociable and adrift forever in your foolish dreams."

Contrast all these light quenching comments with those positive comments that rekindle that flickering inner light.

Remember Ronan Tynan's father's famous remark that inspired him: "Ronan, you're great."

Imagine if all those comments were turned into Positive Affirming Remarks (PARs). Imagine if all those people in power made a different choice and moved from that poison negative Red Platform to the positive Green Platform and looked for what was magnificent and noble and bright and wonderful in people and drew it out of them. Here then is what all those people would have heard from the same people on The Green Platform:

"Socrates, you'll revolutionise philosophy."

"Ludwig, music is your gift. Share it with the world."

"Enrico, singing is what you do best. Sing, because that's what connects you to your life purpose. You will feel joy and bring so much joy to others with your marvellous singing."

"Walt, your ideas will create magic for millions of children."

"Thomas, you're a genius. Your brain will light up the world."

"Leo, you are a magnificent writer. Your books will educate and entertain the world."

"Auguste, sculpting is your talent. Give it your all and you'll see and sculpt beauty from marble."

All that would have happened here was a simple change of platform. From toxic Red to encouraging Green. So don't pay attention to anyone who says you can't get the job of your dreams, write a book, run a marathon, get a degree, a master's degree or PhD.

Every encounter we have with another person is an assignment. Everyone has an inner cup. When you meet another person you put three drops into their inner cup.

These three drops are either positive, uplifting and constructive from someone living on The Green Platform — an Energy Transformer or negative, belittling and destructive from someone living on the Red Platform — an Energy Vampire. We can even do it with an email or a text. And you'll always know. Check your stomach and how you feel afterwards. People will always remember how you made them feel.

Every encounter will be either a rekindling light encounter from a Green Platform Energy Transformer or a light quenching encounter from a Red Platform Energy Vampire.

It's a choice. Your choice. During every single encounter — to contribute to someone's energy or to contaminate it. To give energy or to sap energy. To kindle to flame or to quench.

Research shows us that you cannot get continual high performances from a diet of NBRs.

Positive thinking is powerful no matter what kind of challenge you face so long as your goals are realistic and stretching for you.

With the support given to athletes by the Dublin public, the negative voice in your head has no chance. In every walk of life whenever you see someone who is about to give up or throw in the towel, you can be the one to "blow again into flame and rekindle their inner light," inspiring them to continue on their heroic journey to achieve their life's dreams.

The runner and doctor George Sheehan captures what the race or life is really all about: "It's very hard in the beginning to understand that the whole idea is not to beat the other runners. Eventually you learn that the competition is against the little voice inside you that wants you to quit." That little light-quencher inside.

Ultimately you, yourself will be the one to continue to "blow into flame and rekindle your own inner light." It's a powerful choice and it makes all the difference.

RED PLATFORM: NBRs. Light quenchers. Negative belittling remarks and putting people down.

GREEN PLATFORM: PARs. Positive Affirming Remarks. Blowing to flame and rekindling inner lights. Spotting the brilliance in people before they see it themselves. Always encouraging and uplifting people.

53

Success Has An Address

In the dust of defeat as well as the laurels of victory, there is a glory to be found if one has done his or her best.
Eric Liddell

SUCCESS has an address. It leaves tracks and is different for different people.

September in Ireland is a special month for sporting people — for over 130 years, this is when the All-Ireland football and hurling finals take place.

Every year there is only one winning team in any given competition. Sportspeople often get caught in the trap of a one-dimensional picture of success — the winner. The champion. The one who comes first.

If we look at success at this level, then most sports people are doomed to failure. Thirty-two managers started out at the beginning of the year in hurling or in football or in different sports. Thirty-one of them knew one thing for sure — there was going to be only one winner.

In other words there were for sure going to be 31 losers. So what are the odds?

Well, it all depends on what we see as success. How do we define success when 31 so-called 'failures' is what stares us in the face?

Really, there is no such thing as failure.

There is only feedback. We simply get a result. Failure is the fuel to get it right next time. The key is to fail forward. Make adversity a stepping stone rather than a tombstone.

I love Thomas Edison's response, when someone asked him how he felt having failed 10,000 times to make a light bulb. He said: "I have not failed 10,000 times. I've just discovered 10,000 ways that I know for sure won't work."

He saw his failures as feedback. Eventually he found a way that worked. Every time we switch on a light we can thank God that Edison didn't believe in failure but simply turned it into valuable feedback.

Many of life's failures are people who did not realise how close they were to success when they gave up. The ability to bounce back and learn from every bounce back is a fundamental factor in the lives of all successful people. The most successful person is similar to a person on a trampoline. The deeper they go down the higher they bounce back up.

Kipling put it this way: "If you can meet with Triumph and Disaster and treat those two impostors just the same ..."

What happens to us when we grow up and make a mistake or fail? If only we had the ability to continue to see each other as we see children and give each other the same kind of encouragement.

A child will fall an average of 243 times before that child walks. We say: "Come on, come to Daddy, come to Mammy. Another step. Come on, you can do it." We encourage them all the time.

We don't say: "Look, you're a faller. You'll never walk. So give up this walking stuff. Walking's for others. Not you. Give up. Throw in the towel."

No, we keep on encouraging the child. We learn to walk by remembering how we walked. Not by remembering, videoing and replaying how we fell.

Yet as adults we focus so much on mistakes and failures and what people do wrong. Why not catch people doing something right?

Replay what people do right.

A mistake has the three Gs. It's a gem. It's a gift. And it's there for our growth. The only mistake is not to learn from a mistake.

The three questions you ask about a mistake are:

1. "What can I learn from it?"
2. "How can I grow from it?" and
3. "How can I serve the team or people with the lessons I've learned?"

You've learned the lessons. Don't haul the negative past around with you in a toxic sack on your back. Dump that sorry sack of mistakes. They've done their job. You've learned the life lessons.

Experience is not what happens to us. It's how we experience the experience that matters. How we choose to view the experience determines whether it helps us to change and grow or to make matters worse. It's what we learn and how we grow by learning the life lessons about what happens to us. Life is a series of tests. We meet bigger challenges and we grow longer legs.

When people with high self-esteem fail, they ask those three 'learn', 'grow' and 'serve' empowering questions, learn those lessons and move on with their lives.

When people with low self-esteem fail, instead of asking those three empowering questions, they say: "I failed."

Then they make that failure their identity: "I am a failure. That proves it." They make it permanent.

John Wooden, the great UCLA basketball coach said: "Success is the peace of mind that is the direct result of self-satisfaction in knowing that you gave your best effort to become the best of which you are capable."

This definition of success is different because its underlying rule of never comparing yourself to others, goes against one of the most pervasive conditioned habits in our culture: comparing ourselves to others for the purpose of self-evaluation.

When we do that we direct our focus towards that which we cannot control.

We feel successful when we outscore, outsell or out perform others; we tend to set ourselves up for either failure or self-importance. Neither serves us well over time.

Success is not trying to be better than anyone else — which may be impossible. It involves learning from others, modelling the best skills of others and striving to reach your own level of excellence. I am not better than others today. But I do strive to be better than I was yesterday. It's not how good you are. It's how good you are compared to how good you could be. Your aim is to be the best that you can possibly be. To find that place beyond, which you thought you could not go — and then go there.

Success is also about the significance of every step you take on the journey. Richie Stakelum, the great Tipperary captain of "the famine is over" fame, put it like this to me one day: "Can you look in the mirror tonight and say, 'Yes, I was the best that I could possibly be today?'"

Roosevelt captured the real spirit of Wooden's definition of success with his Man in the Arena speech at the Sorbonne in Paris:

"It is not the critic who counts; not the man who points out how the strong man stumbles, or where the doer of deeds could have done them better.

"The credit belongs to the man who is actually in the arena, whose face is marred by dust and sweat and blood; who strives valiantly; who errs, who comes short again and again, because there is no effort without error and shortcoming; but who does actually strive to do the deeds; who knows great enthusiasms, the great devotions; who spends himself in a worthy cause; who at the best knows in the end the triumph of high achievement, and who at the worst, if he fails, at least fails while daring greatly, so that his place shall never be with those cold and timid souls who neither know victory nor defeat."

The man or woman in the arena will never know the abysmal horrors of the half-lived life.

Only you alone can determine whether you made your best effort, whether you were the best that you could be, whether or not you emptied the tank.

I salute the 31 managers and teams that did not win, who 'failed,' and leave them with some words about success from Ralph Waldo Emerson:

"To laugh often and much;

To win the respect of intelligent people and the affection of children;

To earn the appreciation of honest critics and to endure the betrayal of false friends;

To appreciate beauty;

To find the best in others;

To leave the world a bit better whether by a healthy child, a garden patch or a redeemed social condition;

To know even one life has breathed easier because you have lived.

This is to have succeeded."

Make today your masterpiece in your own special arena. Bloom where you are planted. Your best self will take you to what coach Vince Lombardi calls "your finest hour."

"I firmly believe that any man's finest hour, the greatest fulfilment of all he holds dear, is the moment when he has worked his heart out in a good cause and lies exhausted on the field of battle — victorious."

By victorious he means that your inner self knows that you gave it your all. You were the best that you could possibly be. You gave "your best effort to become the best of which you are capable." That is the true address of success.

RED PLATFORM: To finish at Number 1. Champions. Winners.

GREEN PLATFORM: You were the best that you could possibly be. You emptied the tank. The person in the arena. You gave your best effort to become the best of which you were capable.

54

The Power Of Believing

REMEMBER Henry Ford saying: "Whether you believe you can do a thing or not, you're right." He was telling us that belief comes before performance.

Why have the world's best middle distance runners grown up in the same Ethiopian village? Why are 137 of the world's 500 best female golfers from South Korea? How did one athletic club in Kingston, Jamaica succeed to produce most of the world's best sprinters? What is the secret behind Brazil's mass production of soccer super stars?

Rasmus Ankersen, a 26-year-old Danish ex-professional footballer and performance specialist, quit his job, spent his last pennies booking flight tickets and for six intensive months travelled the world and literally trained and lived with the world's best athletes and their coaches in an attempt to see whether or not Ford was right.

Ankersen tells his story in his book *The Gold Mine Effect* of how he went to a small Kenyan village in the Great Rift Valley that has become a production line of running talent thanks to the famous Irish missionary Br Colm O'Connell.

He is the coach of the 800m world record holder David Rudisha and has trained 25 world champions and four Olympic gold medalists during almost 40 years there.

"What's the secret?" Ankersen wanted to know. "The secret is that there is no secret," replied Br Colm, "it's all about belief."

He was finding echoes of Henry Ford's statement: "Whether you believe you can do a thing or not, you're right."

In 1954, the belief was that you couldn't run a mile in under four minutes. Medically, people believed that your heart would burst. Then, on May 6, 1954, Roger Bannister ran the first sub-four minute mile in 3:59.4 to break the barrier. Actually, he did much more than that. What he really broke was a limiting belief.

Since then, more than 30,000 people have broken that running time. Eamon Coghlan even managed to achieve it when he was 40. In fact in 1999 Hicham El Guerrouj ran the mile in 3.43.13 minutes knocking nearly 17 seconds off the famous sub-four-minute mile.

Belief comes before performance. To achieve your potential, to achieve performance, alter your belief.

When Liam Griffin won the All-Ireland hurling final with Wexford in 1996 he spent a huge amount of time in not just building up belief within the team, but he also created the stuff of legends with the stories of how he broke limiting beliefs within the players. He used every belief building block he could from planting Wexford flags on the graveyards of famous hurlers of the past to visiting holy islands to getting off the bus at the Wicklow border ... anything he could think of to carve out and stack up the building blocks of belief, one by one.

The Clare legend and former Dublin hurling manager Anthony Daly has an Aladdin's Cave full of stories about their All-Ireland wins in the nineties and the steps Ger Loughnane took to break limiting beliefs — including the mythology of Biddy Early's curse — and replaced them with powerful beliefs.

There's a massive 712k ultra-marathon in Australia that goes from Sydney to Melbourne. One year, a 61-year-old farmer called Cliff Young appeared at the start wearing a pair of wellingtons.

"Have you ever run a marathon before, Cliff?"

"No."

"Half-marathon?"

"No."

"Did you ever run a race in your life?"

"No."

"Then why are you here?"

"Coming home from the pub the other night, I thought: 'Wouldn't it be great to run from Sydney to Melbourne? Imagine telling the story to my mates.'"

The organiser thought he was cracked but allowed him to chug off thinking he'd only last an hour or so.

All the way he shuffled along. Then, on April 29, five days, 15 hours and four minutes later, Cliff ran into the Westfield Centre in Melbourne more than 12 hours ahead of the rest of the runners.

When he was asked how he did it, he said he just imagined he was running after sheep all day on his farm like he did when he was a young boy. That way he blocked out every negative thought and limiting belief and even enjoyed the excruciating experience.

Cliff epitomises the words of John Stuart Mill: "One person with belief is equal to 99 who have only interests."

Nikos Kazantzakis who wrote *Zorba the Greek* said: "By believing passionately in that which doesn't exist, you create it and that which has not been sufficiently desired is what we call the non-existent." Here he nails passion, desire and belief. The best way to predict the future is to create it and make it with a burning desire, with passion and with belief.

What is the goal that you passionately believe in? Does that goal ignite a burning desire in your heart? Do you believe you can? Provided your goal is realistic and stretching for you, you can achieve what you believe!

You'll see it when you believe it. Belief comes before performance.

RED PLATFORM: "I believe I can't." Head full of limiting beliefs reinforced by a posse of negative thoughts.

GREEN PLATFORM: "I believe I can." "It's all about belief." Conceive it, believe it and achieve it.

55

In The Zone

GREAT athletes always talk about being "in the zone" after fantastic performances. Finding the zone is that magical moment when performance seems inspired and effortless.

Runners sometimes call it "the flow." Musicians talk about being "in the groove" when the instrument almost plays itself.

Larry Bird of the Boston Celtics basketball team spoke one time of being in the zone and falling down near the basket and virtually from the ground testing a shot from a ridiculous angle because he was in the zone — and it went in. He nailed it. He was astonished.

Ted Williams, the legendary Red Sox hitter, said that when he was in the zone everything was so clear to him he could see the seams on a pitched ball.

Basketball players say that when they are in the zone, the basket seems bigger and shots come easier. You have total confidence and self-belief. You are at the top of your game.

It's when everything flows and is easy.

Rod Laver, the former Australian tennis ace said: "You get a great feeling when you're hitting the ball really well. The ball comes over the net looking as big as a soccer ball and everything seems to be moving in slow motion. You feel as if there's nothing that you can't do with the ball. You get confidence. You're relaxed. Everything is working for you."

Being in the zone is that moment when your performance transcends the normal or the usual. You can feel it. Everything just clicks. You lose all sense of time.

Children get in the zone all the time when they're absorbed in play. But this natural ability to play 'in the zone' is blocked when we become self-conscious around the age of five. We already begin to judge ourselves through the eyes of the people around us.

So the million-dollar question is: "How do we get back in the zone?"

According to the University of Chicago study, one trait that constantly comes up in research is that entering the zone is most likely to occur when we are focused on only one thing at a time.

Total focus.

It is critical to have a clear goal and then to detach from the goal or outcome. Flow is more likely to happen when an activity is intrinsically satisfying, when our attention is on the present moment performance rather than the outcome or goal.

When we are able to become completely absorbed in a flow experience, we return to that pleasant state where what we are doing and experiencing becomes far more interesting than what other people might be thinking.

The portal or the entrance to the zone is the 'now.'

The simplest way to transform any task into a potential 'flow experience' or the zone is to set an intention, purpose or goal in relation to that task.

In any case where that simple task is mundane, repetitive or simply not interesting to us, our intention need not be related to the actual task.

Classical literature is full of great thinkers who thought that the key to a rich life is to welcome the here and now. Despair is always five minutes ahead, never now. These great thinkers encourage us to "enjoy the precious present." The past is history. Tomorrow is mystery. Now is a gift. That's why we call it 'the present.' It's the only place we'll ever live.

Mystics, philosophers and quantum physicists all agree that the 'stuff of now' is the stuff of the zone. Have a clear future goal, detach from it and live fully and passionately in the now with all your heart and all your soul and all your might. Then and only then, you'll hit the zone, the flow, or your optimal experience.

For instance, performing with energy and enthusiasm and excitement, as if it's the most important thing in the world, can turn washing dishes or changing a child's diaper or nappy into the most enjoyable activity.

Wisdom is knowing how to maximise the enjoyment of each moment. Every day is a gift for those who really believe every day is a gift.

The happiest people don't have the best of everything; they just make the best of everything. There are two great days in your life. The day you were born, and the day you discovered why you were born. The day you discovered your unique talent and how you were going to use it to build a better world.

Perhaps an old Buddhist saying best sums up the zone: "The master in the art of living makes little distinction between his work and his play. He hardly knows which is which. He simply pursues his vision of excellence in whatever he does. Leaving others to decide whether he is working or playing."

Happiness is not in things; it's in you when you are doing what you love and loving what you do with total focus and attention in the zone. There is no better feeling.

RED PLATFORM: Doing something but not fully present. Your head full of mental noise, complaining, blaming and judging.

GREEN PLATFORM: In the zone, in the flow, in the groove. Your performance transcends the normal. You can feel it. Everything just clicks. You lose all sense of time. Totally present in the moment with total focus.

56

Sail Away From 'Someday Isle'

HAVE you ever met a person who is the quintessential procrastinator? All those people live in a special island and it has a name. It's called, 'Someday Isle.'

"Someday I'll get that degree."

"Someday I'll eat and exercise properly."

"Someday I'll get that job I love."

Someday Isle.

I knew someone like that and his problem was that every day he said: "I'll start tomorrow." He reminded me of the song: "Tomorrow, tomorrow, I love you tomorrow. You're only a day away."

Instead of 'Seize the day,' his mantra by default was: 'Let the day slip away.'

I told him a story about the five frogs. "Five frogs sat on a wall overlooking a pond. One decided to jump into the pond. How many were left?"

"Four," he said.

"No, five, because deciding to do something and actually doing something is a horse of a different colour. When you see the frog in the air, then that's a decision. A real decision always implies action."

So start.

Begin.

Don't get it right; just get it going. When you make a decision you create the future.

Life rewards Decisive Action Now (DAN) but life doesn't reward Hesitant Action Later (HAL).

Take that first step. Change islands. Take a boat from "HAL Isle" (The island of Someday Islers) to "DAN Isle".

Mark Twain, the great American writer and part-time philosopher, said: "Twenty years from now you will be more disappointed by the things you didn't do than by the ones you did. So throw off the bowlines. Sail away from the safe harbour. Catch the trade winds in your sails.

"Explore. Dream. Discover."

Take the first step. You don't have to get it right, just get going. When you make a decision, you create your future. The time will never be just right. Start with where you are and work with whatever tools you may have, and you will find better tools as you go along.

As the German writer and statesman Johann Wolfgang von Goethe said: "Whatever you can do or dream you can, begin it. Boldness has genius, power and magic in it."

Walk for five minutes today. Then maybe seven minutes tomorrow. In no time you're up to 10 minutes.

Just nail down three days in a row. And it doesn't matter where you are coming from. It only matters where you are going.

In Charles Garfield's studies of peak performers, he made an interesting discovery. He analysed men and women who had achieved only average results at work for many years but who had suddenly exploded into greatness.

He found that at the take-off point every one of them began engaging in what we call 'Blue Sky Thinking.'

In this state, you imagine that all things are possible for you, just like looking up into a clear blue sky with no limits.

What would you attempt to do if you knew you couldn't fail? Begin with the end in mind and work your way forward with a clearly defined plan.

In the absence of clearly defined goals, we become strangely loyal to performing daily trivial things until ultimately we become enslaved by them. Things that matter least take over from things that matter most.

Exercise is important.

A healthy body to live in is important.

Nutritious food is important.

But none of these are urgent.

That's how things that matter least take over from things that matter most. The trivial many squeeze out the vital few. We get lost in the thick of thin things.

So forget the seduction of safety. Break free from your comfort zone and get into your excellence zone. Big ships are safe in harbours but big ships are not built for the safety of harbours.

Remember what is truly important and sail away from the safe harbour of Someday Isle. Catch the trade winds in your sails.

Explore. Dream. Discover that across the water is the island of all your dreams, desires and opportunities called DAN Isle.

Take decisive action now.

RED PLATFORM: "Someday I'll ..." Someday Isle. HAL Isle.

GREEN PLATFORM: "Decisive Action Now Isle." DAN Isle.

57

Fuel Your Passion
With Purpose

I AM at 32,000ft and halfway across the Atlantic Ocean looking out at a never-ending world of sea below me as I write this. The scene reminds me of the first time I flew in a plane. I had a window seat and my nose was glued to the glass looking back down as the plane rose up into the sky out of Dublin.

Gradually the houses got smaller until they looked like little toy houses. Then I saw a football match being played on a pitch in the middle of one of the housing estates. From that point in the sky, it was hard to imagine the passion and the purpose that fuelled the performances of those youngsters running around that field.

I was embarking on a life journey that would see me work as a missionary priest at the other side of the world and I was leaving behind my family, home and friends. Leaving those and my football career behind left a savage ache in my stomach. It was like dying. A mini-death. It seemed as if the plane was going up to heaven and that everything up to now was my life. What if now my life really was over?

What if that was it?

The thought crossed my mind that if that really was it, my life so far, how would I rate it? Did I make a difference? All the petty rows and arguments going on in the tiny city houses below looked very silly from my seat up in the clouds. You just really wanted to come back down and focus on the things that really mattered.

Like living life with real passion. A passion fuelled by a powerful purpose, a burning desire to deliver peak performances no matter what you were doing. To be the best that you could be.

Later in the USA, I met a great friend who elaborated on that theme. He told me that regardless of whether it was sport, business, science, medicine, education, spirituality or public service — you won't get anyone to perform at their peak without passion. He himself was passionate about life and sport.

Many people have passion of a sort, but if their passion isn't fuelled by 'purpose,' then their passion will come and go in bits and pieces. Peak performers fuel their passion with a powerful purpose or a deeper meaning. To be more. To do more. To contribute more.

Passion is fuelled by purpose. Daniel Pink, the author of *A Whole New Mind* and *Drive*, believes there are three keys to motivation.

1. Autonomy

Highly-motivated people are self-directed. They are proactive and in the driving seat, not passive passengers.

2. Mastery

This is all about doing something like practising a skill over and over until you master it and can see progress. You can see and measure the improvement. Repetition is the mother of skill. What gets measured gets done.

3. Purpose

What's your purpose? The 'something bigger' than oneself. The hunger for meaning. To matter. To make a difference. To be less of a go-getter and more of a go-giver.

Simon Sinek has similar ideas about the power of purpose and a shared vision in his book *Start With Why*.

To have a powerful 'why'. What's your cause? What's your belief? Why does your company exist? Why do you get out of bed in the morning? Why should anyone care?

People don't buy what you do. They buy why you do it. The goal is to get people to believe what you believe. If you talk about what you believe, you will attract those who believe what you believe. You don't hire people who want jobs. You hire people who believe what you believe.

I asked this friend who lives with passion: "Where do you get your passion and purpose from?" He said: "Years ago I was at a funeral. At the graveyard, as the third shovel of clay was tossed on to the coffin below in the grave, one of the people there turned to me and said: 'Ah, sure he was a harmless poor divil.' That is no great commendation or epitaph, is it?"

We should want to be fully alive and driven to become better ever day until the day we die. You have only one life. It's not a rehearsal. This is *it*. So before you take that final one-way ticket flight across the great divide, get into that driving seat of your life, achieve mastery as you live with passion where you can see and measure your progress. Fuel your passionate days with purpose and make it fun.

RED PLATFORM: Passive passionless passenger. No progress measurement. No purpose or meaning. Life's a rehearsal.

GREEN PLATFORM: Autonomy: In driving seat. Mastery: Seeing and measuring progress. Purpose: A passionate purpose. A powerful 'why.' Life — this is it, the real thing.

58

Let Go Of All Things Negative

SOME time ago when I was in the US, Dr Pearse Lyons arranged for me to be a guest on the famous Joe B. and Denny Show, a hugely popular sports radio programme in Kentucky.

Joe Beasman Hall, better known as Joe B. Hall, was the head basketball coach at the University of Kentucky from 1972 to 1985. Hall was given a difficult task, to follow in the footsteps of his legendary predecessor, Adolph Rupp. In 1978 he coached the Kentucky Wildcats to their fifth NCAS Men's Division 1 Basketball Championship. He was named National Coach of the Year in 1978 and South Easter Conference Coach of the Year on four different occasions.

Denny Crum, a famous coach of the Louisville Cardinals was in Louisville, and I was with Coach Joe B. in the studio in Lexington. The questions kept coming hard and fast from the two programme hosts and from listeners. Here's a small flavour of how the programme unfolded.

Q1: "How do you get a team of individuals to play as a team?"

A: "When the wild geese fly in V-formation, they are 71 per cent more efficient than when they fly as individuals. A real team has no Egos. Egos are left at the door. A real team has everyone playing with a savage work rate for the team. Together Everyone Achieves More (TEAM).

All great teams have chemistry, trust and camaraderie. That's much more than a weekend of 'bonding.' It's all about trust. Many poor teams have a bunch of talented individuals. Hard work will always beat talent when talent won't work hard. Chemistry, trust and camaraderie are the cement that turns a bunch of talented individuals into a winning team. It's all about the spirit in the team."

Q2: "How do you get rid of negativity? When I hit a bad shot in golf it keeps bugging me. I can't let it go. How do I drop it and move on?"

A: "We do two things in life. We think and we feel. Now we either think and feel about what we want to create and attract in our lives or we think and we feel about what we don't want to create and attract into our lives."

It's that simple.

An event is like clay. We are the potters. Both the artists and the art. It's how we interpret an experience that matters. The meaning we give to the experience.

Feelings follow meanings and actions follow feelings.

So why are you making up a story about your bad shot that makes you feel bad when you can make up a story that makes you feel good instead? Why not just learn the lesson, let it go and visualise your next shot with excellence.

Most of the time most of us are thinking and feeling about what we don't want. We don't want to get sick. We don't want to hit the water. We don't want to miss this putt. We don't want to hit the bunker.

As I explained already, the subconscious won't process a negative. "Don't hit the water," means "Hit the water." The key is to focus on what we want, not what we don't want. Don't carry that bad shot with you.

The negative past is a backpack full of manure. Learn the lessons, and then cut the straps. Dump the backpack. Don't carry it with you. Don't carry that bad shot with you.

Just like one of the two monks in the following story. They were out walking one day by the riverbank when they met a stunningly beautiful young woman. She wanted help to cross the river because she was afraid the strong current might sweep her away. Politely, she asked if one of the monks would carry her across the river.

One monk said: "Of course I will help." He picked her up in his arms and waded across the river. Near the middle, he found that indeed the current was very strong and at one stage he nearly lost his footing. The lady had to hold on to him very tightly in that part of the river before they successfully waded to the opposite bank where he put her down safe and sound.

She thanked him profusely and when the other monk crossed behind them, the lady said goodbye and the two monks headed off on their journey.

After about five miles of walking in total silence, the monk who had not helped blurted out in fury: "I can't believe what you did back there. You carried that beautiful young woman across the river and I saw you holding her tightly in the middle of the river. You got pleasure out of what you did and you're supposed to be a monk, aren't you?"

The other man kept walking and replied in a quiet tone. "Yes, I am a monk and I carried that woman across the river as you said. But when I got to the far bank I put her down. You still seem to be carrying her."

Like the monk, put down that bad golf shot. Let it go. Don't carry it with you all over the golf course. And do the same with any other negative bad stuff you are carrying around with you."

Joe B. said that from then on he would become a "mental golfing monk."

We had great fun on the show and there was a huge response from listeners.

So which monk are you?

Can you release your negative thoughts or feelings so that they don't bother you? Or will you carry these toxic feelings in that familiar backpack with you throughout the day.

We all think in this way until we learn to stop it and drop it. That is the single most liberating thing you can do for yourself. Awareness is the key. Activate your inner observer. Become aware of what you are thinking and then just throw that inner switch on to focus only on what you want to create and make happen in your life. Focus only on the next shot, only on what you want.

Since I wrote this column the famous Joe B. and Denny Show has been wrapped up. Joe B. is 86 years young.

"I really loved this show," Joe B. said, "for 10 years and seven months, every morning I got up, I looked forward to it." Said Denny: "Doing this show, it's really been a lot of fun. No negatives to it, just a treat to do."

It was my privilege to be their guest on two occasions. It was really like Denny said it was: "No negatives, just a treat to do."

RED PLATFORM: Carry the negative past with you like a backpack full of manure. Keep spreading it, whingeing, complaining and contaminating everyone else's energy.

GREEN PLATFORM: Negative past: Learn the lessons and then cut the straps. Dump that toxic backpack. Fill your new backpack with all the positive things you want in your life. Contribute to everyone else's energy.

59

Emotional Honesty —
Essential For Positive Thinking

POSITIVE thinking has been part of every champion's arsenal over the years. I never heard of a top performer in any field who based their success on the power of negative thinking.

Have you ever heard a winner say: "In the final stretch, my head was full of negative thoughts, I clearly saw myself as a total failure — and that's what got me over the line to win the gold medal and break a world record."

Yet that would seem to be the message coming from a book, *The Antidote: Happiness For People Who Can't Stand Positive Thinking*, by Oliver Burkeman. He proposes that positive thinking and relentless optimism aren't the solution to happiness, but rather part of the problem.

He hits on the nub of the problem when he says: "Trying to make your emotions different from what they are, will backfire."

And of course it will.

Here are three steps to genuine positive thinking on The Green Platform.

1. Emotional Honesty.

2. Feel The Feeling Fully.

3. Honour Your Human Experience.

The first step is that you experience your situation as it is. You feel it fully. You honour and acknowledge it.

If it's tragedy, you feel it fully. You cry the tears. You don't pour pseudo-positive pink paint all over human suffering and tell people "All is well," when obviously it's not.

When someone close to you dies for instance, you realise the truth of the saying about the relationship that: "If it wasn't so good, it wouldn't be so bad."

You feel the deep pain of grief. There can be no healing without such a deep feeling. In effect, you give yourself permission to grieve. You don't pretend you're having a great time when you're not. If it's loneliness you turn on the tap. You feel that loneliness.

You must be emotionally honest. That's part of real positive thinking. Positive thinking is not about denial, it's about transcendence.

THE WHITE SPACE: Your Power to Choose

Journey on to a white space where you find the freedom to choose your response to any situation. This is the space between stimulus and response. It's the second step. Recognising and getting into the white space where you take your time and choose the energy with which you want to respond, rather than automatically reacting. That awareness and choice of response is what saves us from being just a bunch of predictable reflexes constantly being triggered by people and events into predictable outcomes. We can consciously wake up, become aware and alert and break that cycle.

THE CHOICE: To Land on the Negative Red Platform or the Positive Green Platform.

The third step is choosing our response at every moment of our day. This is what makes us human. We can respond negatively by throwing in the towel, giving up and landing on that sabotaging Red Platform, or we can respond positively by digging deeper and finding that extra bit of courage and bravery to land on the positive life-changing Green Platform and tap into the field of possibilities that we find there.

We're not responsible for other people's actions, but we *are* totally responsible for our own reactions. It's not what happens to us that matters, but rather how we choose to respond in that 'White Space.'

Circumstances don't make the person; they reveal the person. We're not responsible for the cards we're dealt; but we're totally responsible for how we play them.

So *real* positive thinking isn't looking out at the garden, seeing all the weeds and saying: "I must be positive, there are no weeds. Look at my lovely garden." That kind of denial is what gives positive thinking a bad name.

No. Positive thinking is all about seeing the weeds, having a vision for the garden and then rolling up your sleeves, pulling out the weeds and planting vegetables or flowers.

Positive thinking is not driving down the road and seeing your fuel gauge pointing to 'E' and then getting a Smiley Face sticker and sticking it over the fuel gauge.

The shadow of some positive thinking movements is the belief that there is no shadow. Of course there is a shadow and darkness. Positive thinking challenges us to stand in the darkness and proclaim the light. To see the opportunity in the disaster, the fortune in the misfortune and the bounce-back gift in the setback.

Women's 400m hurdles final 1993 World Athletics Champion Sally Gunnell said: "I taught myself not to have negative thoughts. I just used to stop myself, turn them around and replace them with positive ones."

Before the World Championship final in Stuttgart, she caught a cold that turned into a chest infection. She said: "I can't say I've got a cold, that's just an excuse."

So she kept feeding herself positive thoughts. Not only did she go out and win the gold medal, but she also broke the world record. "I was freaked out to think I'd actually done it. I'd talked myself into winning," she said.

And so can you — whatever your work or fitness challenge is today. You can talk yourself into success and winning or you can talk yourself into failure and losing. It's fully within your power to choose. Your positive thinking should be based, grounded and founded not in denial, but in reality as it is, with total honesty.

RED PLATFORM: No choice. "They make me angry. I can't help how I feel." "There are no weeds. All is well, well, well. I must be positive now on The Green Platform." Denial.

GREEN PLATFORM: I always have a choice. There are weeds. Get a plan for the garden, roll up your sleeves and pull the weeds. Emotional honesty. Transcendence.

60

The Legend Of 'Caballo Blanco'

A LONG long time ago, I was standing at a pedestrian crossing in Orange County, California, waiting for the little green man to light up and give four or five of us the go-ahead to cross the road. Along came this little old wizened nut-brown jogger. He stopped beside me and we began chatting.

"You're a great man to be out jogging, what age are you?"

"I'm 95," he replied.

"Ninety five, and you're out jogging, fair play to you," I said.

"Ah," he replied, "the way I look at it now is that I'm too old not to jog."

Fast forward to another evening in California, this time in Visalia on a Saturday evening in March 2012. I had just finished a week of leadership training and I went into the hotel coffee shop to have supper.

I was reading a book at the time, the cult bestseller *Born to Run*, by Christopher McDougall, about that celebrated ultra-marathon runner Micah True. Micah is remembered as a legend and an inspiration among ultra-marathon runners. He is nicknamed 'Caballo Blanco' (White Horse), and this tall thin chalky dust-covered white man was also known for his big smile and infectious love of running.

Micah lived for a period among the Tarahumara Indians who are nestled in northern Mexico and the canyons of the Sierra Madre Occidental.

He had been involved in ultra-marathons for years, but it wasn't until he became friends with the Tarahumara of Mexico that he became fully alive.

The waiter came over, saw the book and told me that Micah True's family had lived for a time near Visalia. He said that Micah had been born Michael Hickman, and took the name Micah from the courageous and fearless spirit of the Old Testament prophet Micah, and True from the loyalty of an old dog called True Dog. During the week the waiter also worked in a sports shop called Sole'n'Soul.

The Tarahumara call themselves Rarámuri, loosely translated as 'running people.' They're known for evading the Spanish conquerors in the 16th century and keeping their cave-dwelling culture alive and secluded. They're also known for their long-distance running and their superior health without the common western diseases.

It seems the Tarahumara are able to undertake extraordinary feats of long-distance running, 100 miles or further at their ease. They can run over 435 miles in just over two days. Age doesn't seem to matter to them either. They run these extraordinary distances in their fifties and their sixties.

Running is central to their culture and they go everywhere wearing simple thin-soled sandals known as 'huaraches.'

What Micah discovered among the Tarahumara was the sheer joy they got out of running. It's about listening to their bodies, finding an inner peace and enjoying the scenery at the same time.

Micah True boiled it down to having fun. He understood Einstein's answer when he was asked about the secret of his success in mathematics and physics. The great mathematician said: "Keep it simple. Make it fun."

When the Tarahumara Indians run they really seem to enjoy it. There's a great description in the book of an American runner, tense and stressed out struggling up a big hill near the end of an ultra-marathon, and next thing a Tarahumara runner with a rain-poncho and a type of Tarahumara skirt just glided past and gave him a big warm smile. He was just enjoying the scenery.

The same week I was in California, Caballo Blanco went for a long run and never came back. They found his body by a stream on a Saturday evening, on March 31, 2012 in the Gila Wilderness of southwestern New Mexico.

Micah True was the race director of the Copper Canyon Ultra Marathon, a gruelling 50-mile race through Tarahumara lands. The day before his disappearance, True tweeted about the race: "We are messengers fuelled by the message, when the message we carry is of truth, beauty, love, hope, and peace ..."

A Dr Bramble has an interesting story in the book. He has been monitoring the New York marathon results since 2004, and he discovered that starting at age 19, runners get faster every year and hit their peak at 27. After that they start to decline. Then he asks the question: "How old are you when you are back to the same speed you did at 19?"

The answers he got:

"40?"

"Wrong."

"50?"

"Nope."

"It can't be 55?"

"You're right," said Dr Bramble, "it can't be 55."

"It's 64!"

As our wizened nut-brown jogger understood, it seems we don't stop exercising because we get old.

We get old because we stop excercising.

With a car, the more you use it, the more you lose it. With your body, you use it or you lose it. That was also the mighty life-changing message that the magnificent Micah True, 'Caballo Blanco,' got from the warm and smiling Tarahumara people.

RED PLATFORM: Really trying so hard. Clenched fists. Teeth gritted. Head down. Pressure. Hard miserable work to be endured. Destination addiction.

GREEN PLATFORM: Running with freedom. Enjoying the scenery. Having fun. Smiling. Head up. Micah's running message of "Truth, beauty, love, hope, and peace."

61

Powerful
Beyond Measure

U S motivational speaker Marianne Williamson coined a powerful statement that sums up the great, late Ian McKeever.

She said: "Our deepest fear is not that we are inadequate. Our deepest fear is that we are powerful beyond measure."

That was so true of an amazing Irishman, Ian McKeever, who was struck by lightening and died taking a team of young people on a trek up Kilimanjaro, the highest mountain in Africa.

Although I didn't have the privilege of personally knowing Ian, our son Fionn did. One day, when he was still in secondary school, he came home full of excitement.

"Daddy, I'm going to climb Kilimanjaro with Ian McKeever and a team from our school, and we're going to raise funds for charity," he said.

That was the Ian McKeever factor, the mountain-climber and record breaker who was an inspirational mentor to young people.

Fionn was devastated when he heard the tragic news of Ian's death. "I had a chat with him for about 10 minutes about the challenge of climbing Kilimanjaro," he told me.

In Ireland, Ian had climbed Croagh Patrick 35 times in 80 hours in 2008. He had had an extraordinary year in 2007, smashing the world record for climbing the highest peaks on seven continents, including Mount Everest.

Powerful beyond measure.

Adi Roche, CEO of the Irish-based charity Chernobyl Children International, had known Ian for the past 20 years through his fund-raising commitments. To her, he was a hero. In an interview for Irish national television, she said: "He was an extraordinary guy, an uplifting fella. Irish children and the children of Chernobyl will be poorer for his loss but he leaves behind an extraordinary legacy, which is one of incredible self-belief in the power of what's possible and always looking on the bright side of even the darkest situation."

Shortly before his death, he had led a group of 145 Irish teenagers, teachers and fundraisers to the summit of Kilimanjaro, setting a record for the biggest group ever to climb to the summit.

Powerful beyond measure.

Ian was not only a go-getter, he was also a go-giver. By climbing the Kilimanjaro, the group raised money for several charities including Our Lady's Children's Hospital, Crumlin, and Chernobyl Children International.

Ian explained: "These students now realise or will soon realise three great life lessons:

How We Choose to Respond
That we are not judged by the things that go wrong in our lives but how we choose to respond when they do.

Control The Controllables
That the things we cannot do should never interfere with the things that we can.

All The Magic Happens Outside The Comfort Zone
Life really only begins when we step out of the comfort zone.

Any major challenge that gets us out of our comfort zone is going to force us through pain, through a certain amount of suffering but the rewards on the other side are enormous.

Ian understood the new, great and wonderful world on the other side of pain, effort and struggle. He understood that the journey itself is the destination. That it's actually better to journey well than to arrive.

There's no growth without a certain amount of discomfort and deep inner digging. Ian constantly reiterated Edmund Hillary's idea that it's not the mountain we conquer but ourselves.

Ian knew that the comfort zone is the greatest enemy of our human potential and human possibility. He was also aware that to break out of our comfort zone and plunge through that red mist of pain is a two-edged sword.

This comfort zone-bursting pain can deform us or transform us. It can disfigure us or transfigure us. It can make us victims or victors, bitter people or better people.

The choice is ours.

At the bottom of Kilimanjaro, Ian told young climbers: "Get bitter or get better." He had another lovely touch for the climbers at the bottom of the mountain. Knowing that everyone's mind was full of negative personal baggage, he said: "Leave your mental baggage here now. After the climb it's up to you whether or not you want to pick it up and continue to carry it."

When they came down from the mountain, no one picked up their discarded mental baggage. They were transformed, transfigured, victors and definitely better people.

Ian's life showed us that it's not the years in our lives that really matter, but the life in our years.

Powerful beyond measure.

RED PLATFORM: We believe that we're inadequate and we're seduced by the safety of the comfort zone. Years in our lives.

GREEN PLATFORM: We're powerful beyond measure and we're finding all the magic of life outside the comfort zone. Life in our years.

62

Great Expectations Deliver Great Achievements

WITH Ireland's overweight and obesity problems is costing the state at least €1.13 billion annually in healthcare costs and reduced productivity, we need a massive injection of positive expectations about the steps we can take to combat these two lurking killers.

If urgent action isn't taken, Ireland could be on track to become the fattest country in Europe by 2030. We need great expectations of ourselves and of others to deliver great transformations in terms of taking exercise and combating obesity.

People say that perception is reality: but it's not, it's much more. When you believe you *can't* do something, that belief flips an internal switch to prove you right — that you can't actually do it. It's a massive self-sabotage switch whose hidden agenda is to make you right. You always knew you couldn't do it.

On the other hand, when you believe you can do something (provided it's realistic and stretching for you) you flip another internal switch that opens up all kinds of possibilities to make that belief happen in real life.

So the initial belief that you can or can't do something is crucial to the actual doing it or not doing it. "Well, what did you expect?"

Expectations matter hugely and there is a huge difference between toxic negative expectations locked into hard rigid 'shoulds' on the Red Platform and positive flexible, open expectations rooted in expectancy on the Green Platform.

"The difference between a lady and a flower girl is not how she behaves, but how she's treated," said the Irish playwright George Bernard Shaw. Shaw was the author of *Pygmalion*, on which the film *My Fair Lady* was based.

When you treat a flower girl like a lady, something happens. There's a flip of that inner energy switch. Her expectations of herself change and subsequently she changes. In other words, if you have positive expectations you'll dramatically increase the possibility of getting positive results.

This has often been called the "Pygmalion effect", based on the myth of the Cypriot sculptor who married his ivory sculpture that Venus had turned into a woman.

The Pygmalion effect is a form of self-fulfilling prophecy. It means that people will internalise their positive labels and those with positive labels succeed accordingly.

Psychologist Dr. Robert Rosenthal of Harvard University performed an experiment in a school in California that proved how ordinary people could perform at an extraordinary level.

At the beginning of the school year, the principal, Lenore Jacobson, called three teachers into her office.

"You are the best teachers in this school. We have identified three classes, each with 30 of the brightest students, and we're going to assign them to you to teach for the entire year."

She told the teachers to keep this information totally to themselves.

The result?

At the end of the school year, these students not only led the school but also the entire school district in academic accomplishment.

Calling the three teachers into her office, the principal said: "Well, you've had a very good year."

"Yes we have ... it was so easy," replied the teachers: "These children were so easy to teach. They were so eager to learn; it was such a pleasure to teach them."

The principal then told them the truth.

"Actually this was an experiment, and those 90 children were chosen at random. I had no idea what their IQs were at all."

"That's incredible!" exclaimed the teachers.

The principal went on: "And I think I should also tell you the other side of the experiment. At the beginning of the school year, we put all the teachers' names in a hat and yours were the first three names that were drawn."

The Pygmalion effect shows that you achieve not only what you expect to achieve but also what others expect you to achieve.

First, the principal expected a lot. Then, so did the teachers. Then the students, sensing that the teachers expected a lot, in their turn also expected a lot from themselves as well.

Rosenthal repeated this experiment 300 times, and every time he got identical results. To achieve more, you have to expect more from yourself and from others. It really is that simple. But the opposite is also true and that's why so many bright and capable people never perform up to their abilities. For too long, they've been knocked and put down by people around them in a manner that destroys their self-confidence.

So by 2030 let us in Ireland expect to be the fittest and healthiest nation in Europe. Let us take all the actions necessary to make that happen.

Expect more from yourself. Expect more from others. Whether you jog or walk a mile in seven minutes, or 14 minutes or 21 minutes. You can smile because you're off the couch and out in the fresh air. Have great expectations and, like the teachers, you'll see dramatic results.

RED PLATFORM: Expect little. Live down to expectations. Prove yourself right.

GREEN PLATFORM: Great achievements and peak performances always happen in an atmosphere of great expectations.

63

Your Best Reasons To Run

I WAS speaking to a famous doctor recently about the challenge of depression in Ireland today. We discussed the importance of exercise and its benefits in combating this mental health challenge. She said: "We all know what to do. Don't we? It's doing what we know that matters. My patients all know about exercise at intellectual and academic levels. They will give me better statistics than I have myself.

"What counts is the motivation to put on the running shoes, to actually get out the door, to take that first step. But that's where the process breaks down. That's what depression does.

"I want something that people can pin up on their wall, read, re-read and motivate themselves to take exercise now."

A powerful 'why,' purpose or reason will provide you with 80 per cent of the energy to get up, get off the couch and take exercise. Once you have your powerful 'why,' you will go through any 'how.' So, if purpose gives power, what are the 21 reasons, 21 'whys' to get up and just take some form of exercise now?

Here are 21 reasons to run:

1. Second Fattest Is No Fun. Run

As the second fattest country in Europe after the UK (23 per cent of our adult population is obese), and with one in four of our children obese, it makes sense to run, as running is a top calorie-burning exercise. So get up, put on the running or walking shoes, get out and start burning up those excess calories and bring the children with you.

2. Keeps On Working When You're Resting

Exercise revs up your metabolism, even when you are not doing it. Following a good run, you will continue to burn calories for up to two hours.

3. Reasonable cost

You don't need expensive equipment. It won't break the bank.

4. Social Life

Exercise works wonders for your social life, especially when you join a group or a club or just get even one other person to join you.

5. Best Ideas Time

Even when you run by yourself you break routine and you get some time to think, reflect and discover the deeper more creative parts of yourself. So many people get their best ideas while they are out running.

6. Enjoy Nature

Running provides the opportunity to get out and enjoy nature — the trees, the woods, the fields, the flowers, the lakes, the mountains and, if you're lucky, the sea.

7. Runner's High

It increases your feel-good factor and your self-esteem. All those endorphins, serotonin and dopamine flowing through your body combat negative energy and give you a 'runner's high.'

8. Stress Buster

It's a natural stress-buster. You definitely feel better coming back than you did when you went out.

9. Ups Water Intake

It helps you drink more water. About 60 per cent of an adult's body is made up of water. The body needs water to process calories. If you're even mildly dehydrated, your metabolism slows down.

10. More Energy
Exercise increases your energy and your energy lasts longer.

11. Helps Lift Depression
If you suffer from depression or anxiety, make an appointment with a friend, mentor or partner to run or walk or jog at a certain time each day no matter what.

12. Longer Life
Exercise lengthens your life span and gives you a better quality of life.

13. Goals With Purpose and Meaning
It gives you clear goals to focus on. And linking your major runs, walks or mountain hikes to raising funds for a charity also touches the lives of others.

14. Enjoying The Journey — Living In The Now
You can use a run to train yourself out of "destination addiction" and practice enjoying the run itself, the journey. You can learn to live in the now and be one with life. You'll discover that it's better to journey well than to arrive.

15. Excellence Zone
It gets you out of your comfort zone and into your excellence zone.

16. Sets You Up For The Day
Running in the early morning gives you the feeling that you've conquered ordinary human sloth for one more day. It sets you up mentally for the day.

17. Private Victories Matter Most

Some form of exercise early in the day is a private victory that precedes all public victories.

18. Overcomes SAD

Running, especially in the rain, helps overcome seasonal affected disorder (SAD), also known as winter depression or winter blues.

19. Good Humour

Exercise lifts your mood and puts you in good humour. Imagine the benefits that can have for your family and friends.

20. Better Sleep

Exercise helps you to sleep better.

21. Good Soreness — Sore Not Sorry

There are two kinds of soreness — two kinds of pain. The first is bad soreness like the pain of a rotten tooth. The second is good soreness, the soreness in your muscles after a run. So ask yourself: "Do I want to be sore tomorrow, or sorry tomorrow?"

There are also two mental pains. The pain of discipline and the pain of regret. Regret is by far the worst. You may be tempted to say to yourself: "When I feel better about myself I'll go out and take some exercise." No. Don't think about it. Just do it now. Only think about those 21 reasons to run. Go out and run, walk, jog, swim or cycle and you'll feel better about yourself.

RED PLATFORM: Finding reasons or excuses not to take exercise or tackle that job. Knowing what to do but not doing it. Pain of regret. Feeling sorry rather than sore.

GREEN PLATFORM: Finding reasons or excuses to take exercise or do that job. Doing what you know. Discipline that leads to good soreness.

64

The Victory Of Persistence

HERE'S a story I heard many years ago in California. A man heard that there was a diamond vein under his farm. He bought a massive mining drill and drilled for days and weeks and months. He got nothing but rubble. Then one morning he decided he'd had enough, and he gave up. He sold the farm and went off to make his fortune some other way. The farmer who bought the land was a bit of a handyman. He managed to crank up the mining drill and got it working. After about five minutes he hit the diamond vein. He made his fortune.

Meanwhile the other man heard about his friend's good fortune and he also made a fortune — going around the country telling people that just when people are about to make a breakthrough, they give up. So near and yet so far. He became the guru of persistence.

There's always a time just before a tipping point in life where 'the acomodador,' the 'giving up point' strikes and we throw in the towel, but more often than not, we stop when we're at the very point of making a breakthrough.

Paulo Coelho describes that old Mexican word, 'acomodador' well in his book *The Zahir*: "There is always an event in our lives that is responsible for us failing to progress: a trauma, a particularly bitter defeat, a disappointment in love, even a victory that we did not quite understand, can make cowards of us and prevent us from moving on." The 'acomodador' is that giving up point.

Journalist and author Malcolm Gladwell calls the tipping point, "the moment of critical mass, the threshold, the boiling point." The tipping point is that magical moment when an idea, trend, or social behaviour crosses a threshold, tips and spreads like wildfire. It's similar to the 212 degrees when water boils. That one-degree from 211 to 212 makes all the difference. It's the boiling tipping point.

Just as a single sick person can start an epidemic of the flu, so too can a small but precisely targeted push cause a fashion trend or the popularity of a new product ... that is, if we don't give up just before we reach it like the man drilling for diamonds.

When you work on any big exercise goal, your motivation will wax and wane like the tide in the sea. Sometimes you'll feel motivated; sometimes you won't. But it's not your motivation alone that will produce results; it's your action. Persistence allows you to keep taking action even when you don't feel motivated to do so and therefore you keep accumulating results. "Genius is one percent inspiration and 99 per cent perspiration," according to inventor Thomas Edison.

I'm not sure what sort of leader Calvin Coolidge was when he became the 30th president of the United States. But I think he was spot on when he declared: "Nothing in this world can take the place of persistence."

He said: "Talent will not; nothing is more common than unsuccessful people with talent. Genius will not; unrewarded genius is almost a proverb. Education will not; the world is full of educated failures. Persistence and determination alone are omnipotent".

How true and enlightening, even some 85 years down the line. Should you always persist and never give up?

Certainly not. Sometimes giving up is the best option. We need to stop working harder at what's clearly not working. Not to do so is stubbornness, not persistence. And there's a massive difference between them.

So how do you know when to persist and when to give up?

There's no sense in preparing assiduously for the wrong event in life. There are horses for courses. No matter how many hours of practice a Clydesdale horse puts in, he's not going to win the Grand National or the Derby races at Epsom or the Curragh. But he may win the ploughing championships.

To deliver an outstanding performance, is natural talent the answer, or is it long hours of practice?

Malcolm Gladwell, in his book *Outliers*, came up with his "10,000 hours of practice" rule. The rule states that a mere 10,000 hours of dedicated practice brings out the best in you.

But 10,000 hours of training a hen to swim won't do much for the hen, but it'll do wonders for a duck.

He based his theory on a study of musicians by psychologist Anders Ericsson. By the age of 20, the best violinists will have practised an average of 10,000 hours.

That was 2,000 hours more than the 'good' ones and 6,000 hours more than those who just hoped to become music teachers. Master performers had devoted thousands of extra hours of practice to achieve excellence.

Not just any kind of practice, but "purposeful practice" for longer hours was the only thing that distinguished the best from the rest.

"Purposeful practice" means small incremental improvements every day mastering a skill, measuring progress.

Gladwell points out that outstanding performers all get in their 10,000 hours of practice, from the Beatles in nightclubs in Hamburg between 1960 and 1964 to Bill Gates having access to a computer room when he was just 13.

The great Canadian ice hockey player Wayne Gretzky had an ability to read the pattern of a game and then go to where the puck would end up. Incredible anticipation.

"I wasn't naturally gifted in terms of size and speed," he said. "Everything I did in hockey I worked for. That's how I got to know where the puck was going before it even got there."

Golfer Jack Nicklaus said: "It isn't a lack of talent, it's a lack of being able to repeat good shots consistently that frustrates most players. And the only answer to that is practice." It's really the 'T-CUP' approach that matters: To Think Correctly Under Pressure.

How about people like Mozart? A natural musical genius? His first work, regarded as a masterpiece today, was his *Piano Concerto No. 9* composed when he was 21. However, his father, Leopold, also a famous composer, had his son working on intensive composition and performing programmes from the time he was three years old.

Eighteen years of purposeful practice.

How do we get purposeful practice? Words used well have extraordinary power. In 1998, psychology professor Carol Dweck and a colleague took 400 fifth-graders in the US and gave them a series of simple puzzles. Afterwards each student was given their score and each got six words of praise.

Half of the students were praised for intelligence. "You must be very smart at this."

The others were praised for effort. "You must have worked really hard."

After another series of tests the group praised for 'hard work' increased their performance score over the 'intelligent students' by 50 per cent. This massive difference depended solely on just those six words of praise spoken after the first test: "You must have worked really hard."

When the intelligent ones didn't win at something, they saw this as proof that they were failures. When the 'effort-group' failed, they worked hard at learning the lessons from the failure and then they bounced back stronger. Failure was just their fuel to work harder at getting it right the next time.

Which all comes back to what we said at the outset — that success is largely dependent on hard work and persistence. The extra energy required to make another effort or try another approach if this one isn't working is the secret of success.

Mahatma Gandhi recognised the importance of effort when he

said: "Satisfaction lies in the effort, not in the attainment. Full effort is full victory."

There are no shortcuts. You have to put in the hours. Purposeful progress-measuring hours. Hard work will always beat talent when talent won't work hard.

Coolidge really seemed to nail it when he said that: "Nothing in this world can take the place of persistence." Or as Edison said: "99 per cent perspiration." Or Gandhi's: "Full effort is full victory."

If you love your work or your training, bringing joy from deep within you to your work, to the track, to the pool or the gym, then you'll be happy to work hard and put in the hours, because you're enjoying every minute of the journey.

RED PLATFORM: Praising intelligence. Talent not working hard. 1% inspiration should do it. Giving up point — "The acomodador." Stubbornness, working at what's not working.

GREEN PLATFORM: Praising effort. Putting in purposeful practice over many hours. 99% perspiration. Persistence and determination.

65

Spirit Can Raise You Up

I ONCE asked Doug Flynn, the great Cincinnati Reds' baseball star: "What is the essence of a great team?" "Chemistry," he said, "essentially, it's the spirit in the team."

What makes a good team in work or in sport depends on how much "spirit" they manage to generate among themselves.

That's one of the great strengths of the human condition — the indomitable spirit to fight adversity and come out the other side.

Heaven knows we've all had to endure a nightmare time in Ireland since the collapse of the Celtic Tiger. Against the odds in many cases, we haven't just survived but have shown remarkable moral fibre in overcoming all kinds of challenges.

Too many people fail to realise how the human spirit triumphs over so many disasters.

There's a Robert Bly story about "spirit" I heard from the late poet John O'Donohue. Once upon a time there was a man who had 12 cows. One morning he noticed that the amount of milk had lessened overnight from the usual measure of milk. That continued for a week. So he decided to stay up and see what was going on. He figured that someone was stealing the milk from his cows at night.

About midnight, he happened to look up at the stars, and he saw one star that seemed to be getting larger. It came straight down towards his field and stopped a few feet from him in the form of a great ball of light. Inside the light there was a luminous woman. As soon as her toes touched the ground, the light disappeared and she stood there like an ordinary woman. He said to her: "Are you the one who has been stealing milk from my cows?"

"Yes," she said. "My sisters and I like the milk from your cows very much." He said: "You are very beautiful and I'm glad that you like the milk from my cows. So this is what I want to say to you: 'If you marry me, we can live together, I will never hit you and I'll let you care for the cows with me. Will you marry me?'"

She said slowly: "Yes, I will. But there's one condition. I have brought this covered basket with me, and I want you to agree that you will never look into this basket no matter how long we are married. Do you agree to that?"

"Oh, I do," he said. "Of course, I do."

So they were married, and they lived happily together for six months. Then one day, while she was out herding the cows, he happened to notice the basket on the windowsill.

He said to himself: "Well, you know, she is my wife, and this is my house, and the basket is in my house and so it could be considered to be my basket!"

Then he opened the basket and began to laugh and dance. "There's nothing in the basket. There's nothing in the basket! There's nothing in the basket. There's absolutely nothing in the basket. Nothing."

His wife hearing the commotion came into the house and she said to him: "Have you opened the basket?" He began laughing again. "I did," he admitted. "I opened the basket. But there's nothing in it. There's nothing in the basket at all. There's absolutely nothing in the basket. Nothing."

Then she said: "I have to leave now. I have to go back."

He cried out: "Don't go. Don't leave me. Please don't go."

She said: "I have to go back now. What I brought with me in the basket was spirit. The basket was full of spirit. It's so like human beings to think that spirit is nothing."

And then, whoosh, she was gone. How wrong she was.

If this beautiful woman had dwelt a while longer among humans she would have discovered that many humans on winning teams and those who have recovered from horrific accidents will tell her that far from being nothing, spirit is everything.

Janine Shepherd, a former cross-country skier was cycling through the Blue Mountains near Sydney as part of her training regime, when a truck hit her. She suffered a broken neck and back, and severe lacerations to her abdomen.

Her right leg was ripped open, her collarbone and five ribs were fractured, and she suffered serious internal injuries.

Doctors at first thought she wouldn't live. Later they told her that she'd be bound to a wheelchair for the rest of her life and that she'd never have children.

With a spirit full of determination, Shepherd began to go through the slow rehabilitation process until she could walk again and even got her pilot's licence within a year. She now has three children.

She insists that a broken body isn't a broken person: "I now know my real strength never came from my body. Who I am remained unchanged. The pilot light inside me was still alight as it is in every one of us. Although my body might be limited, it was my spirit that was unstoppable."

Janine is one more human who doesn't believe that we're just mere meat-suits bumping into one another and that spirit is nothing. Her basket was full. Her spirit is still unstoppable.

Jack Kavanagh is a windsurfing fanatic and a fluent Irish speaker. When he was 20, on August 31st, 2012, he ran down to the sea in Portugal and dived into an oncoming wave. In that moment his life changed — he broke his neck.

As a result, Jack was left with no feeling or movement below his armpits and with only limited use of his arms and wrists — 15% muscle function. Spending seven months between hospital and rehabilitation centres, Jack had to relearn everything from breathing unaided, to using his arms and hands again with his new functionality to do as much as he possibly could for himself.

After being told he would likely need assistance from two people to do most tasks, he persevered. Within 13 months of his injury he was back in college, living away from home and regaining the control over his life that he had stripped from him only months before. Jack continues to push his mind and body to defy his prognosis and societal notions about what is possible.

They tell him it's unlikely he'll be able to transfer himself from his bed to his wheelchair, or from his wheelchair to a car, without assistance. He's determined to do everything he possibly can to engineer that freedom for himself. He's been told he'll never walk again. But he's determined to try to confound that prognosis.

I was delighted to read in his newsletter that my book *The Green Platform* had helped to rekindle his indomitable spirit during his brave and courageous journey to recovery. He says: "So sometimes when I'm finding the going tough I think about the way children think and try to adopt it myself, that fearless nature in the face of a challenge and unquenchable appetite for life that is such a part of them. Two books that have really helped me: *Fear* by Thich Nhat Hanh and *The Green Platform* by Declan Coyle. Part of winning the mental battle for me is first seeing where I am, then seeing where I want to get to and then putting the steps to get from one place to the next in motion in the 'now' that is between the two."

Although Jack's body is limited, his spirit is unstoppable. His real strength never came from his body, but rather from that pilot light inside him. Who he is remains unchanged. I'm looking forward to meeting him again soon.

This invisible power, "spirit," chemistry or camaraderie is the inner stuff of legends and champions like Jack, Janine, Doug and of all peak performing teams, families and companies.

RED PLATFORM: Spiritless individuals with big Egos watching their personal stats. Massive "me" complexes. Suspicion. "What's in it for me? They wouldn't do it for me!"

GREEN PLATFORM: Unstoppable spirit. Chemistry. Trust. Camaraderie. "How can I serve and be the best that I can be for the team? They would do the same for me."

66

Above All Be
True To Yourself

LIFE doesn't just build character — it reveals it. Some years ago, I suffered a trapped nerve in my shoulder and had to go to a physiotherapist. When I was leaving the treatment room, I noticed a sign on the inside of his door. It said: "From here on out, it's entirely up to you." It brought home to me the truth of those 10 powerful Green Platform words, no word more than two letters: "If it is to be, it is up to me."

A professional trainer I met told his clients that the difference between a dream and a goal was to have an action plan. He gave each person a detailed action plan with a very specific calendar timeline and a 25-point checklist of things to do. Some of the clients were preparing for a marathon and his checklist contained miles to cover each day plus rest and recovery sessions.

However, after he discovered that two of the clients preparing for the marathon were cutting corners during their training, he thought he'd give them 120 per cent of work to do instead.

He explained that if he asked them to do 10 push-ups, they would actually do 12. He wanted the extra two to be voluntary. What he discovered was that rather than doing 120 per cent, two of them were only doing 80 per cent.

"Did you do the six miles today?"

"Well, not fully six, but near enough."

The man actually only did four and a half.

The trainer said: "They're not fooling me; they are only fooling themselves. I'm not talking about training here, I'm talking about character."

Shakespeare understood this fully when he has Polonius bidding farewell to Laertes:

"This above all: to thine own self be true,
And it must follow, as the night the day,
Thou canst not then be false to any man."

Even the most magnificent project depends on the success of the smallest components. Many people downplay small details, dismissing them as minutiae.

Our whole environment is simply an accumulation of tiny details. Ultimately the key to quality and excellence in every aspect of our lives is doing little things correctly, all the time, so that each action contributes to the production of an overall quality result.

Successful people in every walk of life understand the importance of detail. Crime scene investigators know that it's often the smallest, most obscure item that leads to the arrest and prosecution of criminal.

Michael Josephson, founder of the Josephson Institute of Ethics, explains it well in a story about a master carpenter who worked for the same builder for nearly 50 years and announced he was retiring. The builder told him how much he appreciated his work and presented him with a $5,000 bonus. Then he asked if he would build just one more house. He owned a magnificent lot with a spectacular view and wanted to build a dream house there.

The carpenter was bitterly disappointed at the small bonus and extra project, but realised that the building fee would help him buy a small cottage. He agreed to build the dream house.

Even though he'd always prided himself on his uncompromising commitment to quality, his resentment caused him to cut corners, ignore details, and accept shoddy workmanship from his workers. He even looked the other way when some of them substituted cheaper materials and pocketed the difference.

When the house was finished, the builder shook the carpenter's hand and with a huge smile gave him a thank-you card. The carpenter was disdainful, until he saw that inside the card was the deed to the house he'd just built.

The carpenter was ashamed to have misjudged his old friend and betrayed his own values, and he was remorseful that the house he would now live in for the rest of his life had been made so carelessly.

Our character is the house we live in, and we construct it piece by piece by our daily choices. Deceit, irresponsibility and disrespect are like shoddy workmanship. Whenever we put in less than our best and ignore our potential for excellence, we create a future full of creaky floors, leaky roofs, and crumbling foundations.

"Completing the allotted miles is not about training," the professional trainer said, "it's about character." To thine own self be true.

RED PLATFORM: Take short cuts. Cutting corners. Cheating. Forgetting quality. Unreliable.

GREEN PLATFORM: Total commitment to quality. Honesty. Going the extra one or two miles. Excellence in everything. Character.

67

Worry — A Waste Of Time

A FEW years ago Northern Irish professional golfer Rory McIlroy walked off a golf course during a major tournament, obviously bothered by something unrelated to his play. It turned out to have been connected to a toothache.

An essential ingredient of any great performer is the ability to leave personal worries behind and focus on what they are doing, their performance.

As I write this column, I'm sitting in a coffee shop in the United States. A man just asked me if he could join me at my table, as the place is jam-packed. On his tray, he had a large coffee and a mountain of sugary pastries. He was massive. He had a small black goatee and a tight crew-cut. His dark eyes twinkled as he looked at the food. This was a happy moment for him. He looked across at me like a mischievous boy and said: "I'm afraid I'm just a tad exercise-challenged." Then he tucked in.

"Exercise-challenged!"

Don't you love it? What a handy label to avoid personal accountability and responsibility.

Later, when he'd finished and a bit of guilt had set in, we had a great chat about diet and exercise. "I'm a disgrace. I actually look after my car better than I look after myself," he confessed.

We ended up talking about setting diet and exercise goals and getting started; just getting the exercise habit going but all he could talk about were his worries. It turned out that he was a world-class worrier.

Every sentence started with: "I'm worried that ..." He worries about his family, about his health, about dying young. He worries that he's taking too many anxiety pills to alleviate his worries. He certainly isn't worry-challenged. So we took a look at worry.

The word "worry" comes from the Old English word *wyrgan*, which means "to strangle". I told him that people literally worry themselves to death, or at least to heart disease, ulcers or high blood pressure.

I told him that people literally worry themselves to death or to heart disease or to ulcers or high blood pressure. Worry is like a rocking chair. It gives you something to do but it actually gets you nowhere.

Worry is crossing bridges before you get to them — in fact 40 per cent of those bridges don't even exist. We worry so much about things that never happen.

Thirty per cent of our worries are about things that we can't do anything about anyway. "I'm going on a picnic on Saturday. I'm worried about the weather." Now there's a good worry. You can choose and change your inner weather, but not the outer weather.

Twelve per cent of our worries are to do with the affairs of others that really don't concern us at all.

Ten per cent are what the researchers called: "Petty and miscellaneous worries about health, real or imagined."

That means 92 per cent of our worries are a waste of good mental space. That leaves only a mere eight per cent that are genuine worries. Action and worry cannot co-exist. You cannot take action and worry at the same time .

Just as light and darkness cannot co-exist, neither can love and fear, negativity and gratitude, nor worry and action. It's either one or the other.

Once it started to dawn on this man that he couldn't worry and take action at the same time, he decided to make a list of all his worries. He said he'd then follow up by writing down specific actions he'd take to "vaporise" them. Action "vaporises" worries.

I urged him to keep his mind open to peace, joy and happiness so that worries, fear and doubt would have little or no room to dwell in there.

Finally, I asked him: "If you had your life over again would you have more actual troubles and less imaginary ones?"

"Definitely I'd cut out the imaginary ones and have more of the real eight per cent genuine ones," he replied, "and I'll vaporise them with decisive action."

Finally, he asked: "What do I say to all those naysayers who will tell me that I can't do this?"

I left him with a few verses of a poem by Edgar Albert Guest:

"There are thousands to tell you it cannot be done,
There are thousands to prophecy failure;
There are thousands to point out to you, one by one,
The dangers that wait to assail you.
But just get stuck right in with a bit of a grin,
Just take off your coat and go to it.
Just start to sing as you tackle the thing
That cannot be done, and you'll do it!"

Worry will never rob tomorrow of its sorrow, but it will steal away your joy from today.

As the Chinese proverb says: "You cannot prevent the birds of worry flying over your head, but you can prevent them from building nests in your hair."

Your decisive action now delivers that precise prevention.

Take action. Move. Do it now.

RED PLATFORM: Wasting mental space worrying, but doing absolutely nothing about it. Creating and manufacturing in your mind clear pictures of what you don't want to happen.

GREEN PLATFORM: Take action. "Just start to sing as you tackle the thing that cannot be done, and you'll do it!"

68

Something Inside So Strong

SITTING on the top of the pyramids in the film *The Bucket List*, Morgan Freeman says to Jack Nicholson: "When you go up to heaven, the Egyptian gods will only ask you two questions: 'Did you find joy in life?' and "Did your life bring joy to others?'" The Egyptian gods were talking you about finding the purpose of your life. The 'why' of your existence.

Jim Loehr tells a story in his book, *The Power of Story*, about two totally different 'whys' that a top 50 tennis player had. One 'why' seemed to drain her energy, but the other 'why' inspired her. Although she had lots of talent, she was on a losing streak to lesser players and often found herself choking in the white heat of competition. She dreaded the pain and agony she would experience from her next loss, and this would normally last for days.

Her coach and trainers were quite alarmed about her increasing unhappiness. Jim met her and asked her how would she define a successful life. He wanted to uncover the real purpose — the why — behind everything she did including playing professional tennis.

She thought about it for a while, and eventually came up with the following three ambitions:

To be No 1 in the world.

To win Wimbledon.

To never worry financially.

Then he asked if she wanted any of those on her tombstone. She frowned and said: "No, they didn't belong there." She went on to say that they were too "shallow and trivial."

Jim asked her again about her criteria for a successful life. This time she said: "I don't know." So he asked her to spend the evening thinking about it and to give him her answer the following morning.

When he met her again she was glowing, full of energy and fully alive. "My purpose is that I want to be sunshine for all the people I care about, and all the people who watch me play," she said. "When they see me play, I want them to feel joy."

She had found her real genuine 'why' and it transformed her training and preparation. She now understood and believed in her preparation and practice because it would help her to bring her best self to her on-court games.

Now that she was connected to her new and powerful purpose, she was able to infuse her competitive play with passion. She was doing what made her heart sing. She wasn't going to die with her music still inside her. For her fans who came to watch her, she was cheerful both in victory and defeat. In her fiercest moments of competition she was true to her 'why,' her powerful purpose, her inspiring reason. She was continually amazed at the difference in her playing and in her life that her vision of a few lines on her tombstone made.

She was now 'sunshine' for everyone both on and off the court.

Did she win Wimbledon? No, but she won something much better than a trophy. She was true to herself and the crowds that she entertained appreciated that honesty and freedom. And yes, she did break into the top 20.

By getting a new 'why' for her tennis, she created a personal transformation.

If her tennis was to ignite a spark in others, she had to first ignite it in herself in a genuine way. No more head-hanging. No more long-faced expressions of defeat or dejection. No more hangdog 'poor me' faces. She was operating on a new understanding of what it is to live, to be successful and to really and truly win the games of tennis and of life.

Recent breakthrough research enables us to understand the science of purpose at work and the powerful implications it has for the workforce. It has become clear that "purpose-oriented workers" outperform their peers across all key indicators.

Purpose-oriented employees, who work for self-fulfilment and serving others above money and status, are outperforming their colleagues by every measure. People are no longer willing to work in 'a job." They hunger for purpose, meaning and a powerful 'why' to underpin all their 'whats.'

Purpose gives power.

A powerful 'why' will take you through any 'how.' What's your deep inner 'why' in life? What's your deep and genuine purpose? What few lines do you want on your tombstone? Where do you find your joy? Do you bring joy to others? Look for your powerful purpose right now and once you find it, deep peace, boundless energy and the sheer joy of living will follow.

RED PLATFORM: Results. Number 1. Wimbledon. Money. Lots of it. Serious stuff. Not much fun.

GREEN PLATFORM: Purpose. Finding sunshine and joy in playing and bringing that joy to others. "When they see me play, I want them to feel joy."

69

Let Your Dog Be Your Personal Trainer

A FEW years ago I saw on a wall a picture of a dog with a tiny caption underneath the picture that simply said: 'My personal trainer.'

If you have a dog, then you simply have to walk or jog. Your dog will insist on it. Your dog becomes your personal trainer.

Dogs know when they need their exercise and they won't let up until you get up and take them for their 'walkies.' If you've ever owned a dog you'll know that when they want exercise they get exercise. They can be very, very persuasive.

Years ago when we lived in Monkstown, County Dublin we had a white Golden Retriever called Gina. Gina made sure that we walked the nearby Dún Laoghaire pier every day for about 10 years — come rain or shine.

I remember one Sunday taking Gina for a walk up Killiney Hill with Annette, the children and their uncle Warren. That night I sent this email to a friend:

"It's a summer's day in July and we are walking our Gina with eyes and nose black as coal up the nature trails around Killiney Hill. We see her dart and dance and run hither and thither into the grass and over the ferns, hopping, sniffing and tearing off for new discoveries in the undergrowth. So different and exciting for her from the stony hard pier. So full of interest and adventure. She is so joyful and dog-happy.

"We drink in the exquisite views 'from swerve of shore to

bend of bay,' as Joyce would say, and all the time she was mooching and pooching in the long grass."

"Her emotions are all upfront," says Warren. I think that she could teach us wonder, awe and amazement at the simply Kavanagh-like weeds and trees and rocks.

A new day. A new beginning. A new adventure.

Then we moved south, to another town, Bray. That first Saturday, before anything else, we had to take Gina for a walk. That was the day we discovered the famous Bray to Greystones Cliff Walk.

Again, I emailed our friend: "On this summer's sky-blue day, we take off through Bray. We find a pathway, a trail, high up on the hill overlooking the sea. It is a glorious day with the hum and buzzing of bees among the wild flowers. Gina is running along snapping at butterflies with her back doing the Gina-wobble.

"Down below the sea is a Mediterranean blue. We can look down to our left and see flying seagulls against the blue sea backdrop. On and on the path is winding, hugging the cliff. On and on we go through this stunning coastal scenery. The green, violet and purple hills are rising to our right. Full of ferns, fuchsia and flowers. An environmentalist's delight. An ecologist's paradise.

"There are young berries on the leafy briars waiting for autumn. Now and then the occasional smiling walker with a friendly greeting. The sea air is fresh and crisp. You could bottle it and sell it in Beijing or some polluted city.

"We come across a thick log of a tree near the pathway where we sit down to enjoy the view. Gina is pooped or else just grabbing the opportunity to flake out in the shade with her four legs to the east. We walk back to Bray. Gina drinks from a mountain stream and then swims in the sea while we have cold drinks to celebrate our discovery."

If you need a personal fitness trainer you can go to your local gym, or you might just think of enjoying nature's outdoor gym by getting a dog. You'll not find a more persistent, encouraging or persuasive "personal trainer."

RED PLATFORM: No reason to go for a walk. No persuader. No dog.

GREEN PLATFORM: A reason to go for a walk. A very persuasive personal trainer. A dog.

70

Leaders Are Dealers In Hope

"WE need to talk," he said.
"Why, what is it?"
"Obesity."

"It's a hopeless cause," he said to me with a deep mournful sigh, speaking about the rise in obesity in children. "It's just creeping up on us and we're all too busy to tackle it. It's overwhelming."

Or is it?

He reminded me of what that wonderful lady, the American cultural anthropologist, Margaret Mead said: "Never doubt that a small group of thoughtful, committed citizens can change the world; indeed, it's the only thing that ever has."

To tackle this massive obesity challenge we need real Green Platform leaders. Leaders who will organise games, runs, walks, cycles, tennis matches, boxing training, swims or hurling, camogie, hockey, football, soccer, or rugby matches and get as many young people as possible involved, engaged and enthusiastic.

We need leaders to inspire us. Health and fitness leaders to stand up and be counted. To challenge a new generation to be the best that they can possibly be. The growth and development of people is the highest calling of leadership.

Are you a 'Green Platform' leader in your family or in your community? If your actions inspire and influence others to dream more, learn more, do more and become more as a person, then definitely you are.

Though leadership may be hard to define, the one thing common to all leaders is to have an inspiring vision and the ability to influence people to make things happen. Leaders bring out the best in others, and the most successful leaders go even further: They form lasting emotional bonds.

They touch your heart before they ask for your hand. When you meet them, you want to be of service and share in their vision. They get you to believe the same vision that they believe.

Green Platform leaders lead by serving others. Although a person can serve without leading, a Green Platform leader cannot lead without serving. And they don't just create followers; they create other leaders.

There's a huge difference between a negative self-serving Red Platform leader and a serving Green Platform leader.

We can ban fast-food outlets near schools, but every step to combat this obesity in young people will depend on local leadership.

So how do you serve as a Green Platform leader? What does it mean to really S-E-R-V-E? To serve means to:

See The Future. See the vision. Be the vision. See who you can be, what you can do and discover who you can help in the community.

Engage and develop others. Green Platform leaders are readers and learners. They continue to grow and develop as people. Their passion is to enable engagement, not compliance. They're really great listeners, not in-one-ear-and-out-the-other people. They respond to what they hear.

Reinvent continuously. Green Platform leaders have a passion for continuous improvement and innovation. They improve and when the moment is right they innovate. They know when not to train a faster horse; they know when it's time for the horseless carriage: the automobile. They embrace change and know that we change best when we change together.

Value results and relationships. People don't care how much you know until they know how much you care. Results matter.

There are those who make it happen and then there are those who make excuses. Ultimately we get tasks accomplished and goals exceeded through relationships.

Embody the values and living the vision; these Green Platform leaders are the change they want to see in the team or in the community. If you want passion, they are a source of passion. If you want fun, they're a source of fun. They're fit and healthy themselves. They themselves represent the change and the vision they want to bring about in the community.

Living with passion, their burning desire determines their destiny. Look at the passion of great leaders: Gandhi for human rights, Mandela and Martin Luther King for equality and Bill Gates and Steve Jobs for technology.

This passion has more influence than their personality. Passion makes the impossible possible. When anything fires the heart with purposeful passion, impossibilities vanish.

Green Platform leaders know that an army of sheep led by a lion will always prevail against an army of lions led by a sheep.

Green Platform leaders with great passion, a powerful purpose and few skills will always outperform a leader with great skills and no passion or purpose. They know you cannot lead something that you don't care passionately about. They know that you can't start a fire in your team unless there's first a fire burning in you first. They don't light fires *under* people. They light fires *in* people.

Many years ago in China, Lao Tzu nailed the heart of Green Platform leadership:

"Go to the people,
Live with them,
Love them,
Start with what they know,
Build with what they have.
But with the best of leaders,
When the work is done,
The task accomplished,

The people will say,
We have done this ourselves."

A man called Michael Heery is one such Green Platform leader. His passionate vision, hard work and purposeful leadership created the famous St Brigid's Athletic Club in Ballinacree, Co Meath around 50 years ago.

In our communities we need many more inspiring leaders like Michael who have a vision, who live the vision, who talk the talk and walk the walk. As St Francis said: "Preach the gospel, and if it's really necessary use words, too." How Green Platform leaders live their lives speaks so loudly that we can't hear a word they're saying.

They're the hope of the future. Napoleon also summed up what Green Platform leadership is all about when he said: "A leader is a dealer in hope."

RED PLATFORM: Command and control leaders lighting the fires of fear under people. Talking the talk. No credibility.

GREEN PLATFORM: Servant leaders who inspire people to believe in what they believe, lighting the fires of inspiration in people. Walking the walk. Living the vision. Credibility.

71

Grieving – From The Green Platform

IN the weeks I was a guest on *The Saturday Night Show* with Brendan O'Connor on RTÉ and *Ireland AM* on TV3, I received a huge amount of feedback from people asking how to apply the Green Platform tools to different life-challenging situations. Bereavement was high on the list.

Here's one message I got:

"Just saw part of your interview on *Ireland AM*. I wonder how does the power of positive thinking apply to someone who has suffered bereavement. I lost my husband almost a year ago and I find it hard to be positive and see that White Space. I know it's early days but as time goes on the pain never seems to ease."

The experts tell us that we never get over a major bereavement. We just learn to live the best we can with it. To live well with bereavement we need to consciously and continuously choose to live on the positive Green Platform in a manner that's emotionally honest.

Grief happens in instalments. Just when we think we're over it, and we're 'better,' then along comes another 'grief instalment.' Had the relationship not been so good, the grieving wouldn't be so bad. Your deep grief is a signpost pointing to a deep and lasting love connecting you to your loved one.

The usual stages of grief are shock, anger, guilt, denial, depression and then a new acceptance. But everyone's grief is personal and unique. Following a death, bereaved people often find it hard to take care of day-to-day tasks. Their energy levels can become very low.

These people are likely to have some days when they feel they're doing quite well and other days when they may feel overwhelmed by their loss.

The key is to have a Green Platform Recovery Routine. Here are four steps that I recommend:

1. Emotional Honesty — It Is As It Is

You feel the feelings of sadness and loss fully. You acknowledge and honour your human situation. You are emotionally honest. It is as it is. You cry the tears. But you don't pour "positive talk" over human suffering. You don't go into denial. You hold out for transcendence.

2. The White Space

Then you have a White Space. In this space you choose your response. You're not responsible for other people's actions. You're not responsible because someone dear to you dies. But you *are* responsible for your own response. You can, in fact, feel the feeling fully and still choose your response.

3. The Power To Choose — Decision Shapes Destiny

(a) You Can Choose The Red Platform

Many times this appears in our lives as an unconscious automatic reaction. It's the negative reactive platform of despair, the home of the victims, the whingers, the whiners, the moaners, the energy vampires and the "poor me" people. The "I can't help how I feel" people. Always looking backward, blaming, complaining and bewailing

(b) Or You Can Choose The Green Platform

Here you have the 10 most powerful words in the English language: "If it is to be, it is up to me." This is the positive and proactive platform of peace, joy, happiness, creativity, innovation, trust, hope, mindfulness, calmness, daily exercise, meditation, compassion, care, justice, unconditional love, and "do it now" action. It's where you find joy in your own life and always choose actions that bring joy to others.

4. The Outcome

Your quality of life will ultimately depend on which platform you decide to choose.

Green Platform: Hope, joy and inner peace.

Red Platform: Misery, sadness and despair.

In that White Space between stimulus and response you always have a choice. Change is always a choice.

This is the process that sustained Viktor Frankl through his grief in Auschwitz when they killed 38 members of his family. That's when he discovered the last and the greatest of the human freedoms — to choose your response in any given set of circumstances. He consciously chose hope, joy and inner peace. When I met him 30 years later he still radiated that same inner peace, hope and joy. He was happy every day in Auschwitz because he chose happiness every day even though he was swimming in a sea of grief. He called this ability to chose his response: "The last and the greatest of the human freedoms." He said: "When we are no longer able to change a situation, we are challenged to change ourselves." By challenging yourself, you'll play a major role in helping yourself to cope and live well with your new situation.

When we're in grief we often stop doing the ordinary things that made us feel good before the grief, like meeting friends, having warm conversations and taking exercise. We often say: "When I feel better about myself, I'll go for a walk in the fresh air."

Go right now for that walk in the fresh air or go for a swim or a bit of aqua aerobics and you'll feel better about yourself.

But don't leave it to chance. Build it into your daily routine and make it a habit. Don't think about it. Don't talk to yourself about it. Just get up, get out and do it.

Reconnect with your normal network of friends. With your real friends you can talk or remain silent. You can cry, shout or be cranky. They'll understand.

An Indian guru said one time to a grieving man: "You grieve for 40 days. Then when you are ready turn your grief into good works."

Jonathan Irwin is a man who knows all about grief. He lost three sons. His heart was broken three times. His third son Jack had special needs. Jack lived for 22 months — a desperate and painful life. A mix of drugs, physiotherapy, postural drainage, seizures, reflux operations, gastronomy and suctioning. The state refused to take responsibility for Jack unless he was admitted to a children's hospital. But Jonathan, his wife Mary-Ann and their family knew that there's no care like home care.

The only saving grace for Jack and the family was that he was cosy and warm and nursed around the clock by a dedicated volunteer band of five nurses and carers from the neighbourhood. His short life showed his parents the ideal way in which little children like Jack can be nursed.

From their experience evolved the Jack & Jill Foundation's home respite care programme that has now been offered to over 1700 children and their families all over Ireland since 1997. Jonathan has raised over €55 million to fund this amazing caring project.

Like the Indian guru said, he turned his deep grief into great works.

When we're in grief, if possible, show compassion to those who come with a positive intention to console us.

The experts will give you a list of the grieving 'no nos.'

Don't say: "It happened for a reason."

Don't say: "You have a little angel in heaven." (The bereaved person would prefer a little 'divil' on earth.)

Don't begin any sentence with: "At least ..."

Don't say: "Well, at least she had a long life. At least she didn't suffer. At least you have other children."

Around Dungimmon and Ballinacree where I grew up, the traditional funeral greeting we had was "sorry for your troubles," a handshake and sincere eye contact. That was our way. Sometimes around the grave it was just a powerful silent hand on your shoulder squeezing hope, solidarity and support into the depths of your heart, mind and soul.

Other times, saying nothing and just being present with people matters. Just being there. A listening-understanding heart with a warm compassionate presence is often all that's needed. The bereaved go deaf anyway. As a friend said recently soon after a major tragedy: "Just show up and shut up." Sometimes there are no words.

But ordinary people are not grief counselling experts. They are doing their best. Hear the feelings of empathy behind their fumbling words. They made the effort to come and see you out of love. Sometimes in these politically correct times, our fear of saying the wrong thing means that we may avoid the bereaved altogether by crossing the street and saying nothing at all. That can be even more hurtful.

At times like this people of faith get enormous consolation from their belief in a God of unconditional love who is waiting with a wonderful welcome, a radiant smile and a warm embrace for your loved one as soon as she or he crosses that great divide.

Tyrone football manager Mickey Harte's family suffered a huge bereavement when his daughter Michaela was murdered on her honeymoon in a hotel room in Mauritius. Her husband, John McAreavey, was devastated.

"The first number of months, I still felt like I was very much in shock," he said of the death of Michaela. John has also always credited his strong faith and relationship with God, who he describes as 'a personal friend' with getting his life back on track.

However, he has also admitted that the pain of her murder is, at times, "too much of a cross to bear."

"That burden, that weight was just too much for me, too much of a heavy cross to ask someone to bear," he told a packed congregation in St Eugene's Cathedral in Derry as they sat in complete silence.

"When I had those temptations to feel like that and to want to almost wallow in self-pity, to be left with the temptation there is no hope left, there was always something there that came to me to sustain me in those dark times and, I suppose, sustain my determination that I would get through this suffering," he said.

"You could react with bitterness, the anger, or you could choose to transform that suffering to go the opposite way and to transform the suffering into a creative force. I decided the latter was for me."

What a perfect description this is of the Red and Green Platforms and our power to choose one platform or the other. What a powerful choice John made to choose to transform the suffering into a creative force on the Green Platform. Not denial, but rather transcendence.

Together with the Harte family he set up the 'Michaela Foundation — Life Without Limits.' It is inspired by the life of Michaela McAreavey née Harte. It runs summer camps and other initiatives for young people who encourage the practice of all the values Michaela, her family and friends hold dear.

Again, this shows us the power of putting Viktor Frankl's words into action: "When we are faced with a situation that we cannot change, we are challenged to change ourselves."

You can create your own Green Platform Recovery Routine. It can be that walk by the lake, a cycle up the mountain or that cup of afternoon tea and chat with a good friend. You may even reach out when you're ready to help other grieving people. Isn't that what the person you love and you're grieving for would want you to do. Isn't it?

When I lost my brother Noel in a car collision with a stray bullock on the road outside Dunshaughlin when he was just 25 years old, in 1976, and later on when my parents died, these things worked for me.

But your grieving process is unique to you. Try this process, but embrace only what works for you.

RED PLATFORM: Go into grief denial. Stoic indifference. Emotional dishonesty. Close in on self. Stay inside and brood. Snap at people who should know better. Denial.

GREEN PLATFORM: Feel the feeling fully. Crying the tears. Taking time and then choosing to turn grief into good works helping and uplifting others. Getting out for fresh air. Transcendence.

72

From Abducted Boy To Leader Of Men

' I WAS six years old in Southern Sudan when I was abducted from Mass, which was celebrated under a tree," said Lopez Lomong. "They ripped me from my mother's arms, throwing me and other boys into a truck. They blindfolded us, then drove us to a prison camp that trained rebel soldiers."

It was 1991, when Lopez's home village of Kimotong was attacked by rebels in the second Sudanese civil war. The 27-year-old 1,500m runner, one of the "Lost Boys of Sudan" captured the world's attention at the 2008 Beijing Olympics, where, now having also become an American citizen, he led the US team in the opening ceremony as the flag-bearer.

I had the privilege of presenting Lopez Lomong with the 2014 Alltech Annual Humanitarian Award a few years ago. Introducing Lopez to over 2,000 participants from 60 nations, Alltech President Dr Pearse Lyons simply said when he was introducing and honouring him: "The purpose of life is to live a life of purpose."

Then Lopez told his remarkable story. In the prison camp along with 80 other boys, he was crammed into a hut, where he survived on sorghum mixed with sand. The boys were beaten with canes by the soldiers who gave them a clear message: "You dare not escape, or even think of escaping."

However, Lopez escaped three weeks later, with the help of "Three Angels," a story he recounts in his autobiography, *Running For My Life.*

On a moonless night the four children slipped out of the room, crawled on their bellies and slid through a hole in a fence. It was so dark that when he was running he didn't know whether he would run into a tree or not.

"The savannas are very tough. We ran for three days. My legs and feet were bleeding. When I wanted to stop, my angels (the other three boys) carried me."

Eventually the four boys hobbled into the United Nations-sponsored Kakuma refugee camp near Nairobi, Kenya, where he remained for 10 years. Food in the camp was sparse and refugees had to rummage through garbage for scraps.

If running saved Lopez's life from one circumstance, writing saved him from another. He entered an essay competition and his life story won the competition. The prize: a trip to America.

He then discovered that running was more than just a way of transportation and dodging bullets. While in Kenya in 2000 he saw Michael Johnson on a small TV winning a gold medal. That fired up his dream to run in the Olympics.

Feeling compelled to use his talents and his own story to give back to those less fortunate, he founded 'The 4 South Sudan' team to help provide clean water, health care, education, and nutrition to the people of Southern Sudan.

"When I run now, I keep thinking about the children I had to leave behind, those who did not have the opportunity I had," Lopez said.

He had three pearls of wisdom for the audience that day:

Don't be afraid to make mistakes and learn from them.

You are not given opportunities. You make them.

You have the ability and the responsibility to make a difference in our world.

He concluded: "I am just one voice for the thousands of children who rely on us to make a difference in this world. Running is the talent that God has given to me. When you are given a talent, you can put it in your pocket and not use it or you can use it."

Think of the God-given talents you have, and decide to use them! If you desire to start something new today, whether it's a business, or a job, or taking up regular running, just go and start it and you'll change your own life-story for the better. More than that, you'll also change those around you.

RED PLATFORM: Blame your upbringing and your parents for all the problems in your life. Circumstances make the person. It's the cards you were dealt.

GREEN PLATFORM: Circumstances reveal the person. You are responsible for your life and how you play your cards. Setbacks and obstacles are launch pads for growth and development. Your one voice can make a difference in this world.

73

You Can Get Out Of That Rut

H AVE you ever had the feeling that life is passing you by, that somehow you're going around in circles like a hamster on a wheel? I got an email from a lady who had just turned 50 who felt her life was stuck in neutral. "I can't motivate myself anymore. I'm stuck in a rut. How can I use your book, *The Green Platform*, to change?" she asked.

To get out of a rut you have to get so disturbed about your present life that you scream: "Enough is enough." You have to get sick and tired of being sick and tired living a half-lived life of daily quiet desperation.

Like the bowling ball trundling down the bowling lane, it takes a huge whack to make it suddenly change direction. This is the awful thing about getting stuck in a rut. We don't just suddenly see a rut and say: "Ah, there's a nice rut. Let's step into it." Once we're in a rut we need a massive 'whack' to get out of it. A powerful purpose. A passionate 'why.' A worthwhile reason.

The challenge is to choose to change direction. Decisions shape destiny. When you make a choice you create the future. The choices you make in turn make you. The choice to go in a new direction with a new vision of a fit and healthy you on The Green Platform is the most magical and transformational choice you'll every make.

It's not going to be easy, but it'll be worth it. You must do the thing you think you can't do. You think of a place beyond which you think you can't go and you go there.

Like the falcon in a story I heard recently from my good friend Peter Donnelly. Once there was a king who received a gift of two magnificent falcons. They were the most beautiful birds he had ever seen. He gave the precious birds to his head falconer to be trained.

Months passed, and one day the head falconer told the king that though one of the falcons was flying majestically, soaring high in the sky, the other bird had not moved from its branch since the day it had arrived.

The king summoned experts from all over his kingdom but no one could make the bird fly. Having tried everything else, the king thought: "Maybe I need someone more familiar with the countryside to train the falcon to fly." So he said: "Go and get me a farmer."

In the morning, the king was thrilled to see the falcon soaring high above the palace gardens. He said to his courtiers: "Bring me the doer of this miracle."

They brought the farmer to him. The king asked him: "How did you make the falcon fly?"

With his head bowed, the farmer said to the king: "It was very easy, your highness. I simply cut the branch where the bird was sitting."

Such a simple and powerfully motivational solution. He cut the branch. That was the whack for the trundling bowling ball. The sudden and decisive change of direction.

We're all made to fly, to realise our incredible potential as human beings. But at times we sit in fear on our branches, clinging to the things that are familiar to us.

Even though the possibilities on the Green Platform are endless, for most of us they remain undiscovered. We conform to the familiar, the comfortable and the mundane on the Red Platform.

Generally, our lives are mediocre instead of exciting, thrilling and fulfilling. The French poet Guillaume Apollinaire challenges us to leave our comfortable life branch:

"Come to the edge, he said.
We are afraid, they said.
Come to the edge, he said.
They came to the edge.
He pushed them and they flew."

Let us cut the branches of fear that we cling to and wing our ways to our true potential on the Green Platform. Don't limit your challenges. Challenge your limits. Take off. Soar.

RED PLATFORM: Keep sitting on that branch, sitting on your potential to fly, to take off or to achieve your natural potential.

GREEN PLATFORM: Cut that branch and fly. Take off and unleash your true potential.

74

A Life-Changing Conversation

WE all have two conversations running in our lives most of the time. The first one is the inner conversation, or "self-talk." The second is the conversation we have with others.

Are these powerful, inspiring, life-changing conversations or are they just the bland meeting the bland? I was doing a team building and leadership course with eight people recently. The participants were very conscious of the twin challenges we face here in Ireland at the moment: obesity and lack of fitness.

Everyone in the room felt that they were either overweight or not fit enough, and wanted to get out running or at least get into some kind of exercise habit.

There was no doubt that that none of them were happy with their fitness levels. Being too busy and a low level of constant chronic fatigue seemed to be their constant companions.

As part of the process of embedding the tools of the course I get them to commit to a Green Platform Partnership Programme (GPPP). What that means is that every Friday for 15 minutes they'll meet a positive supportive Green Platform Partner and review their week in terms of their positive contribution to each other and their progress in achieving their written goals.

But this team was different.

They also wanted to meet together for an extra five minutes. One woman offered to bring in a weighing scales, to set up a chart and have their own positive good-humoured operation transformation where they weigh in and share their exercise routines from the week.

Their progress has been astonishing. There's nothing as motivational as being able to see and measure your progress. Now they're even sharing healthy diets. They are inspiring, motivating and encouraging each other to change.

They have the chart on the wall and they can see the improvements each week. One of them recently said to me: "We have all changed both inside and out and our conversations have changed as well."

What happens when you have these powerful life-giving, life-changing and life-enhancing conversations? What happens is that there's no room for toxic negative conversations.

Here's a story a reader sent me that illustrates the impact that our inner conversations can have on others.

"One day I hopped in a taxi and we took off for the airport. We were driving in the right lane when suddenly a black car jumped out of a parking space right in front of us.

My taxi driver slammed on his brakes, skidded, and missed the other car by just inches.

The driver of the other car whipped his head around and started screaming at us. My taxi driver just smiled and waved at the other man in a really really friendly way. So I asked: 'Why did you just do that? That man almost ruined your car and sent us to the hospital.'

This is when my taxi driver taught me what I now call: 'The Law of the Rubbish Truck.'"

He explained that many people are like rubbish trucks. They run around full of rubbish (frustration, anger, and disappointment, etc.). As their rubbish piles up, they need a place to dump it and sometimes they'll dump it on you.

Don't take it personally. Just smile, wave, wish them well, and move on. Don't take their rubbish and spread it to other people at work, at home, or on the streets. Life is 10 per cent what you make it and 90 per cent how you take it.

If you are part of a work team, why don't you have a few fierce and powerful "rubbish-free-day" conversations and set up your own "operation transformation." The only thing you need to sort out is: "Who's going to bring in the scales and create the wall chart?"

Have a rubbish-free day.

RED PLATFORM: Negative energy-draining complaining and blaming conversations. Operation or Stay-The-Same.

GREEN PLATFORM: Having powerful, memorable, life changing goal-achieving conversations. Operation Transformation.

75

Green Platform
Steps To Nirvana

S OMETIMES it's the simplest of ideas that get the most profound results. In my work with businesses across the world, one idea that has delivered consistently major results has been a programme called 'The Green Platform 100 Steps To Clear Improvement.'

The thinking behind it was quite simple. Could you look around your business (or your home) and start a process of listing 100 Steps to Clear Improvement.

Brainstorm the first 10 Steps, prioritise them and write them up in a public place. A flipchart or a whiteboard. Some place that is highly visible. Then do them. One by one just cross them off the list.

According to the *Harvard Business Review*, the highest motivational factor for people is when they can see and measure progress. So basically progress has to be seen and it has to be easily measured. So long as the graph is going up, no matter how slightly, people's motivation moves up accordingly.

Years ago I got the seeds of the idea from the Japanese process of 'Kaizen,' which means continuous and never-ending improvement. The Chinese call it 'Gai Byan.'

Some teams would colour code their '100 Steps To Clear Improvement' in terms of priority and I would always put a reasonable but stretching time limit on the 100 Steps. The highest team notched up 176 steps within the allotted time.

While individual steps to clear improvement are important, what's even more important is creating the culture within the organisation of continuous and never-ending improvement. Culture will always eat plans and strategies for breakfast. A positive Green Platform culture will implement strategy with energy, creativity and innovation. A negative Red Platform culture will sabotage the best-made plans of mice and men. The core value of the 100 Steps is in the creation of the positive, can-do, proactive Green Platform culture.

In life, you can make your list of the things you want to do.

Experts vary on whether it takes 21 or 28 days to build up a lasting habit. But one thing is for sure. If you complete your 100 steps you will have built up a great habit to last you a lifetime.

I spent five days in Beijing while I was writing this. You couldn't jog outside because of the smog. I looked across the city from an 18th floor training room at 11.0 am on Monday and you couldn't see the skyscrapers through the haze. To be able to go out and exercise in clear bracing fresh air without monitoring smog measurements is an enormous privilege we have in Ireland.

Let's not take this gift of clean fresh air for granted but use it to benefit our lungs, health and fitness over the next 100 days. One step a day to clear improvement for the next 100 days. Now just imagine how you'll feel at the end of the next 100 days of Japanese Kai Zen or Chinese Gai Byan or if you prefer the Gaelic, Feabhsú Comhleanúnach.

But again, no matter what you call it in whatever language, the word water won't make you wet. Only the experience of water, plunging in to that sea or lake or pool will make you wet. Experience for yourself the 100 Steps. Plunge in.

RED PLATFORM: Stuck in a rut always doing what you've always done. Flat-lining. Always getting what you've always got.

GREEN PLATFORM: 100 Steps to clear improvement. Creating the Kai Zen culture of continuous and never-ending improvement. Doing different things to get different results.

76

From Comfort Zone
To Excellence Zone

JANE COX is one of the most compassionate, caring and loving people I know. Yet she takes no prisoners; she makes things happen. She knows that the "comfort zone" on the negative Red Platform is the greatest enemy of our human potential.

She knows that all the magic in life happens outside the "comfort zone," not in it. So Jane cajoles and inspires everyone she works with to break out of their "comfort zone" prisons; way, way out into the field of all possibilities in their "excellence zone."

Jane is a member of staff at St Catherine's special school, in Newcastle, Co Wicklow. Together with her team, Jane does amazing work with our special needs son Alexander.

He was recently the star of *The Saturday Night Show* with Brendan O'Connor.

You may remember that I wrote about Muhammad Ali and our son "Alexander the Greatest" earlier in the book. Alexander has Mowat-Wilson syndrome, which means that he can't talk, is barely able to walk, cannot eat orally, is doubly incontinent and needs 31 syringes of medications every day among other things.

People have been telling me that when he reached out with one wave of his hand during *The Saturday Night Show* on March 8, 2014 he touched the heart of the nation. Host Brendan O'Connor spoke for us all when he said: "I think he likes me."

Jane is a firm believer that you should never ever do for a child what a child can do for himself. So she's always challenging

Alexander to move outside of his "comfort zone", to walk across the floor, to take another step and find another gear. She encourages him to do another little activity, to stretch that tiny little bit and reach that wall.

With Jane, not taking exercise is not an option. In my book *The Green Platform*, I wrote that when Genevieve and Fionn, his sister and brother, were growing up, "it was often in the world of action and doing. Brush your teeth. Do your homework. Tidy your room. Hurry up. Get ready. Put away the dishes please. Come on. Let's go."

"But as you look at, listen to, touch or help Alexander with this or that you join him in being completely present, not wanting anything other than the moment as it is. He helps transport all of us to a different place in life. The world of 'being' behind all the 'doing.' A higher level of consciousness. Now there is nothing wrong with the doing, but if our lives are only about the 'doing,' and no time for "being," then our lives will be very impoverished. After being in his presence, then we can go back energised to the 'doing,' again."

I was making the point that behind all the doing there's a place of being, a quiet place of peace, joy and silence where the mystics go. It is called "the present". The precious "now". The only place we ever really live.

Jane appreciates Alexander's ability to get us into the now, into the 'being' behind all the 'doing." But she won't allow him to spend his life in the "comfort zone" of being. She is also the guru of doing. She doesn't see Alexander as disabled, but rather differently abled. She understands yin and yang, exercise and rest and being and doing.

She has a list of stretch goals for Alexander, challenging him to be more and to do more. Then when the nurses achieve even a small breakthrough with him, there's much joy, praise and celebration.

We all need a Jane to get us out of our "comfort zones" and into our "excellence zones" to take daily exercise, do that challenging job, or make that phone call.

Even if we don't have a Jane to help us, we can have our own inner Green Platform voice that won't make excuses but will challenge us, cajole us and encourage us to burst free from our comfort zones and go for that walk or do that job. A voice that'll take no prisoners; if only we listen to it.

Jane is right. Outside and beyond the "comfort zone," in our "excellence zone", is where we find the real magic in life.

RED PLATFORM: Wallowing in the comfort zone of just "being." Avoiding the effort and hard work of "doing."

GREEN PLATFORM: A great natural balance between "being" and "doing," between resting and working. Breathing in and breathing out. Naturally.

77

Do It Anyway

ONE of my earliest memories of growing up in Dungimmon on the Cavan/Meath border was the whole community experience of going to the funeral in Ballinacree of a neighbour who had died.

Everyone rallied together to console the bereaved family; and the wake in the house was a great occasion. A celebration of the life of the person who had died, but also with a full and genuine acknowledgement of the family's pain and loss.

They say that Ireland and some part of Africa are the two healthiest places in the world to grieve. Death is not sanitised or repressed. It's felt fully and expressed. There's an emotional honesty where a real healing comes from a real, genuine and wholesome feeling. Tears flow freely, as does the laughter. Tragedy and comedy are so close. Two sides of the same coin.

In one corner of the room, someone is crying and in the other there's outrageous laughter at some story from the life of the person laid out in the bed. For the bereaved family, all these stories and celebrations of the person's life ease, comfort and console their aching hearts.

But one thing that always struck me when I used to hear all the great things about a dead person was this: "Wouldn't it have been great if that person had heard even one of these wonderful things they're saying about them now when they were alive?"

It seems we're completely biased in terms of begrudgery. So quick to put a person down. That is, until they're dead.

So whatever form of exercise or whatever work challenge you've decided to do in the coming year, don't listen to the begrudgers, the put-downers or the belittlers. Maybe your current commitment is stalled. So what. Don't listen to the 'I told you so-ers.' Cut yourself a bit of slack and start again.

I was talking recently to a woman who was an exercise stop/starter. She still managed to get a bit of restarting rhythm and momentum going. She could somehow pick herself up and take off again.

I asked her how she did it.

"Well," she said, "I just say this wee prayer every day. 'Oh God of new beginnings and fresh starts, here I am again.'"

Over the years I've seen so many young people start off in life with high hopes and high ideals but then give up because they got negative feedback or suffered failure or got some kind of setback.

It's so important to keep going no matter what, otherwise many of the things that need to be done in our world just won't get done. Young people have a gift or a talent or a signature strength that the world needs and if they don't deliver, the world isn't getting the help, hope and healing that it needs.

In a book compiled by Lucinda Vardey, *Mother Teresa: A Simple Path*, there's a series of paradoxical commandments entitled "Anyway," that were pinned up on the wall in Shishu Bhavan, Mother Teresa's children's home in Calcutta. The original version of the text was written by Kent M. Keith in 1968.

"People are illogical, unreasonable and self-centred. Love them anyway.

If you do good, people will accuse you of selfish ulterior motives. Do good anyway.

If you are successful, you will win false friends and true enemies. Succeed anyway.

The good you do today will be forgotten tomorrow. Do good anyway.

Honesty and sincerity will make you vulnerable. Be honest and sincere anyway.

The biggest men and women with the biggest ideas can be shot down by the smallest men and women with the smallest minds. Think big anyway.

People favour underdogs and follow only top dogs. Fight for the underdogs anyway.

What you spend years building may be destroyed overnight. Build anyway.

People really need help but may attack you if you help them. Help people anyway.

Give the world the best you have and you'll get kicked in the teeth. Give the world the best you have anyway."

Mother Teresa added: "It was never about you and them anyway, it was always about you and God."

Dream big. Follow you dream. Do what you love and love what you do. Shine a light on all that's positive and wonderful and noble and bright in people before their funerals. In the long run, it's not the years in their lives that matter, but the life, the light and the love in their years.

Most of the time all you need is two words:

"Well done."

"Great job."

"Thank you."

Attention amplifies everything. Say all those wonderful things to them while they're still alive and can appreciate your positive feedback ... anyway. Then watch them grow, develop and flourish here, now, this side of the grave.

RED PLATFORM: If you do good, people will accuse you of selfish, ulterior motives.

GREEN PLATFORM: Do good anyway.

78

To Click Or To Experience Your Experience

S OME years ago, our Christmas present from our son Fionn was not a thing, but an experience. A night at the cinema to see *The Secret Life of Walter Mitty*.

Walter spends a lot of his time chasing Sean O'Connell, a world famous photographer for *LIFE* magazine, looking for the negative of a photograph he wants for the last cover of the magazine.

He finally tracks O'Connell down in the Himalayas where he finds a long-haired Sean with a very full snow-flecked beard snuggled down under a cliff of snow behind a massive long camera lens waiting patiently to take the perfect picture.

"Shishhhh," he says to Walter. "Don't make a sound."

"Why?"

"I'm waiting to get a shot of the famous snow leopard. She is very rarely sighted by any human."

"Why?" says Walter.

"Because a thing of great beauty doesn't need attention."

And they waited... waited... and waited. Suddenly, as if by magic, the snow leopard appeared.

Sean had her perfectly framed in his lens. He silently flicked a finger inviting Walter to take a peek. It was a magnificent sight. A magnificent shot. What a rare and wonderful picture. Time passed. Walter was getting impatient, anxious and frustrated because Sean was just sitting there gazing across the snow-covered valley at the snow leopard. Just drinking in and savouring the scene.

"Are you not going to click?" he hissed. Sean shook his head.

"Sometimes," he replied, "I don't click!"

An absolutely astonishing statement in that context.

He didn't click. He didn't take the photograph of the snow leopard, this rare creature of great beauty.

Why?

Because he really wanted to experience this rare moment for himself. He wanted to savour it and be fully present to the sight of the snow leopard without any artificial mechanical go-between.

How many of us parents at birthdays or sports events miss the experience because we are too busy 'clicking' or 'videoing?'

The great photographer didn't click... and became a great human.

When you are out for your run or walk or taking any kind of exercise, are you ticking it off a list of things to do, or "getting it in," or doing it out of duty? How are you living your experience? Or are you suffering from destination addiction?

You can see or take in reality in three ways, through three lenses or "eyes".

The First Eye

Three women were jogging by the ocean one evening and they took a break to watch a beautiful sunset. One woman saw the immense physical beauty and enjoyed the event in itself.

She was a 'sensate' type who like 80 per cent of the world deals with what she can see, feel, touch, move and fix. This was enough for her. She was 'seeing' with her first eye.

The Second Eye

The second woman enjoyed all the beauty that the first woman did. Like all lovers of reason, technology and science she enjoyed her power to make sense of the universe as she thought about the cyclical rotation of the planets and the stars. Through her intellect she was 'seeing' with her second eye.

The Third Eye

The third woman saw the sunset, knowing and enjoying all like the first two women, but she progressed from seeing, to intellectually explaining to 'tasting or savouring.'

She remained in awe before an underlying mystery, wonder and beauty that connected her with everything else. She was 'seeing' with her third eye.

She had an inner experience. Seeing the way the mystics see. The way Sean saw the snow leopard.

Mystics don't reject the first eye. The senses matter to them. We humans live in our bodies. Nor do they reject the second eye. Reason is important too. But they don't confuse knowledge with depth of understanding, or information with transformation.

The third eye person has always been the saint, the seer, the poet, or the mystic, who grasps the whole picture in the moment, and doesn't interfere with a "click."

How you experience your experience matters. Without a need to always video, text or click, you become what you *really* are — the mystic, the poet, the seer. Thank you, Fionn, for the gift of this visit to the cinema that night, for the experience, and the "present".

RED PLATFORM: Non-stop clicking, texting and videoing but missing the experience, the event, the present. One step removed.

GREEN PLATFORM: Real presence. Fully present in the moment. Not clicking or texting. Tasting, savouring and experiencing the underlying mystery, wonder and beauty of the naked and undefended "now". Presence is everything.

79

Wooden Heart Made Him An Amazing Coach

A YOUNG coach asked me recently what he should do to become a successful coach. We ended up having a chat about John Wooden. To most, Wooden is known as the "Wizard of Westwood," the basketball coach who guided the UCLA Bruins to an unprecedented 10 national championships over two decades. He wasn't just a coach. He was a teacher, father figure, mentor and master motivator who got every last drop and more out of his players.

"What kind of man, what kind of human being was Wooden?" he asked.

Both as a man and a human being, Coach Wooden was immense. In June 2010, he died at the ripe old age of 99. He had no problem dying because he had lived a remarkable life.

In his wallet, Wooden always carried a tattered piece of paper that he'd been given by his father when he was 12 years old. The words on it served as signposts for his entire life. They were called, "Making the Most of One Self." Here's what was written on the note:

- Be true to yourself.
- Make each day your masterpiece.
- Help others.
- Drink deeply from good books.
- Make friendship a fine art.
- Build shelter against a rainy day.
- Pray for guidance and give thanks for your blessings every day.

When he was asked in his late nineties whether or not he had successfully lived up to these principles, he replied: "You know, we're never perfect. But every day I still try to live up to that creed."

Wooden achieved personal, private victories before he achieved public victories. He was truly disciplined. As a leader he lived the life of a leader.

He didn't need words. He didn't just *have* a vision; his life *was* his vision. He lived the vision with joy. He was a happy man.

"Happiness begins where selfishness ends," he used to say. He believed that happiness comes from making and keeping these nine promises:

1. Talk health, fitness, happiness and prosperity as often as possible.

2. Make all your friends know that there is something in them that is special and that you value.

3. Think only of the best, to work only for the best and to expect only the best of yourself and others.

4. Be just as enthusiastic about the success of others as you are about your own.

5. Be so strong that nothing can disturb your peace of mind.

6. Forget the mistakes of the past and press on for greater achievement in the future

7. Wear a cheerful appearance at all times and give every person you meet a smile.

8. Give so much time improving yourself that you have no time to criticise others.

9. Be too large for worry, too noble for anger, too strong for fear and too happy to permit trouble to press on you.

"A coach," he would say, "is someone who can give correction without causing resentment." He didn't see success as merely winning a game. His definition of success went much deeper:

"Success is that peace of mind that is the direct result of self-satisfaction in knowing that you gave your best effort to become the best of which you are capable."

Wooden was truly a Green Platform coach. One to model both in coaching and in life.

RED PLATFORM: Success is winning and nothing else.

GREEN PLATFORM: Success is: "The self-satisfaction in knowing that you gave your best effort to become the best of which you were capable."

80

Attitude, Not Aptitude, Determines Your Altitude

THIS man told me in his email that his inner weather wasn't great. "We spent last autumn, winter and spring training for the club championship and we lost the first round by one solitary point. We're devastated. Any advice on how we can bounce back? There is a 'back door' in the county. But our attitude is all wrong."

Bouncing back is all about *attitude*. It's attitude, not aptitude, which will ultimately determine our altitude.

What is the difference between a disaster and an opportunity? It's our attitude towards it. When confronted with a difficult situation, a person with a great attitude makes the best of it.

Greatness in people often emerges out of a crisis just because of their attitude to it. Daniel Defoe wrote *Robinson Crusoe* while he was in prison. John Bunyon wrote *The Pilgrim's Progress* in Bedford jail. And Beethoven was almost totally deaf and burdened with sorrow when he produced his greatest and most joyful works.

When our attitude puts others first, and we see people as important, then we'll see the world from their perspective as well. Otherwise we'll be like the man who angrily jumped out of a car after a collision with another car. "Why don't you people watch where you're driving!" he shouted wildly. "You're the fourth car I've hit today!"

What's a person's real capability? No one knows, so no one should be instilling an attitude of life-limiting thoughts into others. Many years ago, Johnny Weissmuller, who played the role of Tarzan in many films, was called the greatest swimmer the world had ever known. Doctors and coaches around the world said: "Nobody will ever break Johnny Weissmuller's records." He held over 50 records. Do you know who's breaking these records today? Thirteen-year-old girls! The 1936 Olympic records were the qualifying standards for the 1972 Olympics.

An elephant can easily pick up a one-ton load with his trunk. He can knock a huge tree with his forehead. But you'll see in Africa or India one of those huge creatures tied to a small wooden stake, and he just stays put. Never moves. Why? When the elephant was young and weak he was tied by a heavy chain to an immovable iron stake. He discovers that no matter how hard he tries, he can't break the chain or move the stake. Then no matter how large or strong the elephant becomes he continues to believe that he can't move as long as he sees that tiny stake. His attitude, not his aptitude, is what's making the difference here.

Many of us are like this elephant. We continue to have restraining attitudes in thoughts, actions and results. We never move further than the boundaries of our self-imposed limiting beliefs.

You won't win every game. You won't win every race. You won't be successful all the time at work. But if you've fuelled every moment of training or playing or working with the best that's in you now, then there's no reason why you won't bounce back.

What lies before you or what lies behind you is nothing compared to the bounce-back power that lies within you.

All you need is someone to take personal responsibility for your bounce back and light that fuse. And that someone is you.

RED PLATFORM: You lose the game, the sale or the contract. You fail, fall down and stay down. Blame others for your bad day.

GREEN PLATFORM: Bounce back and be responsible for your own bounce back. You are like dynamite. It's attitude, not aptitude, that determines your altitude.

81

Growing Older No Excuse
For Not Growing Up

THE poet Robert Browning wrote: "Why stay we on the earth except to grow?" Everyone agrees that growing is a good thing, but few people dedicate themselves to the process of growth.

Why?

Because it demands change. And most of us are reluctant to change. We only change when the pain of not changing outweighs the pain of changing. But without change, growth is impossible. Your life doesn't get better by chance; it gets better by "change". If we don't change, we don't grow; and change is always a choice.

Growth demands giving up familiar limiting beliefs and patterns that keep us in a safe but unrewarding world where exercise or goal achieving is something we just don't do.

The Russian writer Fyodor Dostoevsky puts it like this: "Taking a new step, uttering a new word, is what most people fear most." The real fear should be the opposite course. Is there anything worse than a stagnant life devoid of change and improvement?

The reality is that there's no "standing still." Either we're climbing or we're sliding. Don't be afraid of growing too slowly. Be afraid only of standing still — of sliding.

As the poet Ralph Waldo Emerson says: "Do the thing you fear, and the death of fear is certain." Courage is not the absence of fear but the mastery of it.

FEAR is "False Evidence Appearing Real." It's ultimately an illusion that the Ego needs to keep us trapped, blocked and stifled.

Fear is the Ego's fuel; the Ego feeds on fear.

On the negative Red Platform, FEAR is "Forget Everything And Run". On the positive Green Platform, FEAR is "Face Everything And Rise."

Most people resist change, especially when it affects them personally. Another Russian writer, Leo Tolstoy, put his finger on it: "Everyone thinks of changing the world, but no one thinks of changing themselves."

The reality is that who you are as a person, embracing every opportunity for change and growth, is far more important than anything you do, say or teach.

Ironically, whereas change is inevitable, growth is optional. The future is about the four Cs: the Constant Capacity to anticipate and adapt to Continual Change.

Like a sailing boat on the high seas, we can ignore the wind, or harness it. In order to grow, you must embrace the winds of change, harness them and give them direction.

Ask yourself: "What if everything in life really did happen for a reason? What if everything really did have a purpose and it always served us in the long run? What if life was always happening *for* us, not *to* us? What if even the pain and problems had a higher purpose intimately connected to our growth, development and evolution as persons?"

Choose a life of health, fitness and goal-achieving growth where you can see your daily improvement. When the Spanish composer-cellist Pablo Casals was in the final years of his life, a young reporter asked him: "Mr Casals, you are 95 years old and the greatest cellist that ever lived. Why do you still practise six hours a day?"

What was Casals's answer?

"Because I think I'm making progress."

Athletes and business people who reach their potential always think in terms of improvement. People who are determined to 'hold their ground,' and still be successful, are mistaken.

Start growing today. It's not the exercise or the job you're going to do sometime. It's the exercise or that task you're committed to doing now that counts.

Some people keep putting off their goals and dreams. Their motto is always: 'One of these days.' But as we all know from sad experience: 'One of these days,' means 'None of these days.'

Growth isn't automatic. Just because you get older doesn't mean that you're growing. Don't just *go* through life, *grow* through life. You're never too old to set another stretch goal or to dream a new and bigger dream.

It's not the experiences you've had, but the lessons you've learned from them that really matter. US author and physician Oliver Wendell Holmes Sr put it this way: "Man's mind, once stretched by a new idea, never regains its original dimensions." Growth is about never going back.

To keep growing, get into your strength zone. Find what you do well and keep on doing it. Nobody ever commented that Pablo Casals couldn't play the trumpet well, or that Muhammad Ali wasn't a great swimmer, or that Rory McIlroy wasn't a great rugby forward. Strength is always specific.

If you're a runner, run. If you're a swimmer, swim. If cycling is what you love, get on your bike. If you have a gift or a talent, use it. Develop it. Make a better world for people with it. But do it now.

You don't stop exercising and having fun because you grow old; you grow old because you stop exercising and having fun. And when you die, wouldn't it be great if people said: "She never stopped growing until the moment she died."

RED PLATFORM: A fear-fuelled resistance to change and growth.

GREEN PLATFORM: Everything happens for a reason if I'm creative enough to find it. "What can I learn from this? How can I grow as a person from it and then how can I use this growth lesson in the service of humanity?"

82

Visualisation — You'll See It When You Believe It

WE all have within us an awesome power that most of us have never been taught to use. Top business people use it. Olympic champions use it. Peak performers at all levels use it.

That power is called visualisation. "The you you see is the you you'll be."

The daily practice of visualising your dreams as already complete can rapidly accelerate your achievement of those dreams.

The power of visualisation comes from the fact that our bodies understand and respond to clear images much better than words.

We actually visualise all the time. The trouble is, most people visualise negatively. It's commonly called 'worry.' They imagine all the bad things that can happen and feel justified when so many of them do actually happen.

We are like guided missiles. We move in the direction of our regular, consistent thoughts, pictures and images towards whatever we imagine with vividness and strong feelings.

Those types of pictures have a magnetic attraction, so be careful of what you picture with emotion, as you will be pulled in that direction and you'll manifest it.

Visualisation works because it has a measurable, physiological effect on your body. When you visualise doing a movement, play, stroke, shot, or performance at work, there's a measurable response by the specific muscles used in that activity in response to your imagined movements.

For instance, to do a tennis serve in reality, a specific programme of neuro-muscular circuits has to fire in order for that to happen.

However, if you just vividly imagine doing a tennis serve, it's been found that micro-muscular stimulation occurs in those same muscles used to do the serve in "reality."

The mind can't tell the difference between what's real and what's imagined when accompanied by strong feelings.

Combine a vivid imagination with deep emotion and you have an effective tool to enhance your performance. It's truly a case of "The you you see is the you you'll be."

Visualisation of your goals and dreams accomplishes three very important things. It:

Activates Your Creative Subconscious
It activates your creative subconscious, which will start generating all kind of new ideas to help you achieve your goal.

Programmes Your Brain To Be Magnetic
It programmes your brain to more readily recognise and attract the people, opportunities and resources you'll need to achieve your deeply desired goals.

Builds Internal Motivation
It builds your internal motivation to take the necessary actions to realise your dreams.

Athletes call this process "mental rehearsal." Jack Nicklaus won over 100 golf tournaments and won almost $6 million. He said: "I never hit a shot, not even in practice, without having a very sharp in-focus picture of it in my head. It's like a colour movie."

There are some important things to consider when visualising. You need to be inside yourself, or "associated" — not as a spectator watching yourself from the outside. You need to visualise everything out of your own eyes.

If it's basketball, you have to be there at the free-throw line. Seeing the basket. Hearing the noise. As you shoot, you should feel the ball roll off your fingers. You should see it travelling through the air with perfect backspin. You should see your hands out in front of you with the perfect follow-through as you hear and see the ball swoosh through the net.

It's the same for everything you want to achieve in life. Feel it, sense it, hear it and visualise it.

Don't assume anything.

I once suggested to a member of the Professional Golfers Association of America that he visualise 10 perfect shots onto the green before he went to sleep. The following day he reported back. "I only got seven of them onto the green", he said. If he couldn't even visualise 10, what chance had he of improving himself on the real green?

One dramatic example of the power of vivid visualisation is that of Colonel George Hall. He was a US prisoner of war in a North Vietnamese prison for seven years, five-and-a-half of which he spent in solitary confinement. Before his imprisonment, he was a golfer playing off a handicap of four.

Every day Hall played a full game of golf in his imagination. One week after his release from prison, he entered the Greater New Orleans Open, walking with the aid of two walking sticks. He shot 76, right on his handicap, despite not having held a golf club for seven years.

After the game, a reporter congratulated him and said: "That was really what you call beginner's re-entry luck, right?"

Hall smiled and said: "Not really. I never three-putted a green in all my years in solitary". He only ever visualised excellence.

It's called having a set of rituals. Humans are hotwired for rituals. Before performances, Olympic champion swimmer Michael Phelps eats the same breakfast, works through the same stretching routine and listens to the same music.

Here are four steps to using this incredible power of visualisation to improve your performance:

Step 1: Frequency

The more often you repeat a clear mental picture of your very best performance or result, the more rapidly it'll appear as part of your reality. Repetition is the mother of skill. Writing down you dream or goal helps focus the clarity you need for your visualisation.

Step 2: Duration

When you deeply relax, you can often hold a mental picture of yourself performing at your best for several seconds or even minutes. The longer you can hold your mental picture, the more deeply it'll be impressed into your subconscious and the more rapidly it'll express itself in your future performances.

Step 3: Vividness

There's a direct relationship between how clearly you can see your desired goal or result in your mind and how quickly it becomes your reality. The vividness of your goal directly determines how quickly it manifests in your world. The more often you write it, review it, and visualise it, the more vivid it becomes for you. Eventually, it'll become crystal clear and manifestation will rapidly follow.

Step 4: Emotional Intensity, Deep Feelings

In reality, this is the most important and powerful part of the visualisation process. Sometimes, if your emotion is intense enough and your visual image is clear enough, you'll be surprised at how quickly your goal will manifest in your life.

The elements of frequency, duration, vividness, and emotional intensity can help or hurt you depending on whether your visualisations are positive or negative. The power of visualisation is neutral. Like a double-edged sword, it can cut in either direction, making you a success or a failure.

Visualisation brings you whatever you vividly and intensely see or imagine, whether good or bad, positive or negative.

Continually feed your mind with clear, exciting, emotional pictures of your goals and dreams, and what you want to achieve. Your imagination is your preview of the great things life has waiting for you.

Believe it and you'll see it. The you you see is the you you'll be.

RED PLATFORM: Visualising everything that could go wrong. Everything you don't want in your life. "Catastrophising" everything in advance.

GREEN PLATFORM: Visualising clear pictures with strong feelings of what you want and only of what you want.

83

Living Lightly

I T was lashing rain at the bottom of Croagh Patrick, Ireland's pilgrimage mountain, and a young reporter from London was interviewing an old Traveller woman who was about to climb "the Reek."

"What's the point," asked the lady with the microphone, "just tiring yourself going up that big hill?"

"Ah, love," replied the Traveller woman, "you don't understand. It's not a journey up. It's a journey in."

I had a long chat with an old friend from the west coast of Ireland a few weeks ago. He lives by the sea on the western edge of Europe. His normal life has been quite hectic. A very busy schedule peppered with hundreds of emails, phone calls and texts. The noise deafening. The chatter incessant. The onslaught of messages unrelenting.

"How do you compete with this in our information-glutted world of today?" he asked.

He is a modern man who was slowly going under with a tsunami of those emails, speeches, memos, presentations, tweets, voicemails, reports, blogs, phone calls and letters.

Pure mental clutter. Information overload. So much oppressive baggage of the mind. He felt weighed down.

But then he found freedom. He broke his chains. He ripped his mental cage apart. How?

He decided to go for a run on the beach near his home.

"I had the most unbelievable experience tonight," he said. "I was mentally tired, oxygen deprived and feeling fairly miserable. Too many meetings. Too many hours in the car. So much on my mind. Then I put on the running socks and shoes, togs and T-shirt and took off for a run down to the beach. As usual the hardest part was putting on the running shoes. A little gremlin voice in the back of my head told me I should be going to bed instead.

I ran easily for a mile and then it kicked in. A magical feeling. The moon was shining on the sea. The mountains and the woods were off to my left, a dark purple in the moonlight. The white sand was firm under my feet, the fresh salty sea breeze in my face and I was transported into another world. It was pure magic. My mind was instantly uncluttered. I found a kind of freedom. How do you describe it? I was living lightly on the earth. I was in total harmony with my surroundings. I was one with life.

You talk about living simply so that others can simply live, well, tonight I was living simply. This is as simple as it can get. No suit or tie. They say you've never seen a trailer on a hearse; well I didn't need a trailer tonight to carry my stuff. I just didn't have it. Out there on the beach, just running. No one to judge you, evaluate you or criticise you. Detached from any destination, just enjoying the moment, enjoying the journey, enjoying the magic of the moonlight on the water. I was on this earth, running on the sand with a minimum of physical or mental baggage. Just a T-shirt, shorts, socks and running shoes. Life stripped back to the essentials.

I thought of all the expensive stuff in the windows of the shops in Oxford Street in London that I don't actually need. I looked up at the stars, and again at the reflection of the moon on the ocean and back to the woods and the mountain and I knew then what real freedom is all about.

As the poet Patrick Kavanagh put it, I had come "through fields that are part of no earthly estate." Freedom is just another word for nothing left to lose as the song says. They say that the best things in life are free. I don't know what you call it, a runner's high or something, but I do know that it was an amazing feeling.

I felt so thankful for my injury-free body, my mind, my soul and my ability to just run on a beach between the ocean and the moon. I understood fully in that moment that gratitude and negativity cannot co-exist.

And none of this was costing me anything. No fees for the beach. No fees for the moonlight or the ocean. No fees for the views of the woods and the mountain. No booking early to avoid disappointment. Do you understand what I'm saying? Am I making any sense at all?"

I understood. Absolutely.

Years ago I saw a documentary on television about the Masai tribe in Africa. Another young reporter travelled with them as they ran rhythmically for about 25 miles across the savannah grassland. Then they stopped. "Why are you stopping now?" she asked.

"We're waiting for our souls to catch up with us," they replied.

Some years ago I told this story to my running-in-the-moonlight-friend. Then he phoned me about six months later when I was in the middle of traffic gridlock going nowhere fast on the M50 motorway. It was full of traffic cones at that time.

"Where are you now?" I asked.

"I'm up here sitting in a grotto in the middle of the woods overlooking the sea near to my father's house. I rode up here on the bike."

"And what are you doing there?"

"What do you think I'm doing?" he said.

"I'm waiting for my soul to catch up with me."

Like the lady from the Travelling community, another journey — in.

RED PLATFORM: Spend a fortune buying lots and lots of stuff thinking that all this stuff will make you happy.

GREEN PLATFORM: Happiness is living lightly on this earth running on a sandy beach between the ocean and the moon.

84

Mental Health Hero

THE great Irish rugby icon Paul O'Connell is a friend, huge fan and admirer of the famous Ireland and Munster rugby legend Alan Quinlan.

"I have never played, known or seen anyone play rugby like Alan Quinlan. He's the life and soul of the dressing room but, when a match starts, the game takes over his life and his soul. For 80 minutes he will rage against everything in pursuit of a big performance and a big victory... he plays on the edge and for eighty minutes his mind is also on the edge. But this 'edge' is what makes Quinny special — when Alan Quinlan is on the edge he's one of the best players I've had the pleasure of going into battle with," says Paul.

I had the privilege of getting to know Alan over the past while. Alan's rugby playing days are over now, but he is channelling his energy and his famous 'edge' these days into another battle where he is also delivering more big performances and big victories — the battle against depression and mental illness. In an Ireland where we've had 140 documented suicides so far and the prediction for 600 before the end of the year, Alan is challenging us to build mental resilience, to proactively choose a positive mental attitude, to speak up about encounters with depression and to reach out and seek help.

Physical obesity is easy to spot, challenge and change. Mental obesity or mental problems are much tougher to spot. The emotional energy of the world has flat-lined. Over the past 40 years, across almost every developed country in the world the diagnosis of clinical depression has grown nearly tenfold.

This is happening despite the fact that almost every factor we associate with well-being — plenty of food, money, education, safety, access to the arts and health care — is abundant in these societies. Increasingly people are reporting feelings of restlessness, fatigue, stress and that awful misery that leaves them feeling bored, brittle and frustrated.

I had an exceptionally sad day recently at the funeral of a friend of a young man who committed suicide. The family were devastated. Thousands of people came to show solidarity and express their sympathy. A river of devastated people in the wake of a coffin trying to find a rational explanation for an irrational act — this heart attack of the mind. Suicide is becoming far too common now. The family wants no other family to have to suffer what they are suffering.

The priest challenged us all to look after each other, to take time out to listen to one another, to share any problems we had with each other and to take care of each other. He asked us to nourish, nurture and shelter each other, reminding us over and over that, "It's okay to say that I'm not okay."

He continued: "We are all often too busy doing things that don't really matter, to make time for our friends. In these challenging times in Ireland, many people are worried and many people are hurting, but your health is your most important asset and your mental health is more important that your physical health. We often take more care of our cars than we do of our physical and mental health. People are far more important than things — and issues that we think are important pale into insignificance on a day like today," he said.

Soon after that heart-wrenching day, the extraordinary 16-year-old Donal Walsh, who was fighting cancer for the third time in four years, was a guest on *The Saturday Night Show* with Brendan O'Connor. His time on earth was limited. He said he "feels nothing but anger" when he hears of young people committing suicide.

"It kills me because I am here fighting for my life for the third time. That does make me angry and I'm not going to lie about. I have nothing against people with mental illness but these people have to realise there is help everywhere."

He had discovered that his cancer was terminal the October before the interview. "A few months left. There it was. I was given a timeline on the rest of my life. No choice, no say, no matter."

This is his passionate plea to teenagers today: "So please, as a 16-year-old who has no say in his death sentence, who has no choice in the pain he is about to cause and who would take any chance at even a few more months on this planet, appreciate what you have, know there are always other options, and help is always there."

I think it was Brendan's finest interview where he enabled Donal to reach out with such bravery and courage to touch the heart, mind and soul of the nation.

Over the years Donal had raised funds totaling €50,000 for St. John's Cancer Ward in Our Lady's Hospital for Sick Children, Crumlin and in his final battle this grew to €65,000.

Donal took to writing in his last months and told his story of his battle with cancer and what it took each time to fight his way back to living life.

He also wrote about his anger at teenage suicide while he was battling to get as much out of living his life as possible.

The third thing he wrote about was about him 'Climbing God's Mountains' and how difficult that was and how his faith had allowed him to reach the mountaintop and scream from it.

In your own environment, what can you do to be more aware of the moods and needs of others? Can you find time to listen to others who may be feeling a bit down? Sometimes a listening-understanding heart is all that's needed. To let them know that they are not alone.

On May 12, 2013, Donal moved on to his final journey and reached 'God's Highest Mountain,' climbing as he did with a great phrase he said to the priest who gave him his Last Rites in the following conversation:

Donal: "Father, Father Pádraig what is it like on the other side?"

Fr. P: "Donal I'm not sure but I can tell you that it will be a much better place because you are there. Donal, why, are you afraid?"

Donal: "No Father, just a little nervous."

Donal who fund-raised tirelessly while battling cancer has now had the Donal Walsh #Livelife Foundation set up by his family primarily in order to promote his anti-suicide #Livelife message.

The foundation will also assist in his other causes of providing age-appropriate teenage facilities in hospital and hospice care centres.

Paul O'Connell was also a friend, a huge fan and admirer of this other young Munster warrior, hero and legend — Donal Walsh from Tralee. Ar dheis Dé go raibh a anam dílis.

RED PLATFORM: Afraid to say "I'm not okay." Afraid to ask for help when feelings of not being able to cope arise.

GREEN PLATFORM: Donal: "There is help everywhere!"

85

Change Is A Choice

" I CAN'T change," she wrote in an email. "I've tried everything. I want to get fit and healthy, but I don't seem to have the willpower to persist. I keep going back to old ways and old habits. How can I improve my willpower?"

Well, for a start, willpower doesn't work. I've been here in Texas, New Mexico, Arizona and California for the past few weeks and I see the evidence of it all around me. Two out of every three adults here in the US are overweight. Some are actually *huge*.

For the first time in history obesity is a greater threat to health worldwide than hunger. Here in the States they spend 40 billion dollars a year on diets, but for 19 out of 20 people all they lose is their money. Not weight. So do diets not really work? In fact they do.

At Stanford University, they examined the four most popular weight-loss programmes in the US to discover what works and what doesn't. Here's what they discovered:

1. All the programmes worked.
2. If the people used them.
3. But people rarely used them.

So the secret to wellness is not the diet or exercise in themselves, but rather in finding a way to enjoy the food you eat and the exercise you take.

Diets don't work because people don't stick to them. It's as simple as that.

What works is creating new habits that lead to the results you want for the rest of your life. That can change everything for you.

So what steps can we take to get real and lasting change? Here are seven steps:

1. Intention

You must have the positive intention to change infused with a powerful reason.

2. Personal Motivation

Have a picture or an image of your clear goal. See, feel, and believe in the future the goal will bring you. By thinking about the pleasure a good habit will eventually bring you can make the habit itself more enjoyable. Thinking differently actually rewires the brain.

3. Personal Ability

This is all about learning when the crucial moments come and paying attention to the signals of stress. Instead of putting a cigarette in your mouth, have some straws handy. Just take a long drag on the straw instead. For every crucial moment have a new vital behaviour to change your response. Anticipate these moments and make your choices beforehand.

4. Social Motivation

You are the average of the five people you hang out with. Find people who will encourage you and motivate you to make the change. If your friends are all smokers, encourage them all to quit along with you. Otherwise don't hang out with them.

5. Financial Motivation

If you want to quit smoking, add up the cost for a week and then for a year. In 2014, a packet of 20 cigarettes costs around €9. That means if you smoke a pack a day you will spend more than €3,285 a year on cigarettes. Imagine what you could do with the money you have saved.

6. Environment

Stop going to the places where you built up your bad habit. Go to a different place like a swimming pool or a gym or out in the hills for a run.

7. Joy

Bring joy to the process. Keep it simple. Make it fun.

What if you slip up and slide back into your old habit. Now you have a choice. You can become depressed on the Red Platform or become curious on the Green Platform. If you become depressed you'll blame yourself, become discouraged and maybe cut loose on a total binge.

But if you become curious on The Green Platform you will stand back, examine the data, learn from just happened and adjust your plan. Turn your failure into feedback and learn from it.

So it seems that all the programmes work. You just have to work the programmes.

RED PLATFORM: You can bump into a new barrier and become depressed and quit on the Red Platform. Start a programme and then give up.

GREEN PLATFORM: You can experience the same setback, become curious and turn a bad day into good data on The Green Platform. Work the programme.

86

Choose Your Words
To Change Your World

'PEOPLE will do almost anything to get out of exercising. I have been most unsuccessful in encouraging people to run," says US surgeon Jean Rene Dupont.

He was very frustrated. He had arranged for four women and 16 men to join a running programme in Sikeston, Missouri. If they could not run at the same time they worked out together for mutual encouragement and camaraderie. Soon they were able to cover two miles without stopping. "These runners were as highly motivated as any group could be," he said.

No one, including Dupont, understood what happened next. One by one they started to drop out. Each one had a great excuse. Then bad weather came and Dupont found himself running alone. He was stunned by what people would do and the excuses they made to get out of exercising.

So what stops us taking exercise? Mostly it's the stories we tell ourselves, and above all the words we use to make excuses.

However, the right words with the right intention can weave magical changes into our lives.

Words?

We speak of giving our word, keeping our word, choosing our words and living by our words.

Many years ago I remember the cattle dealers on the Fair Green in Oldcastle spitting on the palms of their hands and then slapping hands with shouts of: "You won't break this man's word." A person's word mattered. There were no lawyers, no legal contracts, and no "sign here on the dotted line." There was just a man, his word, a spit on the hand and a hand-slap. Your word was all that mattered.

We use words to wound (cyber-bullying), to hurt, to heal, to pray, to express gratitude, to praise, to encourage, to describe and to question. The real purpose of words is to create bliss in the listener.

It's not the words themselves that create consciousness, or heal the body or change reality. It's the awakened energy behind the words that has the real power. Physicists tell us that the world is made up of energy forms that vibrate at different frequencies, with matter being the densest frequency.

Positive thoughts and words vibrate at a high frequency and magnetically attract matter of the same vibrational density. They call it a 'vibrational match.' The same is true for low frequency negative thoughts and words. What you give out you get back. What goes around comes around.

The latest neurological research reveals that by choosing our words and thoughts with care and concentrating on them for ten to 20 minutes a day we can actually change the functioning in key areas of our brain by as much as 25 per cent.

For example, simply by focusing on words such as 'peace,' or 'joy,' or 'fun, you will begin to feel peaceful, joyful and happier as the emotional centres of your brain switch their neuro-cortical pathways and synaptic patterns.

In their ground-breaking book, *Words Can Change Your Brain*, Andrew Newbery and Mark Robert Waldman explain that once your brain is stimulated by a positive word or thought it slows down its ability to generate messages of anxiety, irritability or depression. You start a positive-reinforcing pattern.

They also show how words, positive or negative, can alter the expression of genes throughout the body, turning them on and off and thereby changing the way we biologically grow.

You can change your brain positively. One new study found that even looking at a list of positive words for just a few seconds improves the mood of depressed person. The bad news is that when people looked at a list of negative words they immediately feel worse.

Surgeon Dupont expressed his frustration above 37 years ago. The good news is that we now know that we can use our thoughts, our words and our inner stories to make things happen, take exercise and achieve our goals in life rather than using them to make excuses. When you *change* your words, you *change* your world.

RED PLATFORM: Use your thoughts, words and inner stories to make excuses

GREEN PLATFORM: Use your thoughts, words and inner stories to make great things happen and totally change your state and the quality of your life.

87

The One Thing

I N the original *City Slickers* movie with Billy Crystal, Curly, played by Jack Palance was the tough, grumpy, old cowboy who almost never spoke. But underneath the rough tough stogy exterior, Curly had the wisdom of the ages.

In a rare heart-to-heart conversation between the two, Curly shared the 'secret of life' with Billy. The secret of life was 'One Thing.' When pressed to name it Curly refused to tell Billy what that one thing was. He told Billy he'd have to find it out for himself.

I had a very interesting conversation about lasting inspirational motivation with a very dynamic woman the other day concerning that 'one thing' when it comes to not just stop-starting things in life, but consistently doing what we say we'll do long after the mood with which we said it is over.

She told me that while I keep telling people: "Give me a 'why' and I will go through any 'how' — in the real world of getting out and taking exercise and continuing to take exercise it is not enough. You need to unpack the 'why,'" she said, "you need to unpack and explain more clearly the power of purpose."

"Most people have short term 'whys,'" she continued, "and the problem with them is that they only work in the short term. Look, for some people they'll have short term compelling goals — they might be a bride or groom, who want to look great on their special day and lose heaps of weight and end up feeling fit and fantastic as they walk down the aisle, but soon after the wedding, because their motivation was based around a time-bound event, a short-term 'why,' the motivation to keep going with their healthier lifestyle, grinds to a halt the day the honeymoon begins.

"So look for your own special motivation to make the changes that are linked to lifelong things that are essential to your happiness and fulfilment. It's not so much about looking great in a swimsuit for your holiday next May, but looking great in a swimsuit when you are 90 and still happy and active!"

Isn't that a fantastic insight into the lasting strength of having a powerful long-term 'why'? I think she nailed that 'one thing' secret of life.

When I asked her how she came up with the long-term lasting 'why,' she told me a story about a friend of hers who only found the motivation to switch to a healthier lifestyle after two heart attacks when he found his 'one thing.'

After the first attack, doctors warned him that if he didn't change a few things he was likely to have a second more serious attack, which he might not survive.

But, even this warning was not enough to change the habits of almost a lifetime — smoking, little exercise and a great love of salt and sugar in his food. For a while everything changed. But, slowly he slid back to his old ways and within six months he suffered that second heart attack and nearly didn't survive it.

But, this time the doctors warned him that he would not live to see his youngest daughter grow up if he didn't take better care of himself. That was the emotional trigger for him; not the thought of his own dying, but the thought of dying and not seeing his beautiful six-year-old little girl grow up. The doctor in one fell swoop had helped him to discover his 'one thing.'

That little girl is now 26 years old, and her father has not smoked since that moment. He has lived a much healthier lifestyle since that terrible, but wonderful day 20 years ago. He found the compelling motivation, the true secret of life, that 'one thing' that made it worthwhile for him to change the bad habits of a lifetime. Just recently he walked her down the aisle on her wedding day. One candle can cast out darkness. One smile can light up a room. One choice can change a life.

Everyone listens to an FM station called WII FM. 'What's In It For Me?' What is your compelling long-term 'why," your one thing, your big WII FM factor that would make it more worthwhile for you to get going and achieve all your life and fitness goals?

But don't ask Curly to tell you your 'one thing.' He won't. He'll tell you to discover that for yourself. Then you too will have Curly's "secret of life."

RED PLATFORM: No one thing. No powerful purpose. No inspiring why. Death coming in dribs and drabs.

GREEN PLATFORM: Finding the one thing, the powerful purpose, the inspiring 'why' that fires your emotional trigger to change, grow and live life to the full.

88

Keep On Going

HE was down in the dumps and feeling fairly miserable. He had finally given up on what he called "this old exercise lark." Too many scars from attempting to take regular exercise in the past and failing to be consistent or keep it up. "I'm back in my toxic cycle," he said.

"Your toxic cycle?"

"Yeah, I stopped exercising. I retreated into my comfort zone. Then I'd feel guilty. When I'd feel guilty I'd snack, comfort snacks — biscuits, crisps, fizzy drinks and all that processed sugary stuff. Is there any hope for me? Can you help me sort myself out?"

Now I know that people decide for themselves and you really can't teach people anything. They have to discover it for themselves. You can lead them to the threshold of their own mind, but they must decide and hold themselves accountable. The key thing is to be able to give up in any moment all that we are for all that we can become. Here's the gist of what I shared with him in seven steps.

1. Pain Is Part of Growing

When times are tough, remind yourself that no pain comes without a purpose. Move on from what hurt you, but never forget what it taught you. Just because you're struggling doesn't mean you're failing.

George Bernard Shaw said: "When I was young, I observed that nine out of 10 things I did were failures. So I did 10 times more work." Every great success requires some type of worthy struggle to get there. Good things take time. Stay positive. Salt rubbed into a wound stings, but it prevents sepsis. Winners usually work ten times harder at what really matters than losers.

2. Nothing Lasts Forever

Every time it rains, it stops raining. Every time you get hurt, you heal. After darkness there is always light. Nothing lasts forever. If things are bad now, it won't last forever either. Just because life isn't easy at the moment, doesn't mean you can't laugh. Something bothering you? You can still smile. Every moment gives you a new beginning and a new ending. You get a second chance, every second. Make the best of it.

3. Complaining Is Mostly Pointless

Those who complain the most, accomplish the least. Most of the time we complain, we complain to people who can't do anything about what we are complaining about anyway. It's always better to attempt to do something great and fail, than to attempt to do nothing and succeed. You don't have to be great to start. You have to start to be great.

4. Your Scars Are Signs Of Strength

Don't ever be ashamed of the scars from your life. They simply mean that the hurt is over. The wound is closed. You conquered the pain, learned a lesson, grew stronger and moved on. Change the way you look at your scars and see them signs of strength and not pain.

The poet Rumi once said: "The wound is the place where the Light enters you." Or as Leonard Cohen sings: "There is a crack in everything. That's how the Light gets in." ⸰

5. Every Small Struggle Counts

In life, patience is not about waiting; it's the ability to keep a positive attitude while working hard on your dreams, knowing that the work is worth it. This could mean 'just doing it.' Putting on those running shoes. Going out the door. The struggle is not found on the path. It *is* the path, where your pain will turn into joy. The joy is in the journey.

6. Choose To Be Positive

Be positive when negativity surrounds you. Smile when others try to bring you down. When other people treat you poorly, keep on being you. Don't ever let someone else's bitterness change you from being the positive person that you are.

7. Keep Going

Don't be afraid to bounce back and get back up. Life is not about falling. It's about how quickly you get back up again. Find the strength to laugh every day and then make others smile. Always look back and see how much you've grown, and be proud of yourself. Create a new 'fit and healthy cycle.' Keep on being you. Keep on going. Keep on growing.

The latest news from my 'toxic cycle' friend is that he has discovered places within himself beyond which he thought he couldn't ever go and he's going there. He's on a 'positivity can-do' cycle now. He told me that it's the difference that's making the difference in his life.

RED PLATFORM: Hoping for painless growth. Keep picking at and scratching open the old mental wounds. Scars signs of weakness and failure.

GREEN PLATFORM: Struggle, effort and good soreness is part of growth. This too shall pass. Tap into your incredible inner reservoir of strength.

89

Self-fulfilling Prophecy

THERE are all kinds of tribal folk wisdom we hear when we are growing up in our families. I grew up in Dungimmon, a beautiful valley between the ancient wisdom hill of Loughcrew, Slieve Na Calliagh, the mountain of the Holy Healing Woman and that famous romantic lake, Lough Sheelin, forever linked with the love story of Orwin and Sabina, whose commitment to each other was stronger than their family quarrels.

Some of this tribal wisdom and 'sayings' we paid heed to. Others we didn't. My mother used to say: "There is so much good in the worst of us and so much bad in the best of us that it ill behoves any of us to talk about the rest of us."

Another thing she used to mention a lot was the power of the Self-Fulfilling Prophecy. "That could be a Self-Fulfilling Prophecy," she'd say. "If you believe you'll fail, you'll fail. If you believe you'll succeed, you'll succeed."

In one of the most detailed studies on the effects of self-belief on performance, the psychologist Albert Bandura, the David Starr Jordan Professor Emeritus of Social Science in Psychology at Stanford University, discovered that a person's genuine beliefs about their capabilities could be a more accurate predictor of their future levels of performance than any actual results they have produced in the past.

It goes back to the power of 'The you you see is the you you'll be.' How you think about yourself in relation to the life challenges you are now facing will have a profound impact on your ability to succeed. The story you are telling yourself inside your head, positive or negative, the little mental movies you are making, will have an incredible impact on your ability to deliver on your health, fitness or life goals.

For instance, if someone believes they are ugly, unattractive and that no one could ever possibly be interested in them, how would you expect them to behave?

If they see someone that they are attracted to, will they approach them with a confident manner, a smile on their face and a glide in their stride?

No.

Because they believe the way they do, they don't and will not take action to disprove their belief. Then they bring about the very condition that they deeply wish weren't so, thereby proving their belief to be true. They'll conclude that's there's just no point in even trying and so their prophecy is fulfilled.

What they don't know is that their Ego-driven mind wants to be right all the time. The Ego loves the: "What did I tell you?" response.

When a golfer is playing away above herself, then all the alarm clocks go off in her head, fraud guilt kicks in and she'll immediately self-correct back down to her usual poor performance telling everyone, "how right they were."

Now there's proof that she was really genuinely a very poor player and thus she achieves one of the mind's primary functions — to prove itself right.

Sometimes that Egoic-fuelled toxic question: "Now who's right?" even creeps into families and teams. Why does the Ego, that false self, always have to prove itself right?

According to the American social psychologist, Leon Festinger, the state of trying to hold two inconsistent beliefs, ideas or opinions is so uncomfortable for the mind that people will subconsciously seek to reduce the conflict by changing one or both of these ideas so that they fit together better.

In other words, your mind wants to be consistent with whatever you previously said to be true. He calls it "cognitive dissonance."

Your Egoic mind is the original "Now, who's right?" person. The "What did I tell you?" person. The "Maybe you'll pay heed to me now" person.

Of course the Egoic mind is at its most powerful when it's in negative mode, the prophet of doom predicting disaster. It knows as well as we know that the best way to create the future is to predict the future.

"See, I told you you'd never amount to anything."

"You're a failure. You're good for nothing."

"You'll never get fit. You're only wasting your time."

Similarly you cannot sit around resenting confident, successful people who are 'getting on well' in the world and be surprised that your mind doesn't want to join them. The mental transition from resentment to admiration is too much. A bridge too far.

The best example of the power of the self-fulfilling prophecy is a story I heard one time from the US clinical neuropsychologist Dr Mario Martinez. He sometimes works with the church to reverse stigmatae, where the blood flows from people's hands like that of Padre Pio in imitation of the suffering of Jesus.

"When I discovered that the human mind could actually rupture skin, and create bleeding," he told me, "then I wondered what else it could do if we harnessed this amazing power?"

He tells a great story about an American football game. Before the game, the groundsman came in to the two teams and apologised to them because he was training in a young assistant, and in a fit of enthusiasm in his first week, the young lad had sprayed the field with weed-killer before the game.

Normally, the weed-killer was only sprayed on the field after the game. The routine was to water the field first, and only after the game, when the players were safely on their way home did they apply the weed-killer. He told them that the side effects of the weed-killer would be quite mild, nothing much, but maybe some of them might get a bit nauseous or maybe vomit, but nothing serious.

After 20 minutes the game was called off. Players vomiting all over the field and feeling nauseous. Then the groundsman came in to the dressing room. He thought it was half-time. He apologised profoundly to the players for misrepresenting what the new young lad had done. As it turned out, he did exactly as he had been told. He only watered the field before the game. He just took the cans of weed-killer out of the shed and put them around at the gable of the dressing rooms to be ready for spraying when the players had gone home.

So there was not a drop of weed-killer on the field. The power of the Self-Fulfilling Prophecy. A real case of you'll see it when you believe it. Their minds 'were right' again.

Maybe we should have listened more attentively to our mothers.

"Eat your greens."

"Chin up."

"That could be a Self-Fulfilling Prophecy."

Family tribal wisdom was alive and well in Dungimmon long before the likes of Leon Festinger or Albert Bandura came along to enlighten us. If you mentioned 'cognitive dissonance' in the yard at home we would probably have assumed that it was some kind of a dose for a calf. But in real life, we knew how it actually worked. How? Because our mother told us. That's how.

RED PLATFORM: If you believe you'll fail, you'll fail.

GREEN PLATFORM: If you believe you'll succeed, you'll succeed.

90

Live To Be Happy
Or Be Happy To Live?

A T the beginning of the year, a friend asked me the following questions: "They say that the purpose of life is to be happy — happy right here, right now. Do you think it's possible that I could make this coming year the happiest and best year of my life? Do you think that I could have an inner peace and happiness like a kind of Green Platform bowl that can contain any amount of grief, pain or suffering — the kind that Mandela had? What role does exercise play in the creation of this peace and happiness?"

This was the opening salvo in what turned out to be a fierce and powerful conversation about happiness and the role of exercise in achieving happiness.

Since the 1950s, hundreds of studies have been done on happiness. Several decades back, the idea was that if we could get good jobs, houses, shopping malls and television sets, we'd all be happier. But somehow it hasn't worked out that way. Far from being a happier society, we see more depression, more anxiety, more young male suicides, more separations and broken relationships.

We're three times richer than we were in the 1950s, but not one jot happier.

"And what about exercise?" he asked.

For a start, exercise is really a lifesaver. According to a January 2015 report in the *American Journal of Clinical Nutrition*, one brisk 20-minute walk a day may be enough to reduce your risk of early death by up to 30 per cent.

Researchers claim that at least twice as many deaths are attributable to the lack of physical activity as to obesity.

According to their research, which was based on data from 334,161 European men and women, a 20-minute daily walk or a comparable exercise will reduce the risk of premature death by between 16 and 30 per cent.

Lack of exercise ranks fourth for risk of death, behind high blood pressure, smoking and blood glucose levels, and it's ahead of obesity.

Ireland's population is more inactive than obese, with 23 per cent of people obese but over 50 per cent inactive.

According to the Irish Cancer Society, exercise can also reduce the risk of cancer. Being physically active, along with eating a healthy diet and not smoking, can reduce the risk of cancer by up to 50 per cent.

But back to happiness.

It's not just reality that shapes you, but the lens through which you look at reality. Change your lens and you change your level of happiness.

The external world predicts only 10 per cent of your happiness; 90 per cent comes from the way your brain processes the world. It's not your experience that matters, but how you choose to "experience" your experience.

Every disaster has an opportunity. Every misfortune has a hidden fortune. Every stumbling block can be a stepping-stone. Change your lens: change the way you look at things and the things you look at change.

The way we've been approaching happiness is scientifically both backward and bankrupt.

A way that'll never work is: "If I work harder, train harder, exercise harder, I'll be successful and then I'll be happy!" That's wrong because we keep changing the goalposts.

The key is to raise your positivity in the present. Your brain at positive performs significantly better than it does at negative, neutral or stressed. Your intelligence rises. Your creativity rises. Your energy levels rise.

According to a recent Harvard study, when your brain is at positive, every single business or sporting outcome improves. People were 31 per cent more productive.

Sales people are 37 per cent better when they're at positive and doctors are 19 per cent faster and more accurate at coming up with the right diagnosis.

Raise positivity in the present and you have the happiness advantage. Your brain releases dopamine which has two functions:

1. It makes you happier.

2. It turns on all the learning centres in your brain.

According to American happiness researcher, author of *The Happiness Advantage*, and speaker Shawn Achor, you can train and rewire your brain to be more positive in the present by doing the following five things for 21 days:

1. Daily exercise
At least 20 minutes a day.

2. Gratitude
At night recall three things that you are grateful for. Our normal night viewing lens is the news that trains our brains to scan for all the negative stuff.

Just by using the viewing lens of gratitude and scanning for three things we are thankful for will, over a period of 21 days, change our brain's way of scanning the world to increase our happiness.

3. Journaling
Write down one positive thing that happened to you today. This will build up the "scanning for the positive" muscles in your brain.

4. Meditation

Slow down. Breathe deeply, breathe slowly and follow your breath. Most of us live in a world of cultural ADHD [attention deficit hyperactivity disorder].

5. Random Acts of Kindness

Just sending one positive email to someone is enough to create ripples of positivity and increase your happiness. The person receiving the act of kindness gets a flood of positive chemicals and the same happens to the person doing the act of kindness. It was even discovered in another study that a person merely observing an act of kindness done by another person received a similar boost in positive happiness-producing chemicals throughout their body.

American author, poet and civil rights activist Maya Angelou put it this way:

"My wish for you that you continue. Continue to be who and how you are, to astonish a mean world with your acts of kindness. Continue to allow humor to lighten the burden of your tender heart."

The purpose of life is to be happy, here, now. And the best way to be happy is to make someone else's life better. "Me, me, me," is the soul's song of suffering. Joy is always about me helping you to have a better day. About *me* contributing to *your* happiness.

"You, you, you" is the soul's song of joy.

Why not try the five steps above for 21 days and watch the way the inner landscape of your brain will change!

I'll promise you that you'll be much more productive, you'll have much more energy and you'll feel so much more joy living the Green Platform.

Your greatest wealth is your ability to manage your inner state. To be happy *now*. To be joyful *now*. To have inner peace *now*.

Elvis Presley, John Belushi and Michael Jackson had millions of dollars, great *financial* wealth, but they did not have the greatest wealth — the ability to manage their inner states.

Your happiness, your joy and your inner peace on the Green Platform — your ability to manage your inner state — is your gift to the world.

RED PLATFORM: Sit down all day. Listen continually to the negative news. Always put yourself first. Head full of negative mental noise judging, complaining and blaming. Suffering from continual doses of 'Poor-me-itus.' What's in it for me?"

GREEN PLATFORM: Exercise. Gratitude. "One positive thing." Meditation. Acts of kindness. "How can I help you?"

Drink from your own well of life experiences. Discover your treasure. Know that you are, in fact, the wise one, the guru you have been waiting for.

Living the Green Platform, continue, as Maya says, to be who and how you are. Author and write your own life-changing stories and astonish this wonderful world of ours with your acts of kindness.

Acknowledgements

IN Africa, they say that it takes a village to rear a child. The poet John Donne said that no man is an island. We are all interdependent.

I believe it also takes a village to write a book. No author is an island. There are so many people who have made so many contributions to this book, and I want to say a very sincere "thank you" to each one of them.

First of all, to the first editor of the *Irish Independent*'s *Fit* magazine, PJ Cunningham, and then to subsequent editors Vicki Notaro and Yvonne Hogan.

For their meticulous proofreading and copy-editing, a huge thanks to journalist Rosemary O'Grady, Barry Cunningham, Vincent Coyle, Jim Martin, Christina O'Shaughnessy in Geneva, and Cathy McCarthy.

A very special word of thanks to Joe Coyle for the design and layout of the book.

To the book editor, PJ Cunningham, a special thanks for all the editing, drafting and redrafting to make it easy for the reader to read, understand and put the Green Platform principles into action in their lives.

Also a special thanks to Annette, Genevieve, Fionn, and Mary, Alexander's godmother, plus Liz, his visiting nurse, who did a lot of the "heavy lifting" around our home to enable me to get a new column out every week. And to Alexander, "the man himself", who cannot speak or walk very well but who managed to step into the pages of some of the columns and got his consistent message of unconditional love across to us all.

Thanks, too, to all of you, the readers, who created what so many people called a "cult following" for the columns. To the parents who cut out the columns and posted them overseas to their children or saved them in cardboard shoeboxes, to the people who stuck the columns on their fridges, and to the teachers who read them out in schools and got the students to put the Green Platform principles into practice in their lives. A huge "thank you" to you all.

And finally a special thanks to the lovely woman from the east coast of Ireland who told me that the columns took her through two of the toughest years of her life when she nearly went under. She survived those extremely difficult years, week by week, column by column, insight by insight.

Every column is a pebble in a lake. We have no idea how far the ripples will extend or who they will influence along the way. So I hope you all enjoy reading these inspirational Green Platform stories as much as I enjoyed writing them. It does indeed take a village to write a book. Thank you so much to all the people in this *Living The Green Platform* village.